THE HERMENEUTICAL SPIRIT II

THE HERMENEUTICAL SPIRIT II

Migrations, Diasporas, and Cultures After Pentecost

Amos Yong
Edited by Rodolfo Galvan Estrada III

CASCADE *Books* • Eugene, Oregon

THE HERMENEUTICAL SPIRIT II
Migrations, Diasporas, and Cultures After Pentecost

Cascade Books
An Imprint of Wipf and Stock Publishers
199 W. 8th Ave., Suite 3
Eugene, OR 97401

www.wipfandstock.com

PAPERBACK ISBN: 979-8-3852-5154-4
HARDCOVER ISBN: 979-8-3852-5155-1
EBOOK ISBN: 979-8-3852-5156-8

Cataloguing-in-Publication data:

Names: Yong, Amos [author]. | Estrada, Rodolfo Galvan, III [editor]

Title: The hermeneutical spirit II : migrations, diasporas, and cultures after Pentecost / by Amos Yong ; edited by Rodolfo Galvan Estrada III.

Description: Eugene, OR: Cascade Books, 2026 | Includes bibliographical references and index.

Identifiers: ISBN 979-8-3852-5154-4 (paperback) | ISBN 979-8-3852-5155-1 (hardcover) | ISBN 979-8-3852-5156-8 (ebook)

Subjects: LCSH: Bible—Criticism, interpretation, etc. | Bible—Criticism, interpretation, etc.—Asia. | Bible—Theology. | Hermeneutics—Religious aspects—Pentecostalism. | Emigration and immigration—Religious aspects—Christianity.

Classification: BS476 Y62 2026 (paperback) | BS476 (ebook)

VERSION NUMBER 02/13/26

Dedicated to

Néstor Medina

Contents

Credits and Acknowledgments

THANKS TO THE FOLLOWING for allowing republication of these chapters of the present volume:

1. The editors (and Aschendorff-Verlag) for: "The Spirit Poured Out: A (Pentecostal) Perspective After Pentecost," in Guido Vergauwen and Andreas Steinbruber, eds., *Veni, Sancte Spiritus! Theologische Beiträge zur Sendung des Geistes/Contributions théologiques à la mission de l'Esprit/Theological Contributions to the Mission of the Spirit—Festschrift für Barbara Hallensleben zum 60. Geburtstag*, Studia Oecumenica Friburgensia 85, Studienzentrum für Glaube und Gesellschaft 7 (Münster: Aschendorff-Verlag, 2018), 198–210.
2. Wipf and Stock Publishers for: "Lydia amid the Jewish Diaspora: Apostolic Migration and Belonging—Then and Now," in Dustin D. Benac, Erin Weber-Johnson, and Glen Bell, eds., *Pathways to Belonging* (Eugene, OR: Wipf & Stock, 2025), 51–57.
3. Sheffield Phoenix Press for: "The Spirit Poured Out in the Last Days: Toward a Pneumatology of Final Creation," in Robby Waddell and Chris E. W. Green, eds., *The Spirit of Prophecy and Reconciliation: Essays in Honor of Rickie D. Moore*, The Bible in the Modern World 84 (Sheffield: Sheffield Phoenix, 2023), 151–66.
4. InterVarsity Press for: "The Spirit, the Common Good, and the Public Sphere: The 21st Century Public Intellectual in Apostolic Perspective," in Todd C. Ream, Jerry Pattengale, and Christopher J. Devers, eds., *Public Intellectuals and the Common Good: Christian Thinking for Human Flourishing* (Downers Grove: IVP Academic, 2021), 21–41.

5. Previously unpublished: lecture presented as "Where Did the Holy Spirit Go? Ephesian Pneumatologies from the Third Apostolic Missionary Journey for a Post-Secular Age" seminar, for "Church with Spirit, in Our Secular Age" conference, StudieCenter Menigheds-baseret Teology (Study Centre for Church Based Theology), Denmark (via Zoom), May 11, 2023.
6. Regnum Books for: "Community Engagement After Pentecost: Apostolic Forays Then and Now," in Wonsuk Ma and Robert Menzies, eds., *Leadership, Spirituality, and the Holy Spirit: Essays in Honor of Younghoon Lee* (Oxford: Regnum, 2024), 151–64.
7. Dr. Samuel George, editor of *New Life Theological Journal*, for: "From the Jewish Diaspora to the Indian (Christian) Diaspora: An Autobiographical Look at 1 Peter's Message to West Asia" (ed. John Alex), *New Life Theological Journal* 9 (2019) 7–18;
8. Professor Lap Yan Kung, editor of the *Asia Journal of Theology*, for: "Diasporic Discipleship from West Asia Through Southeast Asia and Beyond: A Dialogue with 1 Peter," *Asia Journal of Theology* 32 (2018) 3–21.
9. Wipf and Stock Publishers for: "'Not Many of You Should Become Teachers . . .': Whose (Established) Professoriate? Which (Diasporic) Faculty?" in Neal D. Presa and Anne E. Zaki, eds., *Now to God Who Is Able: Vocation, Justice, and Ministry—Essays in Honor of Mark Labberton* (Eugene, OR: Wipf & Stock, 2023), 139–54.
10. The Pennsylvania State University Press for: "Unveiling Interpretation After Pentecost: Revelation, Pentecostal Reading, and Christian Hermeneutics of Scripture—A Review Essay," *Journal of Theological Interpretation* 11 (2017) 139–55.
11. Sheffield Phoenix Press for: "'To Him Who Loves Us and Freed Us from Our Sins by His Blood . . .': A Pentecostal Unveiling of Apocalyptic Love," in Blaine Charette and Robby Waddell, eds., *Spirit and Story: Pentecostal Readings of Scripture—Essays in Honor of John Christopher Thomas* (Sheffield: Sheffield Phoenix, 2020), 117–34.
12. Gateway Publishing for: "Kings, Nations, and Cultures on the Way to the New Jerusalem: A Pentecostal Witness to an Apocalyptic Vision," in S. David Moore and Jonathan Huntzinger, eds., *The Pastor and the Kingdom: Essays Honoring Jack W. Hayford* (Southlake, TX: TKU & Gateway Academic, 2017), 231–51.

Amos is also grateful to Rudy for his contributions to this volume. My graduate assistants Jeanetta Gregory helped with creating the bibliography and Lizette Saldana Buiza generated the indexes. Most importantly, over the eight-plus years that the twelve chapters of this book were drafted and written, Alma accompanied me through three different moves in Pasadena (in large part due to dynamic circumstances around Fuller Seminary's at-one-point planned move that then didn't materialize) plus a two-month displacement due to the Eaton Canyon fire; she has been an amazingly patient, supportive, and steadfast partner in the Yong migrations over this period, and across the almost four decades by now that we have been together.

Rudy is thankful for the Pentecostal Latino church that shaped my early years, a tradition introduced to me by my grandmother. As a child, I would fall asleep beneath the wooden *bancas* of my grandmother's Spanish church, surrounded by the melodies of *corritos* and the rhythmic voices of a worshiping community. These experiences continue to influence the foundation of my faith and my theological reflections. I am also deeply grateful for my wife, Jessica Estrada, who always has encouraged me to be true to myself and believe in the calling that God has on my life. Your unwavering support remains the reason why I write.

And also to Néstor Medina, to whom this volume is dedicated. Thank you, Néstor, for reminding me of my Latino identity when I (Rudy) was a doctoral student. Néstor once challenged me with a question that has echoed ever since: "Where are you in this exegesis? I don't hear your Latino voice in this reading." His question stopped me in my tracks—and has stayed with me ever since.

Néstor, it was wonderful to welcome you as a colleague to Regent University School of Divinity, where you and I (Amos) were faculty together for a handful of years. I remain grateful for your bearing witness to the work of the divine breath across cultures—from Guatemala across North America to Cuba and beyond—disrupting the dominant imperial regimes of our age with the many tongues of immigrant voices in many directions. Thank you for being a bold and unapologetic voice, unafraid to speak the truth with conviction and fire.

We thank Robin Parry and George Callihan, among others at Cascade/Wipf and Stock, for supporting another volume of Amos Yong's *Spirit* books. We especially appreciate Elisabeth Rickard's particularly detailed copyediting of the final manuscript. We remain responsible for all remaining errors of fact or interpretation.

Preface

THIS COLLECTION OF ESSAYS is a sequel to my *The Hermeneutical Spirit: Theological Interpretation and the Scriptural Imagination for the 21st Century* published by Cascade Books in 2017. As the prior volume reprinted previously published or presented essays and articles for the purposes of showcasing one example of pentecostal theological interpretations of scripture, especially but not only Luke-Acts, this book extends that project via another set of previously published or presented essays and articles,[1] but does so in two distinct directions. First, there is a clear shift from the generally "pentecostal" flavor of the prior work to the more dominant "after Pentecost" motif in the present. Whereas "pentecostal" has been my home ecclesial tradition all my life (I continue to retain ministerial credentials with the International Church of the Foursquare Gospel) and I have long theologized explicitly as a pentecostal Christian, all of the material collected in the present volume derives from the period since I arrived at Fuller Seminary in 2014, when I have increasingly deployed the "after Pentecost" theme to register a hermeneutical and methodological strategy that leaps off the Pentecost narrative in the book of Acts.[2] Even if my churches draw their name from the Day of Pentecost in this book, the Lukan account belongs not only to modern pentecostal ecclesial groups but to the church ecumenical. This "after Pentecost" approach includes but is also distinct from a pentecostal one that may be prominent among the growing number of biblical scholars and theologians who do their work amid and from modern pentecostal churches and movements (e.g., the Assemblies of God, the Church of God Cleveland, the Church of God

1. Even as both are part of what is by now one handful of such *Spirit* volumes, the most recent of which is my *The Dialogical Spirit II*.

2. If those interested were to do searches for "after Pentecost" in relationship to my work, they will observe this in titles of my articles and book chapters after 2016 and in my books beginning with 2019, e.g., *Mission After Pentecost*.

in Christ, and others with roots in the early twentieth-century revivals). The present collection of essays, then, expands from the more ecclesially (e.g., pentecostally) generated ethos of *The Hermeneutical Spirit* to a more explicitly theological (e.g., based on the Pentecost narrative) interpretive approach, and in that sense, combined, the two books demonstrate what we might call pneumatic theological interpretation of scripture in both their ecclesial and theological modalities.

Second, however, this collection of essays revolves around the specific cluster of ideas in the volume's subtitle: *Migrations, Diasporas, and Cultures*. While the chapters in parts 3 and 4 of the present volume explore the last two themes—diasporas and cultures[3]—respectively, the migration theme permeates the book. The Pentecost narrative foregrounds those gathered "from every nation under heaven" (Acts 2:5 NRSV), even as the original Greek, ἀπὸ παντὸς ἔθνους might also be translated "from every ethnicity" or "from every tribe and culture," extrapolations consistent with what we read in the Apocalypse about the diversity of peoples gathered around the throne of God. The first two parts of the book therefore illuminate "after Pentecost" readings of particularly the Acts of the Apostles—here mirroring but developing similar readings of the second Lukan book in parts 2 and 3 of *The Hermeneutical Spirit*—and do so also by introducing the migration theme (in part 1) and by exploring apostolic cultural navigation (in part 2).

The three essays in the first part of the book introduce the theme of migration explicitly (in the middle chapter) amid the broader motif of movement. The latter is considered both in terms of the dynamics of the apostolic narrative as recounted in the Pentecost narrative of the book of Acts and then as decipherable theologically in an "after Pentecost" reading of certain theological topics—of pneumatology (chapter 1) and of final creation (chapter 3)—as discernible across other segments of the New Testament. In other words, these chapters combine to provide both an overarching view of the "after Pentecost" movement functioning hermeneutically for Christian theological interpretation and an elaboration of a concrete episode of migration within the Acts narrative. The latter informs the former even as the former provides a central cord of the interpretive lenses in turn.

Part 2 of this book includes three chapters displaying the "after Pentecost" hermeneutic at work in three spheres of apostolic cultural

3. Prefigured in a book I co-edited with Im, *Global Diasporas and Mission*.

engagement. Here, the "after Pentecost" approach illuminates not only the apostolic experience as initiated and sustained by the Spirit of Pentecost but also how our own discipleship in the twenty-first century might be so enabled. In particular the chapters explore issues of the common good and public witness (chapter 4), the nature of the sacred-secular divide (chapter 5), and community engagement (chapter 6), in some ways reading current realities back into the apostolic narratives but, in other respects, retrieving the apostolic witness on these and adjacent areas in view of contemporary challenges and questions. Combined with the chapters in part 1, the first half of this volume exemplifies the "after Pentecost" hermeneutic at work, including theological interpretation of scripture possibilities for considering migration, theology of culture, public theology, theology of the (post)secular, and the like.

The third part of this book turns explicitly to the theme of diaspora, in dialogue with the General or Catholic Letters, especially 1 Peter (chapters 7–8) and James (chapter 9). Each of these two epistles are addressed specifically to the Jewish diaspora (1 Pet 1:1; Jas 1:1), and I read them as, myself, a member of the Chinese-Malaysian diaspora to the West (I have been naturalized as an American citizen since the age of sixteen).[4] Cumulatively, the pages in this part of the volume develop, incipiently, what we might call a "diasporic hermeneutic," one that, as we shall see, is not only catalyzed by the Pentecost narrative but, we might argue, is the on-the-ground conditions that constitute the possibility of the emergence of such an account in the first place. Such a diasporic hermeneutic after Pentecost, we intuit, not only is of urgent relevance in our contemporary global contexts, but holds generative promise for distinctive theological interpretation and application amid the many challenges of racial, ethnic, and cultural marginalization by dominant societies in the present time.

Finally, part 4 of this volume looks specifically at the final book of the New Testament and of the biblical canon from our "after Pentecost" vantage point. These essays were written on the way to my own theological commentary on the Apocalypse,[5] although the themes of hybridity (chapter 10), marginality (chapter 11), and culture (chapter 12) did not get extended treatment in my book (because of the commentary nature of the work). Further, while the task of articulating a theology of culture

4. These essays follow from, historically speaking, my book *The Future of Evangelical Theology*, even as they anticipate a later edited work: Goh et al., *From Malaysia to the Ends of the Earth.*

5. See Yong, *Revelation.*

was the explicit goal in the last chapter of the book, that of hybridity and marginality are more afterthoughts, lifted up here in light of their republication in this book. The tenth chapter does introduce the notion of hybridity, albeit doing so in terms of ecclesial location rather than in terms of cultural or ethnic mixing, but the former is consistent with if not also emergent out of the latter in a world of migration and diaspora (which was also that of the reality of the Seer from Patmos and his readers). The middle chapter of this final section doesn't even mention *marginality*, but such is presumed in its efforts to explicate the submerged motif of *love* and rescue such from the narrative (not to mention historical) underside of the apocalyptic visions of John's Revelation.

In sum, migration, diaspora, and culture are in the pages to come construed after Pentecost. Republication of these articles, essays, and book chapters are a window into reading not only the book of Acts in this after Pentecost modality but also the General Epistles and the book of Revelation as well. They also invite explicitly thematizing the dynamics of migration, diaspora, and culture within the readings and encourage taking them into account for contemporary theological purposes, including those attempting to make sense of global migration and diasporas in the present time. Beyond this, perhaps others might be also inspired to adapt such an after Pentecost approach as a distinctive theological interpretation of scripture hermeneutic for their own purposes, both for reading the rest of the New Testament and even across the biblical canon,[6] and, potentially, as applicable to many other themes and topics evidenced in the apostolic accounts that we continue to encounter and grapple with in our own experience.

Whereas *The Hermeneutical Spirit* represented only my voice, *The Hermeneutical Spirit II* includes that of NT scholar Rodolfo Galvan Estrada III, who brings his expertise on race, ethnicity, and cultures in the ancient world to the volume and provides book-ends to my collection of essays. Rudy has done groundbreaking work on readings of race—more technically: ethnicity—in the Fourth Gospel and is expanding such to engage the rest of the New Testament.[7] In especially the final chapter to this book, he develops his own scholarly agenda in dialogue with St. Paul, thus appropriately concluding this volume that does not otherwise feature any

6. My *Mission After Pentecost*, part I, for instance, is an effort to read the Old Testament in light of both incarnation and Pentecost.

7. E.g., Estrada, *Pneumatology of Race in the Gospel of John*; Estrada, *Latino Reading of Race, Kinship, and the Empire*; Estrada, *Race and the Foreigner*.

substantive Pauline engagement. In fact, Rudy's chapter at least nuances, if not also in a significant sense corrects, prior (mis)readings of Paul as missionary,[8] and instead highlights Paul as (undocumented!) migrant evangelist. Welcome to the ongoing spiral of the hermeneutical Spirit.

8. Including my own, in *Mission After Pentecost*, ch. 7 on Paul's letters.

Introduction

Reading with Brown Eyes

Amos Yong and the Search for Meaning

Rodolfo Galvan Estrada III

The Bible is a difficult book to read. No one tells you this when you receive your first Bible—whether it comes after you join the Christian faith, at your First Communion, or a celebratory event such as a graduation. The Bible should have a warning label that says, "Not everything that you read will appear straightforward—may contain talking animals, paranormal activity, and science-defying physics." I began to realize the challenges of reading the Bible after I converted to the Christian faith. During my early years as a new believer, I thought that it would be easy to read the Bible. I devoured many chapters at a time—during lunch at school, on the bus, on the trolley, and wherever I could find myself alone with the Bible. The stories of Scripture were fascinating, and I often wondered why my church did not preach or teach on all the books of the Bible. Then I began to realize that there was something more to the Bible than what I could glean from a literary reading of its pages. I found the language difficult to understand and many stories culturally and historically obscure. I did not have any commentaries or books, only a dusty concordance left over from my father's library. Without any guidance or knowledge about how to use it, I took what felt like the most natural step—I enrolled in a Bible college located in La Puente, California—just east of Los Angeles.

My experiences at the Bible college were deeply formative, spiritually enriching, and academically enlightening. It was at this institution that I met many friends who are now fellow ministerial colleagues—including the love of my life, Jessica Baez (now Estrada). As a young Latino from the inner city of southeast San Diego, I came to class wearing Nike Cortez shoes, Dickies pants, and Lowrider T-shirts. I was a recent convert and could barely afford tuition, let alone a new wardrobe. So, my attire and urban manners had not yet been "sanctified" enough to fit the norms of that conservative Bible college. And trust me, I did stand out. Though my presence raised eyebrows with the administration, I did not care given my commitment to learning and trying to understand the Bible. My inner city personality enabled me to brush off the judgment and silent criticisms.

Besides standing out as some *cholo* in the classroom, I began to have some cognitive dissonance during these first years. What I was learning in the classroom did not match what I experienced in church. I was challenged to think differently about my experiences, tradition, and how we should read the Bible. Many of the administrators and adjunct faculty of the Bible college were recent graduates from Fuller Theological Seminary, a nearby institution in Pasadena, California. Through them, I was introduced to biblical scholarship. One class, in particular, required me to read cover to cover the *Anchor Bible Commentary* on the book of Romans, by Joseph Fitzmyer. This experience led me to notice starkly how some Latino Pentecostal beliefs, theologies, and readings of the Bible were treated differently, even suspiciously, by those who interpreted the Bible with traditional historical critical methods.

Not until much later in my academic journey did the boundaries and debates between various hermeneutical approaches and epistemological frameworks begin to make sense. As I found, reaching an understanding of Scripture is not simply about utilizing the right hermeneutical method and viewing all subjective experiences and theological convictions as a hinderance to the interpretive process. Nor was I to divorce my experiences, theological tradition, and even community from the process of reading the Bible.[1] This is what my training with the historical method did not teach me. Instead, it taught me that I could read the Bible on its own terms, free from any influences or traditions that guide the interpreter.[2]

1. Estrada, "Is a Contextualized Hermeneutic the Future of Pentecostal Readings?"
2. Krentz, *Historical-Critical Method*, 70.

The traditional historical-critical methods are the default approaches in biblical scholarship. They are the product of the Enlightenment, and they seek to historically reconstruct or discover the author's original intent.[3] Or, as Friedrich Schleiermacher insists, "The goal of hermeneutics is to understand the texts as their original readers understood them."[4] This approach taught me that in order to be a biblical scholar, I had to utilize its tools in order to find the true meaning of Scripture—the authorial intent. Perhaps, one might say, I was never properly taught how to use this hermeneutic correctly. However, Fernando Segovia, a New Testament scholar on the Gospel of John, states that historical criticism is a dehumanizing way of reading Scripture given that it expected all people to read the Bible apart from their flesh-and-blood reality.[5] I felt this dehumanization. Whether explicitly stated or merely implied, I felt compelled to believe that to be a real Bible scholar and interpret the Bible, I could not be a Latino—let alone a Pentecostal.

Now, one would suppose that interpreting the Bible is simply a matter of uncovering the original meaning of the text and applying the biblical text—as if all we did was unpack and repackage the text for a new context. But this is not the way it works. Rather, the meaning of Scripture is always shaped by the horizons we bring.[6] No one comes to Scripture with a *tabula rasa*. We all approach and interpret Scripture with a particular lens that frames and situates our reading. The meaning we derive from the text makes sense because we read the text within the thoughts and ideas that emerge from our own social and cultural context.[7] This includes, but is not limited to, our views on politics, gender roles, social norms, and cultural values. These are the pre-understandings and

3. Though no one person invented the historical approach to reading Scripture, some of its early ideas can be traced to Baruch Spinoza, an early figure of the Enlightenment. While discussing the need to understand the historical context of Scripture, the language, and the author, Spinoza remarks, "If we are ignorant of all these things, we can't know anything about what the author intended, or could have intended." See Curley, *Collected Works of Spinoza*, 183. Virkler, in fact, suggests that the "task of the exegete is to determine as closely as possible what God meant in a particular passage" (*Hermeneutic*, 23). For a historical overview of the historical critical approach, see Barton, "Historical Criticism."

4. Schleiermacher, *Hermeneutics*, 216.

5. Segovia, "And They Began to Speak in Other Tongues," 30; Segovia, *Decolonizing Biblical Studies*, 30–33.

6. Bultmann, "Is Exegesis Without Presuppositions Possible?," 153; Osborn, *Hermeneutical Spiral*, 516–18.

7. See for example, Yong's similar remarks in *Renewing Christian Theology*, 341–42.

assumptions that shape our interpretation of the Bible. What this also means is that when we read, our interpretations will differ from those who live in another historical milieu or those who simply have a different life experience. We all bring "expectations and assumptions" to the text.[8] Or, to put it bluntly, if you never had to migrate and be forced to flee from your home because of political or social unrest, then more than likely you will fail to observe the passages in Scripture that discuss the migration of people. You may only view migration and the challenges of citizenship from positions of privilege and affluence.

My own journey—from a young Latino Pentecostal student at a Bible college—taught me that we must hold space for the rigor of scholarship and the Spirit. But as discussed, biblical interpretation—particularly within the context of the academy—presents significant challenges. Chief among them is the long-standing assumption that the meaning of a biblical text can be discovered through the application of historical-critical tools. This method, grounded in Enlightenment ideals of reason and objectivity, seeks to uncover the so-called original meaning of a text, independent of the reader's context. On the other end of the interpretive spectrum, however, are approaches that prioritize human experience, cultural location, and the inevitable subjectivity of the interpreter. These tensions can be visualized along two axes: the horizontal axis spanning from exegesis to eisegesis, and the vertical axis ranging from objectivity to subjectivity. Traditional historical approaches were situated firmly in the quadrant of exegesis and objectivity, operating under the belief that scholars could arrive at a singular, authoritative interpretation through proper method.

Yet we now find ourselves in a different hermeneutical landscape—one that acknowledges the limitations of exegesis and the inescapable presence of the interpreter in the act of interpretation. Amos Yong, in fact, remarks that the "entire debate about objectivity and subjectivity is driven by modernist modes and habits of thought."[9] He points out:

> The church or believing community as the people of God has never only read their sacred texts from such "objective" vantage points but always engaged these documents from a faith perspective expecting to hear God (not just know about God) in the process.[10]

8. Thiselton, *New Horizons in Hermeneutics*, 44–46.

9. Yong, *Renewing Christian Theology*, 343.

10. Yong, *Mission After Pentecost*, 11.

The pursuit of purely objective reading inherited from the Enlightenment period has given way to a more nuanced understanding that all readings are, in some sense, situated and contextual. We are now at a time in scholarship when the subjectivity of the interpreter has been mostly admitted, and many no longer chase after these lofty, unattainable interpretive goals. Indeed, Michael Gorman remarks that though the traditional goals of finding the authorial intent was "laudable," it is nonetheless "difficult to achieve."[11] Instead, he finds that a more modest and appropriate goal would be to seek a "credible and coherent understanding of the text on its own terms and in its own context," but even this too—as he admits—is difficult.[12] Still, the persistent privileging of Enlightenment ideals of objectivity haunt interpreters today. I know this precisely because any form of biblical interpretation put forth by scholars of color, women, or minoritized communities are often labeled as "contextual" as if some readings are free from cultural and ideological entanglements. As I have come to realize regarding those who incorporate traditional hermeneutical methods—their biblical interpretations are nothing more than "tamed eisegetical readings."[13]

The traditional historical critical approaches to reading Scripture carried over from the Enlightenment period have not been as successful as hoped. Not only did these approaches fail to take seriously the various literary and rhetorical dimensions of the text, but they also failed to recognize the role of the reader. We have theological convictions and spiritual experiences with God that guide and shift our selection and interpretation of Scripture. Experiences, including non-experiences, contribute to the way we read and understand Scripture.[14] For many Pentecostals, reading the Bible is spiritually transformative and not just an academic exercise.[15] We approach the Bible to learn how to live a life of faith. Our desire to learn about God is not just for the increase of theological or historical knowledge. Instead, we read the Bible and explore its rich stories—searching, seeking, and thirsting for God—because we desire to hear the divine voice speak to our present context.[16] The Bible is real for Pentecostals because the same divine experiences we find within

11. Gorman, *Elements of Biblical Exegesis*, 5.

12. Gorman, *Elements of Biblical Exegesis*, 5.

13. Estrada, *Race, Kinship, and the Empire*, 31.

14. Richards and O'Brien, *Misreading Scripture with Western Eyes*, 15.

15. Archer, *Pentecostal Hermeneutic*, 114.

16. Johns, *Re-Enchanting the Text*, xiii, 53–54; Grey, *Three's a Crowd*, 104–14.

its pages are similar to the way God moves and acts in our lives. If you have never had a dramatic spiritual encounter with God, though, or felt the rushing infilling of the Holy Spirit that causes one to speak in an unknown language, then the passages in Scripture that describe such experiences may remain abstract—lacking the depth of a lived experiential significance. This does not mean that non-Pentecostals cannot read these texts responsibly; however, one's non-experiences may limit one in the interpretive process.[17] The charismatic dimensions of the text may be dismissed, overlooked, or outright rejected.

My critical remarks of traditional historical critical hermeneutics should not be misunderstood as an endorsement of a Pentecostal, Spirit-led approach that neglects the cultural and historical context, language, or grammar of the text. Reading Scripture is not merely a matter of following personal intuitions or experiences, as if the nature of the biblical text lacked interpretive boundaries and limitations. This goes too far and can be very dangerous. Even in my own personal experiences, I have observed that those without formal training or familiarity with hermeneutical tools rely heavily on the Spirit to guide their biblical interpretations—not out of a disdain for scholarship—but simply due to an unawareness of its impact or importance. Despite the Spirit's guidance and plain sense of Scripture, though, there are aspects difficult to understand that demand engagement with scholarship. The biblical stories are more complex than one might suppose. There is cultural knowledge that is assumed and knowledge that we as modern interpreters have lost access to due to the distance of time. The sayings and teachings written and addressed to people long ago often become difficult to appropriate for today. Even those who champion the role of the individual in the interpretive process or other new approaches do not assume that the historical critical methods are useless or that questions of historicity are irrelevant. In fact, liberation theologians, Latina biblical scholars, literary critics, and others also admit this point.[18]

17. Spawn, "Principle of Analogy," 49, 63.

18. Gutiérrez, *Power of the Poor in History*, 16; Powell, *What Is Narrative Criticism?*, 2; Elliot, *What Is Social-Scientific Criticism?*, 15; Hidalgo, *Revelation in Aztlán*, 17.

AMOS YONG AND THEOLOGICAL HERMENEUTICS

Though the goals of traditional historical method of hermeneutics and theological hermeneutics differ, my faith perspective leads us to confront the broader complexity of Pentecostal hermeneutics as a theological method. Still, calling myself a "Pentecostal" should not be mistaken for aligning with a singular or unified interpretive tradition. Even more, regarding theological hermeneutics, this also does not suppose that all Pentecostals advocate or utilize a particular approach to biblical interpretation. Jacqueline Grey remarks that "there has been little consensus among scholars on a single reading approach which reflects their community's reading practices."[19] Likewise, Craig Keener asserts that what unites Pentecostal interpreters is "more experiential than methodological."[20] Though it is difficult, and imperative, to not essentialize the Pentecostal movement, let alone Pentecostal hermeneutics, this does not mean that the movement cannot be identified. Said another way, the lack of essential defining characteristics of Pentecostalism does not suppose that a Pentecostal approach to reading Scripture is so fragmented that it is beyond recognition. Not at all.

Given that Pentecostalism is a demographically diverse global movement, no one denomination or continent owns or has the right to define it.[21] As such, the approaches to reading Scripture pentecostally will differ given the contextual differences and needs of its global readers. Within this volume, we are provided with another way forward that broadens our understanding and showcases what it means to read Scripture pentecostally. It is helpful, nonetheless, to provide a brief review of Amos Yong's approach to Pentecostal theological interpretation understood from the vantage point of a biblical scholar. As mentioned earlier, it was the scholarship of Pentecostals such as Yong that helped me break free of the myopic views of traditional historical criticism that had so dominated my academy experience.

I must, however, confess that I am not a theologian by training. I only pretend to be one until I am unmasked when the incongruities of my theological claims are revealed—especially by my students. It is then that I retreat to my enclave of textual ambiguities and the cultural world

19. Grey, "Biblical Hermeneutics," 131.

20. Keener, "Pentecostal Biblical Interpretation," 272.

21. Yong, for example, traces the global diversity and movement of Pentecostalism in *Spirit Poured Out*, 18–22.

of the Bible. All this to say that what follows is a biblical scholar's attempt to explain Yong's Pentecostal hermeneutic—one deeply formative for me ever since I was his doctoral student long ago.

One will immediately notice that for Yong, "Pentecostal" is uncapitalized. This is purposefully done because, as Yong explains, pentecostal refers more to the work of the Holy Spirit than to a specific denomination or tradition. Or, as said in the previous volume of this monograph, "pentecostal hermeneutic is not one that belongs to any church or even movement of churches but one that proceeds from after the Day of Pentecost as recorded in Acts 2."[22] In other words, Yong's pentecostal hermeneutic is historically much broader and did not begin on the Azusa Street revival in 1906. Instead, it began on the Day of Pentecost in Acts 2. To read pentecostally is to read in a way shaped by the experience, relationality, rationality, and dynamic presence of the Holy Spirit, a reading available for all Christians, not just those in Pentecostal churches or denominations.

Yong's approach to reading pentecostally, or more specifically, reading *after* Pentecost appears in his seminal work, *Spirit-Word-Community*, which has become a catalytic text in theological hermeneutics. There, he lays out a systematic approach to this kind of reading. Theological hermeneutics, as Yong explains, differs from scriptural exegesis in that it aims at "interpreting the totality of human experience—and that includes God and God's relationship with human selves and the world as a whole—from a perspective that is specifically and explicitly informed by faith."[23] This differs from the traditional historical critical method within biblical hermeneutics, which concentrates on the world and language of the biblical text. What often goes missing in such an historical approach is the theological dimension—the way the Spirit continues to speak through Scripture to a community of faith.

The theological interpretation Yong puts forth can be understood as a continuous interplay between the Spirit, the Word, and Community as the guiding framework for interpretation. It is a robust "pneumatological-trinitarian hermeneutic," as he describes:

> All three should be understood as moments in the one hermeneutical and methodological movement. The dialectical relationship between Spirit and Word is played out in the context of Community. The dialectical relationship between Word and

22. Yong, *Hermeneutical Spirit*, xi–xii; see also Yong, *Mission After Pentecost*, 13.

23. Yong, *Spirit-Word-Community*, 6.

> Community is mediated by Spirit. The dialectical relationship between Spirit and Community is anchored in Word. Spirit implicates Word and Community; Word implicates Spirit and Community; Community implicates Spirit and Word. None of the three are subordinate to either of the other, and all assume and require each other.[24]

As such, Yong's theological hermeneutic is a trialectical movement. It not only reorients biblical interpretation around the triune God but also positions pneumatology as the theological starting point for the hermeneutical task.

Now, all theology, as Yong explains, is in a sense hermeneutical in that it attempts to know God and reflect upon his self-disclosure in nature, Scripture, and the incarnate Christ. However, as previously mentioned, the preferred entry point in Yong's theological hermeneutic is through pneumatology—or as will be elaborated below—within the person's pneumatological imagination.

Yong's "pneumatological imagination" is the "how" and "where" of theological interpretation. Yong insists that the human imagination is not simply passively shaped and subordinate to the rational mind. Instead, the imagination "mediates the human engagement with the external world, . . . enables human beings to actively construct the world, . . . [and] holds both of these activities—of reproduction and production—together coherently such that one and the same person moves from one to the other subconsciously and fluidly."[25] The imagination, in other words, is both passive and active, thus serving as the place where one has an encounter with the Holy Spirit. A pneumatological imagination, one empowered by the divine breath, is the necessary mediator that enables theologizing. The imagination discerns and perceives more clearly the powers of the world, including its spiritual dimensions, and normatively engages the world and the divine. It is the "synthesizing faculty from which interpretation emerges."[26] And again, this does not suggest that only Pentecostals have this type of imagination. This is possible and available for all as a result of Pentecost in Acts 2.[27] Further, Yong also recognizes that the imagination is imperfect. Yong admits that though

24. Yong, *Spirit-Word-Community*, 18.

25. Yong, *Spirit-Word-Community*, 128–29.

26. Yong, *Spirit-Word-Community*, 144.

27. See Yong, "Pneumatological Imagination," 154; Yong, *Hermeneutical Spirit*, 14.

theological knowledge is pneumatologically mediated, it is also partial, incomplete, and susceptible to error.[28]

Nonetheless, the trialectic of theological interpretation primarily begins with the Spirit, for the Spirit makes possible the relational reality between humanity, Christ, and God.[29] He continues, "pneumatological interpretation of Scripture cannot be for its own sake but must be for the sake of understanding the God of Israel, manifest in Jesus."[30] In other words, a pneumatological approach to biblical interpretation is trinitarian in nature. It may begin with the Spirit but does not end with the Spirit. Additionally, for Yong, the Spirit is also the mediator of rationality as the revealer of knowledge and the mysteries of God. The Spirit is also the power of life in creation.[31] As such, the Spirit engages the interpreter in the never-ending quest for meaning and understanding.[32] As Yong finds, this method "moves through, not necessarily in sequential order, the moment of Word which is also never entirely bereft of either Spirit or Community, and the moment of Community which is also never entirely disconnected from Spirit and Word."[33]

Regarding the act of interpretation, Yong remarks that it is not simply a cognitive affair. Instead, it is an interplay between Spirit, Word, and Community, an activity that is "triadic, trialectical, and trialogical."[34] That is, Scripture, along with tradition, is interpreted in partnership with the Spirit, who reveals all things. More specifically, the "Word" of God as an object of interpretive analysis is not just Scripture. It is the living Word and also the spoken word of the gospel message.[35] Additionally, Scripture embeds the reflective experiences and "subsequent re-interpretations of these experiences."[36] Even more, as we interpret Scripture, Yong agrees that we cannot ignore the fact that "we all exegete our experiences (or lack of them, as the case may be) whether consciously or not."[37] Said differently, "We do not interpret either Scripture or tradition

28. Yong, *Spirit-Word-Community*, 176–84.
29. Yong, *Spirit-Word-Community*, 34.
30. Yong, *Mission After Pentecost*, 14.
31. Yong, *Spirit-Word-Community*, 39–48.
32. Yong, *Spirit-Word-Community*, 77.
33. Yong, *Spirit-Word-Community*, 220.
34. Yong, *Spirit-Word-Community*, 315.
35. Yong, *Spirit-Word-Community*, 264.
36. Yong, *Spirit-Word-Community*, 235.
37. Yong, *Spirit-Word-Community*, 246.

directly, but rather interpret our experience of reading Scripture and tradition," as such, "interpretation thus begins with the self—more specifically, with the discernment of the self, and that always understood as the self-in-community."[38]

For Yong, the world in front of the text and the world of the text are not disengaged. To do so, which is generally the practice of traditional historical criticism, is to become "an illegitimate attempt to break through the hermeneutical circle."[39] In fact, he notes that the "biblicist's insistence that 'this is what the Bible says!' avoids dealing with the fact that all reading is through various experiential and traditional lenses, possibly distorted or ideologized."[40] Nonetheless, he claims, "keeping all three worlds together—the world behind the text and the world in front of the text being connected by the text and the world of the text—is the crux of all interpretive activity; otherwise, we would be fantasizing or dreaming, not interpreting."[41] Yes, theological pluralism is inevitable. This is a reality given the contextual and diverse nature of our communities. However, pluralism has boundaries, "both at the level of authorial intention and at the level of shape of the received biblical canon."[42] As he explains, the Spirit is not creating a new word altogether but "creating new significations of the Word," a point that needs to be distinguished.[43] This is crucial, because as he states, there are certainly some whose imagination knows no bounds. The biblical text, in a sense, provides the contours of our pneumatological imagination.

From this trialectical movement with the Spirit, theology emerges. Or said differently, flowing from the logic of Pentecost, we are able to read and interpret Scripture with a pneumatological imagination—the space and place where the Spirit speaks and reveals. The Spirit and Word come together in our quest for understanding.[44] As such, it also requires that we discern the divine will, "what the Spirit is saying and doing" so that we may "imitate and follow after the Spirit, whether in worship, mission, or socio-ethical activity."[45]

38. Yong, *Spirit-Word-Community*, 247.
39. Yong, *Spirit-Word-Community*, 264.
40. Yong, *Spirit-Word-Community*, 270–71.
41. Yong, *Spirit-Word-Community*, 264.
42. Yong, *Spirit-Word-Community*, 289.
43. Yong, *Spirit-Word-Community*, 226.
44. Yong, *Spirit-Word-Community*, 297.
45. Yong, *Spirit-Word-Community*, 285.

READING AFTER PENTECOST WITH AMOS YONG

Thus far, I have been making mention of the traditional historical critical methods and my struggle with this approach as a Latino Pentecostal. Though trained as a biblical scholar and urged to hide my theological confession in the employment of traditional historical methods in my scholarship, there never was or has been a time that I could ever stop being a Pentecostal, let alone having a pneumatological imagination. In fact, often my own theological convictions and pneumatic experiences led me to rummage the ancient sources, Greek and Latin writers, or reimagine the cultural context and situation in the ancient world.[46] Within my pneumatological imagination, as Yong describes it, I hear the whispers of the Spirit, who provides me with new questions, ideas, doubts, and curiosity. Sometimes my pneumatological imagination begins with the statement, "I wonder what this means," or "I think there is something else going on." In fact, I read the ancient world of Greece and Rome through Chicano *Pentecostal* eyes.[47] In some cases, while I read ancient sources, the Spirit reminds me of my Latino history and heritage, including the Latino Pentecostal Church. It is precisely this experience that has led me to reject the traditional historical-critical methods as the sole arbiters of truth. We do not need to decenter or eschew the role of the Spirit and theological conviction in the interpretive process. Even more, we do not need to pretend that we do not read Scripture apart from a community.

Yet, one thing is certain—reading the Bible is difficult, and it is even more dangerous to assume that we do not have presuppositions that influence our interpretations of the biblical text. Yong warns us about the dangers of an unbounded imagination, but in the end, reading the Bible is never a neutral act. If we do not admit our subjectivity, we will inadvertently impose our own readings of Scripture and presume that they are the "objective" or the "biblical" perspective that ought to be normative for all people at all times and places. We will judge all others who interpret the Bible differently as "misusing" the text, as if those trained in the traditional historical critical methods were the only ones who knew how to read. Additionally, if we do not recognize the limitations of our

46. For example, this is most notable in my essays that were inspired by my spiritual or theological reflections upon my social circumstances. See Estrada, "Racial Significance of Paul's Clothing Metaphor"; Estrada, "Blaspheming Angels"; Estrada, "What Does the Paraclete Have to Do with Dreamers?"

47. Estrada, *Race, Kinship, and the Empire*, 31–58.

experiences and non-experiences, we will miss out on new ways of reading the Bible that not only open us up to different insights but also connect the biblical text to our world today. Indeed, Gorman encourages readers today, especially White readers, to celebrate the God-given diversity in the church and recognize that "Christians from other contexts and perspectives may therefore make us better and more faithful interpreters."[48] This is what Yong means when he discusses the significance of the community. It is within our communities that we read, and it is in community with others that we gain insights into the significance of the biblical text. The Bible was never meant to be read individualistically, as if one alone—apart from others—could find the meaning of the biblical text.

Overall, it was the postcolonial, decolonial, literary, feminist, Black, and Pentecostal theologians and scholars who taught me these points. They taught me not to ignore the flesh-and-blood realities that make us human. They taught me to read the Bible through human eyes. They taught me that the Bible is meant to be read with others—the poor and marginalized, the migrant and undocumented, the orphan and incarcerated. They taught me to read the Bible with the Brown eyes God had given me. These Brown eyes include the legacy and heritage of my ancestors who had their land stolen, were forced to migrate, faced anti-immigrant prejudices, were beaten in public schools for speaking Spanish, or had to endure back-breaking work on the agricultural fields so that Americans could have food on their tables.

JOURNEY AHEAD

In this volume, we will showcase how to interpret Scripture after Pentecost, focusing on the themes of migration, diaspora, and culture with attention to Acts and beyond. Part 1, nonetheless, begins with Pentecostal hermeneutics though a reading of Acts. Chapter 1 introduces a Pentecostal-ecumenical theology along five registers: soteriology, ecclesiology, missiology, theology proper, and pneumatology—arguing that the Holy Spirit remains central to Christian reflection after Pentecost. The book proposes Pentecost as the hermeneutical and methodological engine for Christian theologizing in the present time. Chapter 2 reflects on migration and belonging through the story of Lydia in Acts 16. By situating the apostolic mission in Philippi, the chapter explores how belonging can

48. Gorman, "Majority-Culture Biblical Interpretation," 41–42.

take root amid the contemporary generation of global migrants, how contemporary migrants might find belonging amid global displacement, and how Acts provides a narrative framework for these reflections. Chapter 3 examines the Spirit's role in new creation, tracing a pneumatological and eschatological vision from Pentecost in Acts to Romans and Revelation. This chapter broadens the Pentecostal hermeneutic across the canon and connects apostolic mission to cosmic renewal.

Part 2, with an additional three chapters, turns to public theology and apostolic cultural navigation. Chapter 4 analyzes how Acts models public engagement for theologians today. It assesses apostolic speech and presence in diverse public arenas across imperial Rome, offering a framework for theologians to function as public intellectuals in a pluralistic age. Chapter 5 offers a selective theological rereading of Acts 19, interpreting Paul's Ephesian ministry against the backdrop of imperial Rome from the contemporary horizons of our secular and emerging post-secular landscape. In particular, the focus is on the presence and activity of the Spirit, demonstrating the Spirit's subtle yet enduring activity. Chapter 6 returns to the hermeneutical strategy in the first chapter of this part of the book on apostolic cultural navigation by exploring community engagement "after Pentecost," meaning more expansively across this second Lukan volume. Prioritizing Acts 2, the chapter argues for a pneumatologically informed theology of community that transcends denominational lines and offers insight for contemporary ecclesial practice.

Part 3 moves beyond Acts to consider diaspora theology in the Catholic Epistles. It looks at the themes of the diaspora in 1 Peter and James. Chapter 7, a homily originally preached to a South Asian immigrant church, reads 1 Pet 1:1 through the lens of Asian American identity. It draws parallels between the Petrine audience and today's "perpetual foreigners," offering pastoral encouragement rooted in shared diasporic experience. Chapter 8 builds on this, proposing a "diasporic hermeneutic." It follows 1 Peter's message across three contexts—first-century Asia Minor, late twentieth-century Southeast Asia, and twenty-first-century Asian America—arguing that Scripture invites diverse receptions across time and space, consistent with the Pentecostal spirit of *semper reformanda*. Chapter 9 focuses on James, particularly its instruction to teachers (3:1). The chapter argues for the importance of lifelong learning within diasporic contexts and sketches a theology of teaching shaped by orthopraxy and orthopathy. It highlights how reception of James reflects shifting diasporic concerns across the global church.

Part 4 explores culture and the ecumenical significance of Pentecostal readings. Chapter 10 categorizes Pentecostal contributions to biblical scholarship into three approaches: *authorial* (not overtly Pentecostal), *particularist* (intentionally Pentecostal), and *hybridic* (Pentecostal for a broader audience). It proposes a pneumatological alternative that emphasizes hybridity as inherent to diaspora and migration. Chapter 11 explores the theology of love in Revelation, focusing on Rev 1:5 and other select texts. It reads divine love as relational and trinitarian, enabled by the Spirit and seen from the underside of history. This chapter mirrors chapter 3's broad canonical reading but here centers on love within eschatology. Chapter 12 concludes with reflections on a theology of culture from Revelation. It argues that apocalyptic imagery resists superficial multiculturalism and instead demands deep, performative commitments. A Pentecostal hermeneutic here invites a vision of a global community rooted in the Spirit, completing the volume's arc.

Whereas the bulk of this work collecting Yong's essays are located primarily in Luke-Acts (parts 1–2), and in the latter part of the New Testament (the General Epistles and the book of Revelation in parts 3–4), the Pauline literature is relatively untouched. The conclusion of this volume returns to thinking about missions and migration in the life and ministry of Paul. This essay challenges the traditional portrayal of the apostle Paul as a "missionary," arguing that such a label is anachronistic and rooted in colonial-era constructs. Instead, it proposes that Paul be understood as a first-century Mediterranean migrant whose identity, mobility, and lack of homeland align more closely with the dynamics of ancient migration and undocumented immigrants today. Reframing Paul as a migrant not only reshapes our understanding of his apostolic identity but also invites a reevaluation of modern theological assumptions about the early Christian missionaries. Together, this monograph models how theological hermeneutics after Pentecost—hermeneutics shaped by migration, culture, and diaspora, and open to the Spirit's global work—can enrich the church's witness today.

PART I

The Book of Acts

A Pentecost Hermeneutic of Movement and Migration

Chapter 1

The Spirit Poured Out

A (Pentecostal) Perspective After Pentecost

It would appear that pentecostal theology is coming of age, a century after the Azusa Street revival in Los Angeles sparked a movement that is now practically worldwide in its extensiveness.[1] Pentecostal theology might be defined as critical reflection by the movement's theologians for their churches, perhaps like Wesleyan, Baptist, Reformed, etc., theology can be understood as similar activity by those in Wesleyan, Baptistic, Reformed, etc., congregations for their communities of faith. Yet, if pentecostal theology also takes its name biblically from the Pentecost narrative,[2] it might be arguable that such theological considerations are not to be sequestered to that segment of Christians who attend so-called pentecostal churches, but belong to all who embrace that scriptural and canonical account as their own. If so, pentecostal theology can be nothing less than ecumenical theology, belonging to the church catholic. This is not only a theology of Spirit baptism but a fully Spirit-baptized theology.

1. If theological maturation is evidenced by scholarly journals (e.g., *Pneuma: The Journal of the Society for Pentecostal Studies* and *Journal of Pentecostal Theology*), book series with established theological publishers (e.g., T&T Clark Studies in Systematic Pentecostal and Charismatic Theology), or Cambridge Companions (e.g., see Yong and Robeck, *Cambridge Companion to Pentecostalism*), then pentecostal theology can be said to have come of age.

2. In this essay I capitalize Pentecost and its cognates when it refers to a concrete event (e.g., Day of Pentecost) or noun (e.g., Pentecostalism), but not when used adjectivally (e.g., pentecostal theology).

This essay sketches the possibility of a pentecostal-ecumenical theology along five registers: soteriology, ecclesiology, missiology, theology proper, and pneumatology.[3] It will be seen, however, that the pneumatological motif persists from beginning to end, consistent with the Pentecost message that features centrally the person and work of the Holy Spirit. Pentecostal theology, then, is pneumatological theology that is a critical reflection not just after Easter but after Pentecost.[4] Luke-Acts thus becomes the point of entry, like Romans was to Reformation traditions. This is not intended to replaces theologies of the first or second article of the creed, but to fulfill the promise of a fully trinitarian theology. Let us see how this unfolds.

PENTECOSTAL AND PNEUMATOLOGICAL SOTERIOLOGY

Why start here? Among many other places to begin in the Pentecostal narrative (Acts 2) and among many other reasons that might be given in response, I might say, why not begin where the stakes appear to be highest, when Luke records the response to Peter's preaching of the crowd that had gathered: "Now when they heard this, they were cut to the heart and said to Peter and to the other apostles, 'Brothers, what should we do?'" (2:37). Peter's response provides in miniature what might be considered the soteriology of the Pentecost message: "Repent, and be baptized every one of you in the name of Jesus Christ so that your sins may be forgiven; and you will receive the gift of the Holy Spirit. For the promise is for you, for your children, and for all who are

3. These five themes might seem to be arbitrary. However, they follow the logic unfolded in my earlier *Spirit Poured Out on All Flesh*. The present essay can be read as a condensed account, albeit one informed, deepened, and even developed in and through a dozen years of hindsight (not to mention more than a dozen other monographs since).

4. Apologies for the many self-references in what follows; this essay brings together in a limited space work that I have been doing for the last two decades, so the discussion is streamlined, with the footnotes devoted to guiding those interested in further reading.

far away, everyone whom the Lord our God calls to him" (2:38–39).[5] Three sets of remarks are apropos here.[6]

First, pentecostal salvation, or salvation in these times that are after Pentecost, involves joining with the person of Christ, experiencing the forgiveness of sins, and receiving the gift of the Spirit. These are surely discrete but yet also related, even if the nature of their interrelationship might be understood variously. While classical Pentecostals might want to insist, especially drawing on other texts even in Acts, that the gift of the Spirit is subsequent to salvation, indeed granted to empower the witness of believers, the salvific gifts here that include the Spirit also surely do not have to operate with a narrow soteriological understanding. Salvation understood broadly might begin with the forgiveness of sins, but persists in and throughout "the last days" (2:17a) and culminates in the eschaton.[7] From that perspective, the gift of the Spirit can involve the power to witness, among other aspects, but that does not minimize the latter's salvific nature. Make no mistake then about this soteriological dimension of the pentecostal reality, as Luke immediately records that Peter "testified with many other arguments and exhorted them, saying, '*Save yourselves* from this corrupt generation'" (2:40, italics added).

Second, note the promise of the Spirit is "for you, for your children, and for all who are far away" (2:39). On the one hand, there are no spatial limits to the Spirit's outpouring. If the message of the coming reign of God (1:3) was intended to be spread "in Jerusalem, in all Judea and Samaria, and to the ends of the earth" (1:8), then it makes sense that the gift of the Spirit would be made available also to those at the brink of the (known) world. On the other hand, the promise is not first and foremost about geographic expanse (even if this is not neglected in the broader Acts narrative) but about temporal extent: "for your children" and theirs also! This temporal

5. Oneness Pentecostals insist that the entirety of the Bible's salvation message is wrapped up in this text. I would put things differently: that one can enter into the drama of salvation history from many scriptural pathways, this being no more or less important than any others. However, since ours is a pentecostal theological approach, such a ramp serves our purposes at this juncture. For more on the Oneness reading of, and debates about, this text, see Fudge, *Christianity Without the Cross*. My own account leans on and resonates more from Macchia, *Baptized in the Spirit*.

6. As will be clear as we proceed, I read Acts not first and foremost as an exegete in the classic senses of that notion, but as a theologian; mine is therefore a theological interpretation of Acts, one inflected by my pentecostal location and perspective. For more on such a pentecostal and also pneumatological and trinitarian hermeneutic, see my book *Hermeneutical Spirit*.

7. Now, see also Macchia, *Justified in the Spirit*.

and historical sense is actually also included within and embedded in the *eschatou tes ges* ("ends of the earth") so that the extent of the Spirit of Pentecost knows neither synchronic (the farthest reaches of the world) nor diachronic (the ends of time, even after innumerable generations of children) bounds.[8] In other words, the redemption wrought by the Pentecost event is cosmic in scope (cf. Rom 8:18–25, 37–39).

Last but not least, the pentecostal and pneumatological soteriology encompasses "everyone whom the Lord our God calls to him" (Acts 2:39b). Peter here is only repeating—albeit not merely as a repetition—what he has said earlier, adapting from the prophet Joel: "Then everyone who calls on the name of the Lord shall be saved" (2:21; cf. Joel 2:32a). Everyone is invited to repent, which involves invoking the Lord's name, and the possibility of such repentance and calling is itself dependent on the triune God's prior invitation, one now lavishly sounded in the Pentecost event. In contrast with the floods of destruction that visited the ancient cosmos, from the right hand of the Father (2:32–33) the Son inundates the world with the life-giving winds of the Spirit, thus fulfilling the prophetic pronouncement of old: "I will pour out my Spirit upon all flesh, and your sons and your daughters shall prophesy, and your young men shall see visions, and your old men shall dream dreams. Even upon my slaves, both men and women, in those days I will pour out my Spirit" (2:17b–18a). These are all-inclusive, even if binary categories: there are none who are not sons or daughters, none beyond those young or old, none in a third realm beyond slave or free. Such a pentecostal soteriology thereby is unconstrained and unrestricted in this "time of universal restoration" (3:21).

PENTECOSTAL AND PNEUMATOLOGICAL ECCLESIOLOGY

Does Luke in general or his book of Acts more specifically have a doctrine of the church? Perhaps there is no developed ecclesiology. Yet, arguably the Day of Pentecost outpouring re-establishes the people of God according to the new covenant, who are indwelt by the Spirit rather than circumcised according to the flesh. If the disciples were interested in restoring the ancient Israelite theocracy (1:6), the heavenly response was the blowing of the divine breath upon the face of the earth. Luke's

8. See Westhelle, *Eschatology and Space*, 132.

second book is thus both the "Acts of the Apostles" and the "Acts of the Holy Spirit." Whereas the Pauline letters acknowledge the body of Christ also as "the fellowship of the Spirit" (2 Cor 13:13), it is Luke's story that reflects most extensively the vitality of the divine breath in the work of the new people of God.

A pentecostal church is described at the end of Acts 2: "All who believed were together and had all things in common; they would sell their possessions and goods and distribute the proceeds to all, as any had need. Day by day, as they spent much time together in the temple, they broke bread at home and ate their food with glad and generous hearts, praising God and having the goodwill of all the people. Also, day by day the Lord added to their number those who were being saved" (2:44–47). Much has been said about the communal character of the church, and about its being constituted by worship, fellowship, and witness. The point is in part that the church exists as a social body, facilitating mutuality in the economic sphere and organizing human life in material, political, and spiritual ways, each distinct from, but yet interwoven with the others.[9] Herein lies the institutional dynamic of the church, which is generative of specific forms that arise and wane, which come and go, but always animated variously by the Spirit. There are no people of God apart from the Spirit's presence, even as there is no witness by, in, or through the members of this body and fellowship apart from the Spirit's gifts (see 1 Cor 12). There is a symbiosis, then, between the Spirit's impelling initiative and human response and activity, whether of individuals or of the church manifest as congregation, parish, community, or other collective and cooperative form.

Such symbiotic synergism is clearly depicted in the Pentecost event: "Suddenly from heaven there came a sound like the rush of a violent wind, and it filled the entire house where they were sitting. Divided tongues, as of fire, appeared among them, a tongue rested on each of them. All of them were filled with the Holy Spirit and began to speak in other languages, as the Spirit gave them ability" (2:2–4). The Spirit works, but creaturely reactivity and participation is presumed and involved. In other words, the Spirit's achievements and accomplishments are mediated through creaturely organs, bodies, and agents. Also, it is not just that the Spirit's manifestation catalyzes tongues-speech, but that such glossolalia resounds with linguistic particularity—"in other languages"—reflecting

9. For more, see Yong, *Who Is the Holy Spirit?*, part 3.

thereby the work of the Spirit as embracing rather than bypassing the culturality and sociality of human creatureliness. The languages that come forth do not eliminate but encapsulate the contingencies of human historicity. This is not far from the older and more historic sacramental ecclesiology that sees the church, its priesthood, and rituals as channels of redemptive grace. The overriding emphasis here, however, is on the ongoing vivaciousness of the divine breath, not on any specific rite or medium, but on human life in its socio-historical variability and tangibility.[10]

Of course, the point is not to build an entire ecclesiology on Acts 2. Yet, the ecclesiological implications of the Pentecost outpouring ought not to be neglected. Certainly Acts 2 is followed also by an extended narrative that is rich with implications for the doctrine of the church.[11] Foregrounding Acts ecclesiologically does nothing to minimize more explicit teachings about the church in the rest of the New Testament, but might shed some new light on that material from such a pneumatologically robust set of perspectives. My suggestions recognize that multi-directional ecclesiological dialogues and explorations are already ongoing—e.g., pentecostal theologians are already thinking about ecclesiology in light of pentecostal spirituality and practice; ecumenical theologians have begun to reflect on the work of the Spirit in relationship to the church; and ecclesiologists of all stripes are poised to consider the church from such a pentecostal and pneumatological vantage point[12]—and hope that they will only continue to flourish and even proliferate.

PENTECOSTAL AND PNEUMATOLOGICAL MISSIOLOGY

It might be argued that the missiological turn is most organic to the overarching telos of Acts, particularly in terms of its providing a synopsis of early Christian evangelistic efforts moving out from Jerusalem into Judea, Samaria, and the furthermost parts of the earth: Rome, which is where Acts 28 ends up, therefore represents the imperial and therefore most distant outer realm from a Jerusalem-centric point of view. In effect, however, the shift from pneumatological ecclesiology to pneumatological missiology is one that moves to the other side of the same coin, so to speak.

10. I discuss parallels between pneumatological and sacramental ecclesiologies in my "Spirit, the Body, and the Sacraments."

11. See Robinson and Wall, *Called to Be Church*.

12. E.g., Green, *Pentecostal Ecclesiology*; Peterson, *Who Is the Church?*

The church—as the body of Christ and as the fellowship of the Spirit—is what she is in and through mission. Three domains of the church's mission understood in light of the Spirit's work can be elaborated upon here,[13] building upon the preceding as well as developing some new trajectories.

First, it has already been noted that pentecostal communal and economic life has a missional aspect: "day by day the Lord added to their number those who were being saved" (2:47). Those who enjoy the fellowship of the Spirit are missional not only when they go outside of the community, but when they live in solidarity with those most vulnerable within. From this perspective, pentecostal missiology involves not just theories regarding evangelism and church planting, as important as these are, but also social, economic, and related considerations. As such, a pentecostal and pneumatological missiology is inherently public and political, addressing both what the church is as a social body and what its members do both within the community and on its margins in relationship to outsiders. Public and political theology as herein understood involves both how Christians ought to engage the state or be responsible citizens and how the church exists as a body politic, bearing witness in word and deed to Jesus as Messiah in the power of the Holy Spirit. Yes, Spirit-empowered believers witness within a polis, but they are also a political space and form defined by allegiance to Jesus Christ rather than to Caesar.[14]

Second, pentecostal missiology engages not only the economically vulnerable, but also those marginalized because of sensory impairments, deprivations, and disabilities. This missiological horizon is counter-intuitive for a number of reasons, but may be warranted on further consideration. If Pentecostals themselves, because of their emphases on divine healing, have not been welcoming to people who live with (and are not cured from) disabilities, then a fully charismatic ecclesiology embraces—or ought to embrace—rather than sideline members who are considered weaker or impaired.[15] If one wonders where people with disabilities are in the Pentecost narrative, they are actually widespread in the wider Lukan text as recipients of the gospel wrought by the Spirit whose work is bound up with *all flesh*.[16] If so, we are lacking a disability missiology, or a missiology of disability. The Spirit whose sounds are heard, whose rushings are

13. See Yong, *Missiological Spirit*.

14. Developed in Yong, *In the Days of Caesar*.

15. See Yong, *Bible, Disability, and the Church*, esp. chs. 3–4.

16. E.g., Parsons, *Body and Character in Luke and Acts*; cf. Lawrence, *Sense and Stigma in the Gospels*.

felt, and whose potency is palpably imbibed, catalyzes for those with ears to hear and eyes to see (pun intended!) fresh articulation and formulation from this pentecostal site.[17] In sum, Luke's pentecostal theology envisions the flourishing of all flesh, not necessarily their curing, but in their health and salvation as those on whom the Spirit descends and inhabits.

Third, for our pneumatological-missiological purposes, the many languages of Pentecost resounded by the Spirit's outpouring herald the divine intention to redeem the many cultures of the world and perhaps also their religious forms. The pentecostal gift empowers rather than inhibits the diversity of voices and the specificity of their linguistic expressions: "each one heard them speaking in the native language of each. . . . 'And how is it that we hear, each of us, in our own native language? . . . In our own languages we hear them speaking about God's deeds of power'" (2:6, 8, 11). A pentecostal missiology renders urgent, then, theologies of cultures (as carriers of languages) and, by extension, theologies of religions, in order to explore further how the eschatological fellowship of the Spirit will involve those from every tongue, tribe, people, and nation before the throne of the Father. Cultures are the matrices of social life within which embodied creatures like *homo sapiens* are formed, so it might be expected that the cosmic pentecostal deluge enters into the linguistic fabric of such spaces precisely in order to purify and redeem them. To the extent that culture involves a religious dimension, pentecostal missiology now involves this depth domain of the human experience.[18]

PENTECOSTAL PNEUMATOLOGY AND TRINITARIAN THEOLOGY

We have already covered much ground in sketching a pentecostal soteriology, ecclesiology, and missiology, or at least strands pertaining to these loci. The running thread throughout so far, as is obvious, is the pneumatological: the person and work of the Holy Spirit. How else might we understand this Lukan pentecostal "character"? Here we come to one of the key *theological* questions: the trinitarian one. I will attempt to untangle briefly the issues in three directions.

17. See Yong, *Theology and Down Syndrome*; cf. Conner, *Disabling Mission, Enabling Witness.*

18. I have written extensively at this juncture, including but not limited to: *Beyond the Impasse*; and *Hospitality and the Other.*

To begin, the Spirit of Pentecost is the Spirit of Jesus, the Galilean who is at least the mediating conduit of the Spirit from the Father (2:32–33). This same Jesus is the one who said at the end of the first Lukan book: "I am sending upon you what my Father promised; so stay here in the city until you have been clothed with power from on high" (Luke 24:49). To be sure, Jesus is who he is as the Messiah or the anointed one: It was God who "anointed Jesus of Nazareth with the Holy Spirit and with power [and] he went about doing good and healing all who were oppressed by the devil, for God was with him" (Acts 10:38). This is consistent with the gospel portrait of Jesus' life and entire public ministry. Luke records that his public appearance involved such pneumatic expression and charismatic confession: "Jesus, filled with the power of the Spirit, returned to Galilee," and when he arrived at the synagogue, he read from the scriptural scroll, "The Spirit of the Lord is upon me, because he has anointed me to bring good news to the poor" (Luke 4:14a, 18). Thus there is a kind of trinitarian mutuality between the Son and the Spirit, at least in these Lukan texts: The Son pours out the Spirit, but does so as the one anointed by the Spirit.[19]

To speak about trinitarian mutuality, however, is to involve Son and Spirit with the Father. The Spirit of Jesus is also the Spirit of God. If the classical tradition defined these relations in terms of generations and processions and insisted either on the primordiality of the Father (the Eastern tradition) or on the crucial centrality of the Filioque (the Western churches), a Lukan-pentecostal account is amenable to these formulations, albeit it resists being wedded to either.[20] Yet, the Spirit of Jesus poured out at Pentecost can be also comprehended not just in terms of the Joel prophecy from the Hebrew Bible, but also in relationship (a) to the "wind from God [that] swept over the face of the [primeval] waters" (Gen 1:2), (b) to the divine breath that "renew[s] the face of the ground" (Ps 104:30b), and (c) to the divine blowing through which the "wilderness becomes a fruitful field" (Isa 32:15). While the Law, the Psalms, and the Prophets testify to Jesus (see Luke 24:44b), the redemption Pentecost accomplishes in and through the face of Jesus as the Spirit-inspired and empowered one exists in both continuity and discontinuity with the achievements of the divine breath as recorded in the pages of ancient Israel's sacred texts. As such, the Spirit of Pentecost, of Jesus, and of the church is distinct from, albeit also related to, the divine winds—the

19. See my essay "Christological Constants in Shifting Contexts."

20. See also my essay "I Believe in the Holy Spirit."

breath of Yahweh (and of the Father)—fluttering at cosmic creation, hovering over Israel, and discerned across the pages of the first covenant.

The specific nature of the difference or distinction might be difficult to clearly elaborate. One feature is the eschatological opening, which is enlarged through "the last days" of the Acts narrative in light of Jesus' life and message about the impending divine reign, and culminating in the apocalyptic symbolism that may be just as obscuring as illuminating.[21] Yet, part of what makes the pneumatological motif complex is its multiple and overlapping semantic fields. If the Spirit of Jesus and of God in the Christian Testament is also the divine wind of the Hebrew Bible, then we can appreciate that this same wind is creaturely breath in both testaments (Gen 1:30; 2:6).[22] Luke's Pentecost story does not make much of the divine breath as life-giving, but instead focuses on the divine wind as witness-empowering. Nevertheless, such inspiration de-emphasizes the deity's transcendence and accentuates instead the divinity's immanence, on, in, and through creaturely flesh. Hence on this side of eternity, there is an ongoing need for the discernment of spirits—not just evil spirits from the Holy Spirit, but of the divine spirit and its creaturely animations. In the end, even acknowledgment of the name of Jesus is less than definitive, as "Not everyone who says to me, 'Lord, Lord', will enter the kingdom of heaven, but only one who does the will of my Father in heaven" (Matt 7:21). The fruits of the Spirit (Gal 5:22–24) then become important indicators that the message and reality of the divine realm Jesus heralded is at least partially present.[23] The point is that the economic missions of the Son and the Spirit are related but distinct even in the present dispensation, albeit also converging eschatologically so that God, the Father, "may be all in all" (1 Cor 15:28b).

PNEUMATOLOGICAL THEOLOGY AS ONGOING TASK

A pentecostal theology oriented around the Spirit of life cannot have a premature conclusion "now [while] we see in a mirror, dimly . . . [and]

21. Which I elucidate in my *Revelation*.

22. For more on *pneuma* in the New Testament as ambiguously divine and human, see Moule, *Holy Spirit*, 7–12.

23. The ideas discussed in this and the preceding paragraphs are complicated aspects of trinitarian theological reflection; further unraveling can be found in my work on theological hermeneutics: Yong, *Spirit-Word-Community*. See also the more succinct account in the concluding chapter of my *Dialogical Spirit*.

know only in part" (1 Cor 13:12a). Hence this final section gestures toward the kind of theological vision that a pneumatological imagination ought to instigate. Our efforts so far suggest that a pentecostal theology is a pneumatological theology. However, this does not mean a theology of the Spirit only, but a theology inspired by pneumatic elements and perspectives. Thus we have observed a pentecostal and pneumatological theology of salvation, of the church, and of the church's mission, for instance. In these last few paragraphs, we anticipate other venues for pneumatological distillation and development.

One direction is simply a reconsideration of the historic theological loci from such a pentecostal-pneumatological-and-trinitarian frame. In this case, we do not begin with God the creator or redeemer (the first article of the Creed), but with God the Spirit that was poured out at Pentecost in order to inaugurate this final "time" of the coming divine reign. Such an account would be also a thoroughly eschatological pneumatology and theology, a theological vision that begins with the anticipated reign of God ushered in by the Spirit and works "backward," even, toward a pneumatological theology of creation, a pneumatological anthropology, a pneumatological hamartiology (theology of sin), a pneumatological (Spirit-) christology, and a pneumatological theology of revelation, etc.[24] The contours of such a constructive program can be discerned from the preceding forays into pneumatological soteriology and ecclesiology, for instance. Theological dogmatics in such a scheme therefore would be propelled pentecostally, infused pneumatologically, and oriented eschatologically. The person and work of Christ now can be considered in each of these loci also as charismatically messianic. The goal is a fully trinitarian theological conception rather than one in which the Spirit's person and work is compartmentalized in (minimally) select spheres.

Another approach extends the many tongues of the Spirit metaphor beyond its cultural (and religious) domain so that Pentecost's multivocal linguisticality opens up otherwise to plurimorphic discursivity. What this might mean is that the Spirit's redemptive work could be operative not just amid so-called natural languages (in their cultural modalities), but also through humanly constructed discursive sites such as academic disciplines or scientific fields of inquiry. The latter are not less constituted by culturally formed practices that require years of initiation and socialization, even as such social undertakings are also always liable to be

24. My own efforts in this direction can be found in *Renewing Christian Theology*.

distorted by sin and thereby destructive of human life and community. Yet, in principle such an extension of theological imagination after Pentecost suggests that the many (modern scientific) disciplines or fields of inquiry can be discerned also, each in its own "tongue," as declaring or "speaking about God's deeds of power" (Acts 2:11). From this perspective, the multiplicity of discursive sites emergent from within the human community, unfolding historically over space and time, can bear witness to and through the ends of the cosmos (to the degree that our analytical instruments can detect these edges).[25] As all truth is God's truth, then the methods and disciplines that enable access to that truth become testimonies of and by the Spirit to the wondrous works of God.[26]

If a pentecostal perspective thereby opens up both to a pneumatological theology and a pneumatological understanding of and engagement with many other realms of human knowing, then in principle any scope of inquiry could benefit from such an approach. One example is that I have been motivated, despite being musically challenged, to look at praise and worship from such a pentecostal and pneumatological perspective.[27] I want to suggest that musicality's soundscape insists on more pneumatic modes of engagement and analysis, and therefore gains from the kind of pneumatologically oriented sensitivities generated by the pentecostal field. This is not to say that only enthusiastic charismatics can be musicologists, but it does boldly wager that a pentecostal lens might make a difference both for understanding theologically the phenomenon of sound and music and for gaining leverage on how such assessments return to make a difference for theological reflection. Pentecostal and pneumatological lenses hereby operate dialogically and dialectically: to engender perspective on the focus of inquiry which then returns to inform the theological task. If the Spirit brings new life from out of the old, then a pentecostal and pneumatological theology ought also to spawn new understandings from familiar sites.[28]

25. I make this argument in *The Spirit of Creation*, esp. chs. 1–2; see also Yong and Smith, *Science and the Spirit*.

26. Thus I have been working with Dale M. Coulter on a common project: (published later as) *The Holy Spirit and Higher Education*.

27. See Ingalls and Yong, *Spirit of Praise*, including my concluding chapter to this exploratory volume.

28. Thanks to my graduate assistant, Hoon Jung, for proofreading this essay; any error of fact or interpretation remains my own responsibility.

Chapter 2

Lydia amid the Jewish Diaspora

Apostolic Migration and Belonging—Then and Now

From the beginning human beings have been on the move, crisscrossing and forging new migratory treks whether from "out of Africa" as one theory of ancient human origins hypothesizes or from and to multiple regional locations across Eurasia (in one of the other prominent evolutionary models). Movement suggests push and pull forces, navigated further via the complexity of human needs, desires, and curiosities.[1] Yet any new location is "home" for a period, no matter how long the stay for individuals or their groups. What does "belonging" mean or how is "home" made for *homo peregrinator/migrator*, human beings as perennially wandering and traveling creatures?[2]

In this short essay I want to explore this question by looking at the book of Acts, particularly a section in chapter 16 on the story of Lydia.[3] How might we understand "belonging" through her eyes particularly, and also against the backdrop of the apostolic mission in Philippi? We

1. I write in part from out of my own experience as a 1.5-generation Asian American (born in Malaysia but raised since the age of ten in the USA); see my *Future of Evangelical Theology*.

2. I have published a few essays on migration, e.g., "Im/Migrant Spirit," and "Informality, Illegality, and Improvisation."

3. I have drawn inspiration for this essay from a sermon I preached far away from my home: "Pentecostal Witness in the Neighborhood," Assembleia de Deus, Gramado, Brazil, July 15, 2023; for more on the centrality of the Acts narrative to my work as a pentecostal theologian, see Yong, *Who Is the Holy Spirit?*

will conclude with some reflections about how belonging can take root amid the contemporary generation of global migrants and how we can encourage belonging across the challenges of the worldwide diaspora of peoples.

LYDIA THE MIGRANT

While Luke is not first and foremost attempting to convey theological perspectives on migration and belonging through the Lydia story, I believe these lenses open up some aspects of his narrative for our purposes.[4] Here is what we are told in the book of Acts:

> [11] We set sail from Troas and took a straight course to Samothrace, the following day to Neapolis, [12] and from there to Philippi, which is a leading city of the district of Macedonia and a Roman colony. We remained in this city for some days. [13] On the sabbath day we went outside the gate by the river, where we supposed there was a place of prayer; and we sat down and spoke to the women who had gathered there. [14] A certain woman named Lydia, a worshiper of God, was listening to us; she was from the city of Thyatira and a dealer in purple cloth. The Lord opened her heart to listen eagerly to what was said by Paul. [15] When she and her household were baptized, she urged us, saying, "If you have judged me to be faithful to the Lord, come and stay at my home." And she prevailed upon us. (Acts 16:11–15)

Let me make a few observations about Lydia given our migration focus.

First, Lydia appears to have been a gentile and a migrant, from the city of Thyatira in the middle of Asia Minor, to the port Macedonian city of Philippi, a route less accessible except (as even Paul and Luke—note the "we" in v. 11—traveled) by ships over sea. Second, as "a dealer in purple cloth," she was a textile merchant (perhaps retailer and wholesaler),[5] effectively seeking to either expand or transition her business from Thyatira to Philippi. Third, even if the lack of mention of a husband does not definitively indicate she was a widow or even unmarried, that members of her household were baptized and that the apostles were able to accept

4. Other treatments of Luke-Acts from a migration perspective include Stenschke, "Migration and Mission According to the Book of Acts"; and Barreto, "Gospel on the Move."

5. Reimer, *Women in the Acts of the Apostles*, 105–9.

her invitation to *her* home strongly suggests she was the head of her own household. Finally, for now, being a gentile "worshiper of God" meant that they existed within a liminal ethnic, religio-cultural space,[6] and in this hybridized identify may have moved for many, including specifically religio-cultural, reasons, like that of finding a Jewish community to worship with.

Now, even if it is true Luke might have wished to argue that Lydia, "because of her gender, ethnographic, and occupational profile would be considered unsuitable for acceptance into the inner core of church participation,"[7] this does not minimize also the following: that the migration of a putatively single woman or mother and her household across seas is not easy; that if she had been motivated by religious pursuits, she was effectively a doubly marginalized person: first because of her gender and second because of crossing cultural-religious boundaries via her religious affiliation with God-worshiping Jews; and that alongside any religiously inspired reasons for migration there may have also been, for such an individual (and her household), challenging economic and financial circumstances that further fueled the major move to re-establish the business in another, perhaps more favorable—even a "leading city"—location. And even if she may have been a relatively successful and independent businesswoman,[8] that does not mean that her making her way as an immigrant to a foreign city was easy. All of this is consistent with one such as Lydia joining with the group of praying women that the text indicates was piously sought out.

6. Barreto, *Ethnic Negotiations*, 133–39, discusses Lydia's "ambiguous identities" in light of Luke's discussion of Timothy's ethnically mixed heritage in the preceding pericope (Acts 16:1–5) in order to highlight how this portion of the Acts narrative sheds light on early Christian hybridity, wherein indigenous messianic communities navigated between local autonomy and Roman imperialism: "Neither accommodating nor resisting the encroachments of Roman power" (187).

7. Gruca-Macauley, *Lydia as a Rhetorical Construct in Acts*, 277.

8. Calpino summarizes Lydia this way: "While not one of the elite of Philippi, Lydia was a woman of some means who was an independent householder who also made the religious decisions for all those attached to her οἶκος, and she could decide to whom she wished to offer hospitality, all without recourse to male oversight." *Women, Work and Leadership in Acts*, 223.

MIGRATION AND THE JEWISH DIASPORA

It is important here to comment further on the fact that this group of women meeting by the riverside was also part of the Jewish diaspora in the first-century Mediterranean world. These "Jews of the dispersion," as they are called variously across the New Testament (e.g., John 7:35; Jas 1:1; 1 Pet 1:1),[9] had either migrated or, because of prior political and other circumstances, found themselves making a living outside of Palestine. Yet they had kept their Jewish customs and commitments, and some of them found means to travel back and forth to their homeland, oftentimes when there were major Jewish feasts and festivals, like such as the Pentecost feast in Jerusalem that the book of Acts says included and involved "devout Jews from every nation under heaven" (2:5).

Our migration lens further illuminates these facets of the Lukan narrative regarding Lydia. First, the Jewish diaspora attempted to maintain Sabbath but, in this case, gathered outside the city; even if the reasons for this location are not mentioned (maybe because the Jewish community in Philippi was an exceedingly small one at this time), it is not inconceivable that there were also "local restrictions and anti-Judaism (Acts 16:20–21)"[10] sentiments and other impediments to the establishment of a synagogue within the city (which Paul went looking to find, as the text suggests, and ended up "outside the gate by the river, where we supposed there was a place of prayer"). Second, this nascent Jewish site of prayer (and perhaps other religious practices) drew, so far, only women; the diaspora men may have been busy trying to make it even on the Sabbath (diaspora peoples adapt their customs when these have measurable impact on their financial and economic survival), although in any case, this was surely a fledgling community, negotiating their immigrant status and circumstances as people of faith.

For our purposes, there is benefit to extrapolating from this passage to Paul's later letter to the Philippian church. When set side-by-side, we note that the latter's membership was predominantly if not only gentile (all of the names of the congregation mentioned in the letter are Greek), consistent with Paul and his team accepting Lydia's invitation and

9. On the diasporas of the James and Peter texts, see, respectively, my essays "Not Many of You Should Become Teachers . . ." (also chapter 9 of this volume); "Homily: From the Jewish Diaspora to the Indian (Christian) Diaspora" (also chapter 7 of this volume).

10. Keener, *Acts*, 3:2384.

thereafter establishing the *ekklesia* in that city not with the Jews but within Lydia's home (and perhaps also in conjunction with the home of the jailer whose household is also baptized [16:34]);[11] that the gentile women among them continued to bear the marks of struggle (e.g., the reference to Euodia and Syntyche in Phil 4:2), perhaps not qualitatively different from what Lydia herself had to traverse as an immigrant; and that these gentile believers had to carefully if not also apologetically engage with members of the Jewish community at Philippi who appeared to have been hostile to Paul's efforts to build up the messianic community there (see Phil 3:2–3). Here we see further the challenges of diasporic immigration, how marginalized (sometimes doubly so) communities have to struggle to survive, not to mention flourish, while relating to and interacting with their neighbors (often the dominant cultural hosts).

APOSTOLIC BELONGING THEN AND NOW

To belong has to be self-claimed and confessed. One cannot be forced to belong to others or to any group. One commits oneself to or finds oneself belonging to a community. Hence belonging has a fundamentally testimonial character: I narrate how I have found myself accepted by others in some or other respect. Not feeling like one belongs perpetuates distance between us and any others in that space, or moves us along in search of "home."[12]

Whatever success she may have had as a seller of purple cloth in Thyatira, Lydia nevertheless left that city in her search for "home." She sought this at least in part, however tentatively, in a new location (at Philippi) and with a new community (with the community of Yahweh that worshiped the God of Abraham, Isaac, and Jacob). This led her to the river outside of Philippi. Unlike the slave-girl who followed Paul and his friends to the place of prayer outside the city and made money for her owners by heralding the gospel evangelists (Acts 16:16–17), the more or less affluent (we don't quite know) seller of purple goods was

11. While the jailer appears to play a secondary, if any, role in the establishment of the Philippian messianic community, Lydia's ecclesial leadership was insufficient to prevent Paul's incarceration, and she was "unable to shield the missionaries from anti-Jewish attacks" in this colonial city (Reimer, *Women in the Acts of the Apostles*, 263).

12. I have learned much about this aspect of *belonging* as testimonial (rather than impositional) from John Swinton's work on disability, including his "From Inclusion to Belonging"; see also Swinton, *Becoming Friends of Time*.

not looking only for economic boon and financial opportunity; instead, she resonated with what she heard shared by Paul and his friends, to the extent that she then invited them: "'If you have judged me to be faithful to the Lord, come and stay at my home.'" This relevantly cautious invitation is to have been expected especially if Lydia was a widow so as to avoid causing scandal about having men in her home. Yet the more important point for us is that she and the members of her household—perhaps even a "community of work and faith,"[13] if indeed she was (now) an unmarried independent businesswoman with other partners and collaborators—however long they had been in Philippi, had not yet fully experienced *belonging* within their house. After Paul and his colleagues were released from the Philippian jail to her house (16:40), they encouraged the brothers and sisters there in the faith. Although Lydia is not mentioned again (she also does not appear in Paul's letter to the Philippians), her house had become the gathering site for the new people of God at this prominent city and, perhaps more importantly for our purposes, her abode had become a place of belonging even for traveling evangelists like Paul and his fellow missioners and all who embraced the gospel through their (and Lydia's) witness at Philippi and the surrounding regions of this Macedonian city.[14]

The Jewish women who had gathered regularly on the Sabbath by the river outside Philippi were also in need of belonging. Like Lydia, they were multiply marginalized due to their gender (as women in a patriarchal world), ethnicity (e.g., as Palestinians in the Macedonian region and, in the case of Lydia, as someone from Asia Minor in a principal city of Macedonia), and religiosity (e.g., as Jews in a Greco-Roman world and, in the case of Lydia, as a God-worshiper in Caesar's world). Perhaps more of these Jewish women might have found themselves belonging in the new ecclesial community that emerged at Philippi if they had been widows (as we surmise Lydia was) and been unencumbered by commitments to their husbands. Yet we know that by the second or third century, a synagogue had been established in this important Macedonian city,[15] perhaps from out of the faithfulness of this initial group of women who sought a

13. Reimer, *Women in the Acts of the Apostles*, 111.

14. I make this point also in light of David Lertis Matson's argument, engaging in part with the Lydia and jailer stories at Philippi, that "the pattern of the household mission legitimates the Gentiles as equal members of the new salvific community by stressing their full acceptance at table with Jews." Matson, *Household Conversion in Acts*, 188.

15. Keener, *Acts*, 3:2384n799.

safe place for prayer and other Jewish religious practice on the Sabbath as it was the custom of Yahweh-worshipers across the diaspora. Meanwhile, they persevered at this site despite having to congregate outside the city gate, since it was during those weekly moments that this immigrant community found also sustenance—relationally, interpersonally, and spiritually—in their home away from home.

What else then can we say about *belonging* for diasporic or immigrant groups today? I believe we can do not much better, and surely no worse, than to follow in the apostolic footsteps narrated in this Lukan text. First, Paul and his compatriots had to be specifically led by the Spirit to cross the borders into Macedonia (Acts 16:9–10), which means that they themselves were now in foreign territory, doubly emphasized, and it was in this context that they sought out welcome, particularly among others who would have known of the God of Abraham, Isaac, and Jacob. While this was consistent with their conviction that the deity's presence was no longer limited to the Jewish temple but was now made available any and everywhere by the Spirit of the resurrected Messiah sent in Yahweh's name, their own tenuousness as cultural, ethnic, and border-crossing migrants should not be understated. This invites any of us who also might be on marginal sites and in liminal positionalities to seek and search out others who are looking for belonging and to announce that this is finally provided by the God of Jesus Christ who alone fulfills our every and deepest longings.

Second and more even more importantly, if that can be imagined, every space in which the Spirit of the living Jesus is invited can be a home and thereby site of belonging, even and especially for hybridized immigrants of diasporic communities that may be continually on the move.[16] Whether it is individuals like Lydia who may be continually unsettled or groups like Jews of the dispersion however long ago or recently separated from their cultural lands (or places of birth), "the city that has foundations, whose architect and builder is God" (Heb 11:10) is anticipatable wherever God in Christ is present by the Holy Spirit. Thus, even the ancient Israelites who were taken into captivity by foreign invaders were told to "seek the welfare of the city where I have sent you into exile, and pray to the Lord on its behalf, for in its welfare you will find your welfare" (Jer 29:7).

16. See also my essay "From Every Tribe."

The early apostolic believers were promised that the gift of the Spirit would be available to them, their children, and "all who are far away" (Acts 2:39b). Wherever from Jerusalem to the ends of the earth, the Spirit is available to all persons (Acts 1:8; 2:17), to fill their spaces, times, and habitations with the divine presence.[17] Thus, will those from every nation, people, tribe, and language experience belonging to the divine reign in their homes, their cultures, and their lives, whether Jewish and God-fearing gentiles in the first century or those trekking global migration routes in the twenty-first.[18]

17. See also my "The Lukan Commission: The Spirit, Im/migration, and the De-Construction of Empire—Acts 1:6–8," in Yong, *Kerygmatic Spirit*, 52–62; cf. also Yong, *Hermeneutical Spirit*, for more on the book of Acts in relationship to these various themes covered in this essay.

18. As I am finishing this essay, I am also finishing Day, *Azusa Reimagined*, wherein she urges a community of belonging from out of the early modern pentecostal revival which nurtured spaces of belonging for black and brown, male and female, and poor bodies, thereby constituting a supportive vision for how marginalized, oppressed, and migrant bodies can find home.

Chapter 3

The Spirit Poured Out in the Last Days

Toward a Pneumatology of Final Creation

The Christian theological tradition instinctively recognizes that the three articles of its central confession—the Nicene Creed regarding the Father, the Son, and the Holy Spirit—unfold a narrative of creation (the Almighty God), redemption (Jesus Christ), and the world to come (the Spirit).[1] As such, a theology of the Holy Spirit, pneumatology, is intrinsically also a theology of the coming reign of God: an eschatology, more precisely.[2] Christian eschatology, however, can be and has been framed variously: about the repair of a broken (fallen) world and the restoration of the primordial creation on the one hand, or about the full maturation of the created order through arrival of the so-called *last things* that are ahead of us on the other hand, just to name two constructs. But if the historic tradition associates the Father with the doctrine of creation and the Son with the doctrine of redemption, an emerging pneumatological paradigm, what some call a theology of the Third Article,[3] might overcome such correlationist conceptualization. I will suggest in this essay that eschatology is not merely associated with the Holy Spirit but can be substantively reconsidered in pneumatological perspective.[4]

1. See Yong, "I Believe in the Holy Spirit."
2. Also Yong, "Coming Spirit of Theology."
3. E.g., Habets, *Third Article Theology*.
4. The overarching frame of such a project can be found in Yong, *Renewing Christian Theology*, ch. 2 and passim.

What emerges is a way of thinking about the last things in terms of final creation, more specifically, a teleological understanding of new creation that sees the origins, renewal, and zenith of all things in light of the work of the divine Spirit.

Rather than develop the basic thesis about the Spirit and new creation in a more abstractly articulated manner in the genre of systematics,[5] or even in a more interdisciplinary mode in dialogue with the sciences,[6] our goal in this essay is to shore up the scriptural underpinnings of such a theological vision. We proceed in three steps: first, developing the pneumatological credentials of our eschatological and cosmic frame via the Pentecost narrative in the book of Acts; next, exploring further what might be called a pneumatology of fallen-and-being-redeemed creation through Paul's letter to the Romans; and finally, extrapolating from the pneumatologically inspired call of the Spirit for all creation to "Come" and be renewed in the Apocalypse. We will conclude by returning, briefly, to take theological stock of what we have gained in search of a teleological and eschatological pneumatology of final creation that is in some respects a renewal and restoration of the old but in other respects a heralding of the new.

One set of caveats before proceeding. My training is neither in biblical studies nor in exegesis, but in religious studies and theology. As such, those working in the latter domains might consider that the approach charted here is arbitrary, privileging some texts and leaving others aside. Further, some biblical theologians who might chance upon this piece at this point might feel it imbibes the "proof-texting" method from a prior generation. Yet biblical scholars like the one to whom this volume is dedicated were among the first to inspire for me the possibility of reading scripture pentecostally.[7] (As noted in the acknowledgments to this volume [above], this essay first appeared in a Festschrift devoted to Rickie Moore.) This essay thus ought to be read at least in part as an outgrowth of the question: What does a pentecostal hermeneutic look like?[8] More

5. E.g., Yong, "*Creator Spiritus* and the Spirit of Christ."

6. The rudiments of which have already been sketched in Yong, *Spirit of Creation*.

7. Rickie Moore's early essays, "Canon and Charisma in the Book of Deuteronomy," and "Deuteronomy and the Fire of God," were foundational for my imagining a pentecostal hermeneutic; these have been reprinted in Moore, *Spirit of the Old Testament*, chs. 2 and 3.

8. I do not capitalize *pentecostal* when used as an adjective, whether as related to the Day of Pentecost narrative in Acts 2 or to the modern movement that goes by that name; I capitalize such when used with regard to nouns.

precisely, I present a pentecostal perspective now also through the lenses of the emerging theological interpretation of scripture conversation that invites systematicians like myself undertaking responsible readings of the biblical canon—perhaps acceptable even to at least some in the biblical studies guild—from a more or less confessional perspective.[9] I will in the rest of these pages further clarify when appropriate the methodological warrants of this exercise from within this hermeneutical space. In the end, though, I grant that my own ambitions as a pentecostal and systematic theologian are to return repeatedly to the scriptural traditions to situate any speculative or dialogical considerations squarely within the Christian communal endeavor, and hence will also point to other such forays I have made previously as relevant to the task at hand.[10]

THE SPIRIT REDEEMING THE FIRST CREATION: ACTS 1–3

As a pentecostal theologian, I begin with the book of Acts. Yet I begin here also as a Christian theologian since Luke's second volume belongs not to one family within the Christian community but to all. Further, I start here also in recognition that the Christian experience is defined not only with regard to Jesus in his incarnation, death, resurrection, and ascension, but also vis-à-vis the one whose condescension and ascension were undertaken fully as the anointed one, the Christ, who then poured out of his Holy Spirit upon "all flesh" (Acts 2:17b). In short, I begin with Acts 2 because Christian identity cannot be found except in and through both Easter *and* Pentecost.[11] There is a sense in which a pentecostal approach literally begins with Acts—consider for instance a way of reading the Lukan Third Gospel (written first) in light of the Pentecost event

9. See my book *Hermeneutical Spirit*.

10. Although quite influential in my scholarship—see also Moore and Peterson, *Voice, Word, and Spirit*, and its imprint in my *Mission After Pentecost*—my most treasured memories with Rickie remain those moments earlier in my scholarly sojourn when he prayed with me, and I felt the presence of the Spirit touch the depths of my being through his prayers; it is this Spirit about which I write in this essay, scripturally informed as Rickie's pneumatology certainly is, but also affectively mediated through the perlocutionary effects of powerfully spirited prayers offered up by Rickie on my behalf.

11. See my *Spirit Poured Out on All Flesh*; a more theoretically and theologically substantive formulation of this pentecostal and pneumatological starting point is Yong, *Spirit-Word-Community*.

(written second)[12]—even if we don't arrive at Acts directly but through the Gospels, in terms of the canonical layout and the Hebrew Bible preceding that.

But to say that Christian identity, theological and otherwise, is pentecostally initiated is also to say that such identity is eschatologically oriented from the beginning. The divine breath poured on at Pentecost arrives "in the last days" (Acts 2:17a). This is not so much the last days inferno that consumes the world found in other parts of the Christian Testament (e.g., 2 Pet 3:10); rather, it is the time when "everyone who calls on the name of the Lord shall be saved" (Acts 2:21). More exactly, as Peter says when speaking to the crowd gathered at Jerusalem on that Pentecost event (as recorded by Luke), it is the time when the gift of promised Holy Spirit will be made available "for you, for your children, and for all who are far away, everyone whom the Lord our God calls to him" (2:39). *Far away* in this text in all likelihood included the gentile mission that is to be unfolded in the rest of the Acts narrative,[13] and which is implied to be continued among the (gentile) readers of this book beyond the account. By extension, but also with regard to the promise that the gift of the Spirit is for empowered witness so that "you [the twelve apostles and other believers] will be my witnesses in Jerusalem, in all Judea and Samaria, and to the ends of the earth [*eschatou tes ges*]" (1:8), the "ends of the earth" are to be understood not only geographically but also temporally or, more emphatically, eschatologically (from the Greek *eschatou*). Hence that the promise of the Spirit's outpouring has implications and applications across the spaces *and times* of the fullness of days that achieves God's final redemption.[14] Put starkly, authentic Christian existence is always pentecostal in the present dispensation, which means it is both pneumatological and eschatological: full of the Spirit in the present time of God's renewal and restoration that signals the passing away of the older (first) creation and the dawning of the coming (second and new) creation.

Hence this Lukan eschatological pneumatology—or pneumatological eschatology—involves both present and future dimensions. In the next segment of the Acts narrative, after the healing of the man at the Beautiful Gate (3:1–10), Peter now speaks to the crowd that had gathered around Solomon's Portico to marvel at this miracle: "Repent therefore,

12. I attempt such elsewhere; see Yong, *Who Is the Holy Spirit?*

13. See Keener, *Acts*, 1:987.

14. See Westhelle, *Eschatology and Space*, 132.

and turn to God so that your sins may be wiped out, so that times of refreshing may come from the presence of the Lord, and that he may send the Messiah appointed for you, that is, Jesus, who must remain in heaven until the time of universal restoration that God announced long ago through his holy prophets" (3:19–21). Three aspects of this text ought to be highlighted for our purposes. First, there is a historical contingency foregrounded in this Petrine invitation: Human repentance is called to participate in this eschatological work of the Spirit of God. Such creaturely involvement can be identified also in the Pentecost event itself when the outpoured divine breath nevertheless includes and does not bypass human responsiveness and agency: "All of them were filled with the Holy Spirit and began to speak in other languages, as the Spirit gave them ability" (2:4). Second, the culmination of God's eschatological work inaugurated on the Day of Pentecost anticipates both a future return of Jesus and a universal restoration; clearly, then, until the parousia, the time of the last days involves both present and future domains, with the latter engulfing all creation.[15] And this leads, third, to the cosmic renewal that is merely a reiteration, as the text says, of prophetic promises from of old. In the Pentecost sermon that springs off the prophecy of Joel, its apocalyptic cast is suggestive of a divine redemption that spans "the heavens above" and "the earth below" (Acts 2:19). The point is that the Spirit's eschatological renovation not only stretches to the edges of the earth and salvages men and women, sons and daughters, young and old (in case one misses the point, these are sweeping, all-inclusive, and public categorizations[16]), but also involves the creation itself, in and through its convulsions.

A pentecostal reading that begins with the Acts narrative identifies God as the spirit of the *coming* creation.[17] In this we note that the Spirit is both present in some respects (insofar as the world and its creatures now bear witness to the wondrous works of God [2:11], for instance) but also ahead of us in other respects (related to ongoing human repentance and creaturely reception, for instance). This means also that all things—the creation (considered theologically and pneumatologically) and the cosmos (considered apocalyptically)—are also being renewed in the present even as they await full redemption and restoration in the future. As recorded in the first volume via account of the preaching of John the

15. See Lennartsson, *Refreshing and Restoration.*

16. As I argue further in my *In the Days of Caesar*, esp. ch. 3.

17. See also Moltmann, *Coming of God.*

Baptist, "Every valley shall be filled, / and every mountain and hill shall be made low, / and the crooked shall be made straight, / and the rough ways made smooth; / and all flesh shall see the salvation of God" (Luke 3:5–6; see Isa 40:3–5). Creation itself, its valleys, mountains, and hills, will be caught up in the salvation of God wrought by the Spirit anointed Messiah, and this will culminate in and through that same messianic baptism of all flesh in the divine breath.

THE SPIRIT OF THE GROANING CREATION: ROMANS 8

If a Lukan (Acts) perspective on the creation teases out intimations of the Spirit's present dawning renewal of the world, then the turn to St. Paul opens up to both implicit (mostly) and explicit (in a few cases) statements from across his letters about the cosmos and humanity's place in it.[18] For our pneumatological purposes, however, we will zero in on the Epistle to the Romans, and in particular the pneumatologically charged eighth chapter.[19] We will focus on a textual portion at the heart of this dense passage where we read about the Spirit's work intertwined with the responses of the creation, and use this as a lens to open up other segments of the book relevant to our task.[20] Let us dive right into what Paul writes:

> [19] For the creation waits with eager longing for the revealing of the children of God; [20] for the creation was subjected to futility, not of its own will but by the will of the one who subjected it, in hope [21] that the creation itself will be set free from its bondage to decay and will obtain the freedom of the glory of the children of God. [22] We know that the whole creation has been groaning in labor pains until now; [23] and not only the creation, but we ourselves, who have the first fruits of the Spirit, groan inwardly while we wait for adoption, the redemption of our bodies. [24] For in hope we were saved. Now hope that is seen is not hope. For who hopes for what is seen? [25] But if we hope for what we do not see, we wait for it with patience. [26] Likewise the Spirit helps us in our weakness; for we do not know how to pray as we ought, but that very Spirit intercedes with sighs too deep for words.

18. For starters, see Whiteley, *Theology of St. Paul*, the second chapter on the doctrine of creation.

19. See Wood, *Paul's Pentecost*.

20. Elsewhere I have discussed Rom 8 in terms of Paul's pneumatological soteriology—see my *Spirit of Love*, ch. 7—but here we shift to what might be understood as a Pauline pneumatological theology of creation.

> 27 And God, who searches the heart, knows what is the mind of the Spirit, because the Spirit intercedes for the saints according to the will of God. (Rom 8:19–27)[21]

Clearly, this passage speaks directly to any efforts to think about the creation pneumatologically or to consider the Spirit in relationship to the world. Read initially on its own terms, we see here a creation longing, groaning, and hoping for redemption, in effect with the Spirit, albeit as manifest through the creaturely flesh that is human bodies. Hence the Spirit also groans for the broken world, even if deploying human vessels, vocal cords, communicative signs, or embodied sighs.[22] The goal is the liberation and deliverance of a decaying creation, and this finds current and eschatological manifestation in and through the groans of the Spirit sounded through creaturely flesh.

However long creation has been in bondage to its labor pains we are not told. Yet the beginning of the letter indicates that "the wrath of God is revealed from heaven against all ungodliness and wickedness of those who by their wickedness suppress the truth" (1:18).[23] This may suggest that judgment commences from the heavenly location that ancient cosmologies presumed to be the divine above, but more relevant for our purposes is the implication that the manifestation of wrath from the heavens leaves the creation deluged in the pain of ungodliness and wickedness. That being the case, it is unsurprising that Paul moans: "There is no one who is righteous, not even one" (3:10)! The groaning of the *entire* creation is synchronized, in this respect, with the universality of creaturely subjugation and suffering under sin.[24] Human creatures are slaves to sin and dead under the law (Rom chs. 6–7) in part because they inhabit an unjust and wicked world. Human destinies toward destruction are bound

21. Much has been written on this text, including a growing number of voices distilling an ecological theology or a theology of the environment from its interstices; compare for instance the more standard exegetical treatment such as Ware, "Paul's Hope and Ours," with what is representative of the latter developments: Bauckham, "Story of the Earth According to Paul."

22. Pentecostal readings might prefer to understand the groans in this text with reference to speaking in tongues—e.g., Bertone, "Experience of Glossolalia and the Spirit's Empathy"—but that possibility does not foreclose other expressions.

23. I have been helped in what follows on the connections between Rom 1 and 8 by Kraftchick, "Paul's Use of Creation Themes."

24. For more on creation and the fall in pneumatological perspective, see Yong, *Renewing Christian Theology*, ch. 10.3.

up with the world's dissolution because all are frustrated under sin and its consequential judgments.[25]

Hence it is also the case that creaturely deliverance cannot emerge from within the cosmos but in effect must come from without. And it is precisely the divine response in Christ that makes possible the gift of the Spirit: "God's love has been poured into our hearts through the Holy Spirit that has been given to us" (5:5). There is hope for a decaying creation only "if the Spirit of him who raised Jesus from the dead dwells in you" since it is only that Spirit "who raised Christ from the dead [who] will give life to your mortal bodies" (8:11). Yet this gift means that creatures are now, in this time between the times, enabled to groan indeed in and through the life-giving Spirit (8:26–27).[26] For this same reason the apostle turns in the latter part of this missive to urge his Roman readers: "I appeal to you therefore, brothers and sisters, by the mercies of God, to present your bodies as a living sacrifice, holy and acceptable to God, which is your spiritual worship" (12:1). The Spirit's work in human hearts brings forth concomitant bodily behaviors and practices that represent the material creation's forward surge toward the coming reign of God. For as it is also written, "the kingdom of God is not food and drink but righteousness and peace and joy in the Holy Spirit" (14:17), and this in turn brings forth the blessing: "May the God of hope fill you with all joy and peace in believing, so that you may abound in hope by the power of the Holy Spirit" (15:13). If the new creation is to arise from out of the ashes of the old, it must involve the contributions of creatures caught within the snares of the first creation,[27] and such can only happen through pneumaticization by the divine breath.

It is thereby the praying and groaning that heralds the final redemptive purposes of God, and that constitutes creaturely participation in the divine breath's orchestration of "all things work[ing] together for good for those who love God, who are called according to his purpose" (8:28b). The result is that if creaturely sin and wickedness drew divine wrath from and across the heavens, then pneumatic breath unleashed through the resurrected Christ blows through the creaturely dust of the ground. "He who did not withhold his own Son, but gave him up for all of us, will he not with him also give us everything else" (8:32), and does not this

25. This indissolubility is pronounced in the title of Gaventa, *Apocalyptic Paul.*

26. Heufelder, *Spirit Prays in Us.*

27. This theme of creaturely response to the work of divine cosmic renewal is also emphasized by Byrne, "Ecological Reading of Rom. 8.19–22," esp. 92–93.

everything else include also the very life-giving divine breath? If that is the case, no wonder Paul can exclaim in a crescendo of praise: "*In all these things* we are more than conquerors through him who loved us. For I am convinced that neither death, nor life, nor angels, nor rulers, nor things present, nor things to come, nor powers, nor height, nor depth, *nor anything else in all creation*, will be able to separate us from the love of God in Christ Jesus our Lord" (8:37–39, italics added)! Creation as a whole, including each and every level of its diverse reality, will be transformed, with nothing left out or excluded, thus signifying also its thoroughly interwoven web of life and being.[28] It would appear that the divine breath that pulsated over the inchoate primordial waters (Gen 1:2) will eventually fill and baptize all creation into the divine love.[29]

To be sure, such a pneumatological reading of Roman's creation theology cannot err on the side of a fully realized eschatology. Instead, the emphasis is on present groaning even if such goes forth in anticipation of the coming glory. Whereas the Pentecost narrative looses the many voices, the Roman epistle suggests that these remain barely discernible and often no more than muted exhalations. And yet by the power of the Spirit, these "sighs too deep for words" somehow orchestrate the last gasps of the decaying creation that is passing away and usher in the glorious new creation that is on its way. A Pauline theology of redeemed creation inflected pneumatologically thus involves both the realization of the present ordeal but also grasps the teleological promise echoed through the pangs. Redeemed creation anticipates a dynamic finalization. The groanings and sighings of creation are being pneumatically transmuted so that "from him and through him and to him are all things" (11:36).

THE SPIRIT OF THE NEW CREATION: REVELATION

Of course, any theology of new creation would be drawn to the final canonical book of Revelation, not least because its last two chapters unveil a new heavens and new earth, including a new Jerusalem.[30] Yet the

28. Such is emphasized via a feminist reading of Rom 8, inspired by the metaphors of groaning and labor pains in the text; see McGinn, "All Creation Groans in Labor"; a Roman Catholic reading includes Rom 8 as nurturing hope for the *deification* of all things: Edwards, "Final Fulfilment," esp. 183–85.

29. Macchia, *Justified by the Spirit*, develops a theology of the Spirit-baptized creation.

30. Toenges, "'See, I am Making All Things New.'"

apocalyptic eschatology unveiled in this book only culminates in these images and is certainly not reducible to them. Instead, the whole provides a theology of the old creation being transfigured anew. What happens if we read this transfiguration pneumatologically?[31] How might such a pneumatological angle illuminate the final creation?[32]

Of course, the first question that is unavoidable concerns the legitimacy of deploying—some might worry about *imposing*—such a pneumatological lens. How might we justify, even if preliminarily, such an approach?[33] An initial response observes that the visions of the book appear to present themselves as pneumatologically framed. Each of the four major sections is introduced via pneumatological references. Thus the manifestation of Jesus in the prologue was given to John while he was "in the spirit on the Lord's day" (Rev 1:9), even as John's seeing of the throne room and the events that "must take place after this" is facilitated while he "was in the spirit" (4:1–2). Later, the final destruction of Babylon is also unveiled to John "in the spirit in the wilderness" (17:3a), anticipating the unfolding of the New Jerusalem in the final vision (21:9).[34] It would appear that while this is a revelation of Jesus Christ (1:1a), the greetings from this one (1:5) and "from him who is and who was and who is to come, *and from the seven spirits* [cf. 3:1; 4:5; 5:6] who are before his throne" (1:4b, emphasis mine) unmistakably includes the divine spirit (who is referred to in the singular and the plural—seven—alike).[35] This prophetic set of visions—the book also is called a "prophecy" (1:3; 22:7,

31. One version of which is my essay "Kings, Nations, and Cultures on the Way to the New Jerusalem" (also chapter 12 of this volume).

32. Consider the following paragraphs as supplementary to what is otherwise environmentally focused in Waddell, "Revelation and the (New) Creation."

33. The following is a very succinct summary of what is developed more extensively in my essay "Unveiling Interpretation After Pentecost" (also chapter 10 of this volume); see also Waddell, *Spirit of the Book of Revelation*.

34. Not surprisingly, pentecostal exegetes have approached the Apocalypses as divided at least in part by these pneumatological references; see, e.g., Skaggs and Benham, *Revelation*, 14–15; Thomas, *Apocalypse*, 2–6.

35. For more on Revelation's pneumatology, see Bauckham, *Climax of Prophecy*, ch. 5. Note though the argument that *pneuma* in Rev 19:10 refers less to the Holy Spirit than to "essence" of this book; hence, *tes propheteias* should be "the prophecy" or the Revelation book itself, leading to the translation: "For the witness to Jesus is the spirit [essence] of the prophecy"; see Wilson, "Revelation 19:10 and Contemporary Interpretation," 201.

10, 18)—then, can also be understood as given by charismatic unction through "the spirit of prophecy" (19:10b).[36]

More importantly for purposes of articulating a pneumatological eschatology of new and final creation is what might otherwise appear to be the cryptic call at the end of the Apocalypse: "The Spirit and the bride say, 'Come.' / And let everyone who hears say, 'Come.' / And let everyone who is thirsty come. / Let anyone who wishes take the water of life as a gift" (22:17).[37] A pneumatological perspective, however, would emphasize the nature of the divine word and breath here together intoning the call into the new creation: "Together the Spirit and the Bride (Jesus) call people to experience the life that only God gives."[38] Read canonically for the moment: The breath that carries the words that organize the chaos of the primordial waters into a cosmic temple for the deity again reverberates in purifying and transforming the disordered cosmos so it becomes fit as the divine dwelling place.[39] Creation ruptured is being pneumatically mended, as signified by this eschatological invitation of the divine breath.

Read apocalyptically within the scope of these visions, the calling of the Spirit reiterates what has rung from the start. If the visions are addressed to the seven stars that are also the "angels of the seven churches" (1:20), and if and the seven spirits of God are associated with the seven stars (3:1), then it is the divine spirit who speaks in and through the churches. Thus, each of the stars-angels-churches is addressed, after which the admonishment goes forth: "Let anyone who has an ear listen to what the Spirit is saying to the churches" (2:7a; also 2:11a, 17a, 29; 3:6, 13, 22). Two points need to be registered in this regard. First, the initial addresses of this apocalyptic message are the seven churches, and the divine Spirit both warns them but also urges them to faithfulness, an urging that persists amid the apocalyptic fires that burn through the rest of the visions in the book until arrival at the apex that is the new creation. As such, the point of this as a pneumatic communiqué is that the Spirit wishes to guard and enable the perhaps harassed and persecuted but also tempted and tried people of God to remain faithful to the heavenly telos

36. See also Bauckham, *Theology of the Book of Revelation*, ch. 5, where the spirit of prophecy is discussed in more detail.

37. Interestingly, Rev 22:17 does not even appear in the scripture index of Stephens, *Annihilation or Renewal?*, while his book answers the question in the title by exploring both continuities and discontinuities between the first and the second (new) creation, brought about by a "profound change" (p. 256), in effect.

38. Gorman, *Reading Revelation Responsibly*, 122, also 167–68.

39. Kilcrease, "Creation's Praise."

while navigating the violence raging across the first creation.[40] Hence the objective of these visions is less to inform than to propel and even transmigrate, from the remnants of the old creation that is passing away—hemorrhaging through earthquakes and other "natural events" of mass destruction, effectively!—to the glory of the God of the new creation.[41]

The second point is related to the first. To the degree that the prophet was commanded repeatedly to write down what he saw and heard (1:11, 19; 14:13; 19:9; 21:5), to that same degree does the prophecy then have the capacity to address any other readers that might open the scroll or (for later generations) turn the book's pages. In that case, however, the invitation of the Spirit remains, not only the welcome posture of the final scene (in 22:17) but also the message of reprimand and perseverance in the earlier section of letters. What emerges is that no matter the circumstances of any individual reader or even group of hearers—thus Revelation opens with "blessed are those who hear and who keep what is written in it" (1:3)—the call of the Spirit comes fast and furious up front (seven times to the seven churches), and then appears intermittently through the visions in all their horrific twists and turns before arriving at the ultimate destination of the new and final creation at the end of the book. Readers of the visions are not just invited but even carried by the Spirit to participate in the work of repairing the cosmos and to prepare its rehabilitation as the final resting place of God and the people of the deity.

"The Spirit and the bride say, 'Come,'" thus expects that creatures who long for God's delivering judgment (see 6:10) will respond to the movements of the divine breath. The "seven spirits of God sent out into all the earth" (5:6b) have been seeking its renewal and restoration. The descent of the "holy city Jerusalem coming down out of heaven from God" (21:10b) indicates that the work of divine wrath (see above) is completed so that the judgment experienced before as alienation and estrangement now accomplishes the "healing of the nations" (22:2b). The (seven) spirit/s have finally reunited the cosmos with her creator, consummating the relationship through the nuptial feast of the Lamb (19:7–9).[42]

40. See Herms, "Invoking the Spirit and Narrative Intent in John's Apocalypse."

41. See Carroll, "Creation and Apocalypse."

42. See also McIlraith, *Reciprocal Love Between Christ and the Church.*

IMPLICATIONS FOR A PNEUMATOLOGICAL ESCHATOLOGY OF FINAL CREATION

In this final section, I return to my primary voice as a systematician and venture some summary remarks in light of the foregoing and perhaps look ahead to how these ideas can be further developed. I organize these reflections and anticipations along three registers: the soteriological, the anthropological, and the ontological. Consider these both as supplementing prior more theological and philosophical treatments with insights derived from these scriptural considerations on the one hand,[43] and yet as precipitating fresh insight for theological dialogue in the global context of the present millennium on the other hand.

The preceding suggests that a pneumatological eschatology of final creation is fundamentally soteriological in nature. This means that the Bible is concerned with creation—nature or the cosmos defined scripturally—not for its own sake but for the sake of its being brought back into relationship and reconciled with the divine. Creation and its creatures are alienated and estranged from God and from one another, so that the eschatological outpouring of the Spirit is designed to mend the divides—between male and female, young and old, the haves and the have nots, and, perhaps most importantly for our purposes, between human and other creatures—so that all is restored to communion with the divine.

This soteriological reconciliation of the final creation thus is the culmination of a biblical drama, initiated in the scriptures' opening pages and concluding at the end. There is, in other words, a teleological scope that unfolds from the first creation, through its cursedness, and on to its second re-creation. The world that was originally pronounced *good* (Gen 1) but was then tarnished by sin (Rom 5:12) will be renewed and "nothing accursed will be found there any more" (Rev 22:3a). The point is that the biblical drama is headed toward restoration of the old and arrival of the new.

The one caveat to be registered about the soteriological trajectory toward the second creation is that the salvation of the world—the cosmos as a whole—is qualitatively considered rather than quantitatively reconstituted according to at least the scriptural witnesses attended to in this essay. This means that the emphasis is not salvation from out of the first creation but its transformation and carrying forward. The second

43. Besides my efforts in *The Spirit of Creation*, I have worked also on pneumatology of creation in *The Cosmic Breath*, although here, my scriptural engagement is predominantly in dialogue with the Genesis traditions.

creation emerges as a renewal but not displacement of the first. The drama of redemption thus involves a restoration and refurbishment rather than an annihilation and altogether new second creative act.[44]

Part of the reason for the emphasis on the renewal rather than radical reconstruction and re-creation of the cosmos is that, as we have seen from our scriptural reflections, human creatures are involved. This suggests that a pneumatological eschatology of final creation has soteriological and also anthropological dimensions. Human creatures groan and sigh most palpably—or at least most noticeably for our own discernment—aspiring for the glory to come. If the dust of the ground also yearns for liberation of death and suffering (see Gen 4:10), then creaturely breaths, interwoven with the earth (Gen 1:30; 2:7), whisper or sound out these longings for redemption. Human fleshliness, in all of its weakness (Rom 8:26a), nevertheless participates in the creation's thrust toward its final deliverance and emancipation.

This means that the breath—*ruah* and *pneuma*—of life is not just a transcendent aspect of creatureliness but in some fundamental respects immanent within and intrinsic to creation itself.[45] Matter and spirit are thus not binaries, certainly not dual in any ontologically bifurcated sense; rather, in living creatures as a whole and in human beings more specifically, the material and the spiritual are intertwined. The transcending dimension of the spiritual then is found not merely in the original creation but in its teleological destination. Transcendence of the spirit has a dynamic and forward-moving direction, oriented toward eschatological perfection. What transcends is, from this pneumatological perspective, therefore ahead of us, luring us forward, after which we are gasping and groaning, if not also grasping ephemerally.

This teleological (to use non-theological language) and eschatological (here: theologically speaking) character of human creatureliness means that the present decaying creation is in some real sense self-aware it is being renewed by the future second creation. Human creatures know, however, not apart from but in and through their subjectivity embedded between the creation that is passing away and the one that is arriving. Hence, there is not epistemological objectivity in the sense that we stand off from the process of new creation's coming; rather, we are caught up

44. And this despite the rhetoric and language of cosmic destruction and annihilation in 2 Pet 3, which may not in itself deny the goodness of creation; on this point, see Adams, "Retrieving the Earth from the Conflagration."

45. Here I adapt arguments I have developed elsewhere: *Spirit of Love*.

in the pneumatic birth pangs of the final creation and witness to such via our own groans and sighs.

If human creatures are temporally constituted toward a teleological communion with the divine, then creation itself is dynamic and eschatologically oriented. Hence, a pneumatological perspective anticipating the emergence of final creation can be understood ontologically, not only in terms of being but also in terms of becoming. This is neither an attempt to adjudicate being versus becoming, nor is it meant to get caught up in the contested metaphysical disputes about substances versus processes; instead, it is an attempt to consider how the scriptural witness that involves this eschatological horizon invites a teleological understanding of creation and the cosmos that recognizes its animation toward the divine future rather than an orientation only toward statically conceived primordial or original creation. This brings the biblical theologian of eschatology and theology of creation to the precipice where the scriptural witness and even Christian mission meets philosophers, scientists, and other theoretical disciplines.[46]

Our goal in this essay is to open up preliminary biblical reflection on theology of creation from a pneumatological perspective. In doing so, we have uncovered that the lines between spirit and matter are not as hard and fast as how modernists and naturalists might like to understand them, and that both spirit and matter have a teleological orientation that theology recognizes in eschatological—present and arriving—terms. If the comings and goings of the divine wind cannot always be clearly traced (see John 3:8), nevertheless we might identify echoes of such in the cries of human creatures, and detect cues of such in environmental and ecological strains. These aspirations and asphyxiations amid the strangulations that constitute this present decaying world are charismatic and pneumatic pointers to the second and new creation that is now seen only "in a mirror, dimly" (1 Cor 13:12). So even as we humans pray, "Veni Espiritu Sanctu," we embrace the gift of that Spirit's invitation to enter into the final creation.[47]

46. See Yong, "*Missio Spiritus*."

47. A prior, much more underdeveloped, version of this paper was presented at the "Come Holy Spirit: Global and Cosmic Yearnings," Annual Study Days of the Studienzentrum für Glaube und Gesellschaft, University of Fribourg, Fribourg, Switzerland, June 19–20, 2017; thanks to Walter Dürr and Andreas Steingruber for the invitation to participate in this event and for hosting me and my wife on its occasion. I am grateful also to my graduate assistant, Hoon Jung, for his reading of a previous draft of this paper; the remaining errors of fact or interpretation are my own responsibility.

PART II

Apostolic Cultural Navigation

The Common Good, the (Post-Secular) Spirit, and Community Engagement

Chapter 4

The Spirit, the Common Good, and the Public Sphere

The Twenty-First-Century Public Intellectual in Apostolic Perspective

THE INTERSECTION WHERE THEOLOGIANS meet up with public intellectuals has waxed and waned over the past century.[1] In this chapter, I revisit this crossroads from my own milieu as a pentecostal and evangelical scholar whose more recent work has been in the arena of theological interpretation of Scripture.[2] In the latter context, I have been asking, to put it crassly, what would the apostles do?[3]

Applied to the consideration of the work of the public intellectual, at least as historically manifest, the apostolic narrative invites reconceptualization of the assignment as one involving engagement with a plurality of publics in a variety of discursive activities, directed toward the coming divine reign. The following elaborates on this hypothesis in three steps (corresponding to the three sections of this essay): (1) assessing what

1. On the waning of the public intellectual, especially in the North American context, see Jacoby, *Last Intellectuals*; Posner, *Public Intellectuals*; the fortunes of the theologian attempting to work in this milieu have been affected within the arc of this broader "decline" (Posner's account).

2. I develop what I call a pent-evangelical theological vision in Yong, *Future of Evangelical Theology*.

3. My book *The Hermeneutical Spirit* takes up this conversation in dialogue predominantly with Luke-Acts, the latter of this ancient biblical author's two books being a narrative about the early Christian or apostolic experience.

may be perceived as a paradigmatic account of apostolic public speech; (2) presenting observations about the plurality of apostolic engagements with the variety of public squares encountered across imperial Rome and sketching their implications for contemporary public theologians embarking on the public intellectual vocation; and (3) culminating with an exploratory consideration of apostolic speech-acts and their implications for rethinking the theologian as public intellectual and as performer of public intellectual work in the present era. This essay is motivated by this question: If public intellectuals can be critics, scientists, or professionals, and even also theologians, what are the theological norms operative for public intellectual work?[4]

Before proceeding, I note that my thinking about the theologian as public intellectual builds on my prior work as a political and public theologian.[5] These are not identical dimensions of theological labor, but they can be and are related. My bringing these together may be suggestive also of ways in which the traditional understanding of the public intellectual might be theologically enriched. My objective is neither to reduce the theological character of public intellectual work to a branch of political or public theology nor to say that all political or public theologians ought also to be public intellectuals. Rather, I propose that one way to revitalize theological discourse for public impact includes considerations developed within the subdisciplines of political and public theology. More precisely, and now linking back to this essay's broader thesis, the wager here is that my own political and public theology encapsulated in the moniker "many tongues, many political practices,"[6] can also spark new imaginative possibilities for theological embrace of the public intellectual task. This could help clarify how we might work together and in common, from our diverse locations. Rather than being directly persuasive about the common good—what some might take the telos of the modern public intellectual to be—the apostolic effort was focused on heralding the divine rule. Such a focus can be considered a complementary theological anticipation of the goal of public intellectual work.

4. See Michael, *Anxious Intellects*, part 2.

5. Political theology and public theology are not identical; my own thinking about the former, however, has been as part and parcel of the latter; see Yong, *In the Days of Caesar*.

6. This is found in Yong, *In the Days of Caesar*; see also my "Many Tongues, Many Practices."

"THE CROWD GATHERED": PENTECOST AS PUBLIC (INTELLECTUAL) PHENOMENON

At the outset, let me hazard discussing the work of the public intellectual without attempting to define such, not only because I think its present forms are unpredictably malleable, but also because I hope to venture an explicitly theological thesis, one that seeks to (re)inform the efforts of those aspiring toward such work by retrieving the apostolic testimony. In doing so, I risk being anachronistic: what the apostles were doing two thousand years ago can hardly be said to be like what the modern public intellectual essays. Yet I press on precisely because the fluidity of the phenomenon of public engagement invites normative consideration, which for theologians involves scriptural assessment at some level. And it is here, perhaps surprisingly, that the ancient author known as St. Luke may prove more helpful than initially surmised.

Luke—here I go with the traditional consensus about the authorship of the Gospel of Luke and the Acts of the Apostles, which argument for the thesis of this theological (rather than historical or exegetical) essay does not depend on—was certainly not writing for the public in any contemporary sense of that notion. Yet it is well known that he situated his narrative in public space, in fact, in the widest of such spaces, that of imperial Rome. Clearly the first few chapters of the Third Gospel locate the narrative squarely in this public and political realm, when he identified these events as occurring "in the days of King Herod of Judea" (1:5); "in those days [when] a decree went out from Emperor Augustus that all the world should be registered" (2:1); and "in the fifteenth year of the reign of Emperor Tiberius, when Pontius Pilate was governor of Judea, and Herod was ruler of Galilee, and his brother Philip ruler of the region of Ituraea and Trachonitis, and Lysanias ruler of Abilene" (3:1).

If the entirety of the Jesus story for Luke unfolds on this political ground, his sequel, which explicitly builds on the first book (see Acts 1:1), brings the story to the farthest edges of the known world. "And so we came to Rome"—as one interpreter translates Acts 28:16[7]—introduces the final scene of that book by situating the closing events at the heart of the Pax Romana itself. The phrase communicates how Luke envisioned his story as encompassing the social and political world as he and his contemporaries knew it. In short, if Luke is not a political or public theologian in any modern sense, and even if he can in no way be said to have

7. Walaskay, *"And So We Came to Rome."*

been a public intellectual, he was equally as certainly recounting how the lives of Jesus (the gospel) and his followers (Acts) were inevitably political and public vis-à-vis the circumstances of their own times.

Against this backdrop, I wish to attend more carefully to Luke's account of the Day of Pentecost—after Jesus' ascension, the leading event framing the experiences of the earliest disciples. Of course, I do so in part because that has been the site of much of my work as a constructive pentecostal theologian over the years—to which references will be provided in due course—but I now return (again) to this text, given my (re)discovery of its relevance for our topic. Note the geopolitical cues such as that which situates Luke's Pentecost narrative: that then and there "there were devout Jews from every nation under heaven living in Jerusalem" (2:5). In the following scenario, Luke intends to communicate that not only these Jews but also proselytes or gentile converts to Judaism (2:10) came from across the known world. The list of sixteen "nations" (2:9–11) is shorthand for the ancient Hebraic lists of Seventy Nations, which are means of encompassing the whole human family.[8] Luke's cosmic horizon is unmistakable—thus he is concerned to stipulate clearly that the present time of his writing and of those who are reading his words is "the time of *universal restoration* that God announced long ago through his holy prophets" (3:21, emphasis mine)—and it is just as clearly of political and public scope.

Yet Luke was not content merely to locate the Day of Pentecost in this sociopolitical and public space; the characters he introduced also communicate with public intent. St. Peter, the leading spokesperson for the apostles, is presented as addressing those who were "from every nation under heaven": "Peter, standing with the eleven, raised his voice and addressed them, 'Men of Judea and all who live in Jerusalem, let this be known to you'" (2:14). To undergird his message authoritatively, Luke specified that Peter drew from the prophetic tradition in this way: "This is what was spoken through the prophet Joel: 'In the last days it will be, God declares, that I will pour out my Spirit upon all flesh'" (2:16–17). To be doubly clear about Joel's prophecy (and Peter's intent), the "all flesh" is elaborated to include sons and daughters (who among the human family is not one or the other) and young and old (any of us are younger or older), so that the all-inclusiveness of those upon whom the Spirit is being poured out is undeniable.

8. See my essay "As the Spirit Gives Utterance . . ."

The conclusion of the ancient prophet is also brought forth in addressing the known (Petrine and Lukan) world: "Then everyone who calls on the name of the Lord shall be saved" (2:21). And beyond that, Luke explicated that Peter himself drew his sermon to a close by saying that to those who repent and are baptized among the hearers (and readers of this text, by extrapolation): "The promise is for you, for your children, and for all who are far away, everyone whom the Lord our God calls to him" (2:39). If three thousand persons responded to Peter's Pentecost message (2:41), the possibility remains that any and all who might still hear this invitation can be (ongoing) recipients of this divine gift. Luke's description of what happens in the aftermath of this mass baptism leaves no doubt: "And day by day the Lord added to their number those who were being saved" (2:47).[9]

I have two sets of comments, coming forward into our own time and addressing our present concerns. First, let us make explicit the connections between the universality of the Pentecost account and the broader-than-ecclesial dimensions of the contemporary public intellectual domain. Of course, we have always recognized Pentecost has a cosmic vista, but we have not usually comprehended such breadth of scope with the political and public spheres of life, surely not with the realm wherein and within public intellectuals trade. So, to be clear: Luke is not developing a theology of public intellectualism. However, his Pentecost vision—which is summarized in Acts 2 and provides the narrative arc for the entirety of the apostolic enterprise—includes the sociopolitical dimension, and, in that sense, can be said to have public purchase, including, when brought forward into our late modern context, public intellectual implications. Put alternatively, Luke's Pentecost theology directed toward those "from every nation under heaven" may have more to tell us about a contemporary theology of public intellectual activity than we may have previously surmised.

Brought forward then, Luke's apostolic narrative invites contemporary messianic disciples to embrace the public aspects of their faithful witness and then also urges Christians to explicate their theology of discipleship as involving public dimensions. In the twenty-first century, the age of transnational migration and internet, the local is also the global and vice versa. Christian witness in general and theological speech in particular are then also local and global concurrently, even if in different

9. My book *The Spirit Poured Out on All Flesh* is based not only on Acts 2:17 (from which the title derives) but also on the cosmic horizon of the Pentecost message.

respects. To be thus local and global together prompts theological reflection and articulation to be attentive to the pluralism of their audiences, both intended and not. Just as the apostolic witness on the Day of Pentecost was both particular and universal through many tongues and in multiple directions, so also contemporary Christian witness is and should be carried out. The apostolic speech was heard in many languages. In the third millennium, this involves simultaneous resounding across borders, cultures, and continents whether through Google translator or other media. Today's public intellectual already has a global audience,[10] so theologians drawn to this charge will also need to do so globally. As Peter spoke locally but with cosmic reach, so also today's theologians may write and speak to the church, but their words will be amplified, through digital and other means, globally.

Second, then, we might ask more about the normative character of such a Lukan political and even public theologian that might also be relevant to the public intellectual project and how such might be developed. Surely the cacophony of *glossolalia* prompted bewilderment, astonishment, and perplexity (2:6, 7, 12), but also the crowd's recognition that "in our own languages we hear them speaking about God's deeds of power" (2:11). From this, the public invitation was to salvation in Jesus' name (2:21), effectively repentance, baptism in Jesus' name, forgiveness of sins, and reception of the Holy Spirit (2:38).

The immediate implications of such pneumatic inundation is the formation of the economic community of mutuality and reciprocity: the three thousand "had all things in common; they would sell their possessions and goods and distribute the proceeds to all, as any had need" (2:44–45).[11] It is clear that Luke does not have any contemporary notion of a "common good" in mind in telling of the Pentecost event. Instead, his account is about the outpouring of the divine wind, one that inaugurates the so-called last days, which is itself much less the "end times" of speculative prophetic charts than it is about the messianic reign of justice and shalom foretold by Israel's prophets such as Joel. Yet the latter is surely—and by extension so is Peter's and Luke's Pentecost miracle—about the renewal of the human polis in all of its brokenness. So although Luke does not develop a Pentecost theology of the common good that syncs up nicely with our current understanding, he does present, through Peter in

10. See Desch, *Public Intellectuals in the Global Arena.*

11. See my reading of Acts in this socioeconomic direction in Yong, *Who Is the Holy Spirit?*, part 2.

this specific case, a vision for human renewal, redemption, and well being informed by the visitation of the divine wind.

But if Luke is not a political or economic theologian in our understanding of these terms, his Pentecost message was not merely idealistic or otherworldly. Instead, the coming of the divine wind had material consequences of the sort that anticipated the renewal and right-wising of the common realm.[12] The implications for contemporary Christian faith are that its witness is inevitably public and political. Christian theological speech, by extension, also has a public and political character with performative and practical implications. Christian theologians may not be public intellectuals with any intentionality approximating the common understanding of the latter, yet their witness to the divine rule can and should herald a common and public goodness.[13]

"LISTEN TO WHAT I HAVE TO SAY!" APOSTOLIC SPEECH AS PUBLIC (INTELLECTUAL) DISCURSIVE ENGAGEMENTS

In this section, we look at two categories of apostolic speech given in public contexts: (1) among crowds in general and (2) to narrowly circumscribed audiences (of one, even). Building on the preceding discussion, I have two objectives for what follows. One is to canvass how the public character of the Day of Pentecost phenomenon is disclosed pluralistically in the rest of the apostolic witness described in the book of Acts. The other is to draw out implications for our thinking about and engaging the public (intellectual) aspects of contemporary theologizing. We shall see that the many-tongues/nations aspect of the Pentecost narrative can be observed as carrying out the apostolic message in many public contexts and for various purposes related to the inauguration of divine reign. Therefore, the contemporary (public) theologian is invited to address—and, therefore, has to be prepared, or has to ready herself or himself, to engage with—these multiple spheres and arenas in terms of the here-and-coming divine rule.

12. Arguably, the numinous or the "mystical" generates collective action and even activism! See, e.g., Marschner, "Ritual and the Holy in Social Struggles."

13. For more on Acts' missiology of Christian witness, see Yong, *Mission After Pentecost*, 171–80.

Apostolic Exchanges with Large Groups

We cannot be exhaustive in our treatment, but apostolic exchanges with the masses might be grouped into two subcategories: (1) those that are noticeable for how they advance the Pentecost message and (2) those that provide more expansive perspective on apostolic strategies for engaging a pluralistic public sphere.[14] With regard to the former, observe first that the apostles, incarcerated for healing the man at the Beautiful Gate, were delivered from prison by an angel and instructed to "go, stand in the temple and tell the people the whole message about this life" (5:20). While carrying out precisely this errand, they were questioned by the authorities. We find confirmation that this "whole message" concerns Jesus—his life, death, and exaltation, his offer of repentance and forgiveness of sins, and his gift of the Holy Spirit (5:30–33)—consistent with that pronounced by Peter on the Day of Pentecost.

Later, in the city of Samaria, Philip "proclaimed the Messiah" to the gathered crowds (8:5–6), including "the good news about the kingdom of God and the name of Jesus Christ" (8:12). Further, as relevant at this kerygmatic juncture, in Antioch in Pisidia, "almost the whole city gathered to hear" (13:44) Paul and Barnabas where and when they announced clearly how the Jewish rejection of God's offer of eternal life meant that this would now be made available to the gentiles, "so that you may bring salvation to the ends of the earth" (13:47, here quoting from Isa 49:6).

A number of summary comments are here warranted. First, the apostolic witness in the public square is decidedly theological, concerning the good news of eternal life available in Jesus Christ. Second, however, this gospel is messianic, meaning related to the anointed representative that represents and inaugurates the divine plan to renew Israel, and hence the world-to-come is thereby interlaced with the present life in all its depth and density. Finally, this messianic renewal extends from Israel to the world of the gentiles, so that divine salvation has universal and cosmic horizons.[15]

14. Bock, *Theology of Luke and Acts*, 336–40, rightly notes that the Lukan "crowds" function mainly as a foil in the book of Acts, as indicative of how the people accept or, mostly, reject the gospel; nevertheless, I would maintain, our own theological reading of this narrative can appropriately seek to mine normative insights for contemporary public engagement.

15. See, e.g., Chung, *Public Theology in an Age of World Christianity*; Chung, *Hermeneutical Theology and the Imperative of Public Ethics.*

All of this reiterates what we have already seen in the Pentecost event, but here I wish to observe further their implications for contemporary public theological (and intellectual) work. The theologian as public intellectual ought to be no less than resolutely theological. Such explicitly theological talk risks marginalizing the public and intellectual relevance of that message in a contemporary pluralistic and secular world, so *how* such speech is conducted is as important as *what* is said.

We will return to this momentarily. In the meanwhile, it is important to highlight that the soteriological content of theological speech concerns not just the spiritual or postmortem world to come but also includes this messianic dimension that seeks to renew the present order in anticipation of the impending divine reign. From this perspective, the public theologian (and intellectual) is invited to comprehend more thoroughly and expansively the complexities of contemporary political life in order to be able to take up the present opportunities and challenges more intentionally, strategically, and effectively.[16]

This is perhaps one reason why theologians today may be less inclined to the public intellectual vocation, simply because the lifetime taken to master one discursive field—theology in this case—impedes getting up-to-snuff on any other domain of inquiry, whether the political, the economic, the social, or the environmental. My point is not to condone theologians' speaking irresponsibly into these other spheres just because "doing one's homework" is so difficult, but to acknowledge that it takes time, patience, and laborious effort to gain the necessary knowledge and skills to navigate from the theological to substantive interface with these public domains. Many theologians may feel called indeed into the public intellectual arena, but invariably few prove themselves to be chosen.

The next subset of examples of public apostolic speech complicates further the pluralism of the common space but also provides cues for the theological vocation in a pluralistic world. Here what Luke describes as happening in Lystra, Athens, and Ephesus recites how apostolic speech intermingles with a plurality of religious and philosophical discourses. In Lystra, the healing of a man crippled from birth led the crowds to view Barnabas and Paul as manifestations of Zeus and Hermes (14:11–12), and this motivates them to bear witness to the city's inhabitants by deploying natural theological ideas about God as creator and sustainer of the world

16. Ramachandra, *Subverting Global Myths*, e.g., attempts to take on public issues like terrorism, religious violence, human rights, multiculturalism, science, postcolonialism.

and its nations rather than delving more strictly into messianic or more Israel-centric themes.[17] We see similarly at the Areopagus that among Epicurean and Stoic interlocutors (17:18), Paul draws upon the religious, poetic, and philosophic resources available within that broader Greco-Roman milieu (17:28) to present a more natural theological argument regarding the divine Creator who makes himself known and available to the world, even if in this case Paul concludes with a direct allusion to the coming divine judgment mediated through God's resurrected agent (17:31).[18]

Finally, along these lines, at Ephesus, the home city of "the great goddess Artemis" (19:27), we see a businessman upset that Paul's (and his colleagues') preaching had dampened sales of the Greek deity's paraphernalia. Subsequently a raucous crowd (that included some provincial officials) gathered at the theater and threatened harm when the town clerk calmed them down by clarifying, among other things, that the accused Christians "are neither temple robbers nor blasphemers of our goddess" (19:37). The point to be made is a negative but important one: that whatever else had been understood as the content of Paul's message, his opposition to idolatry (see 17:29) and preaching of the gospel did not include denigration, desacralization, or demonization of Artemis.[19]

What then are the implications for contemporary public (intellectual) theologizing? There is surely the rhetorical dimension that ought to be addressed, in particular recognizing local contexts (such as that of Ephesus wherein Artemis predominates) within global flows. There is also what I might call the kerygmatic dimension: how to communicate theologically and respectfully in a pluralistic space. More substantively, public theologians hence need also to be comparative philosophers and comparative religionists in some respect, having knowledge about other wisdom and related traditions, so that their discursive articulations can operate in these common—and thereby pluralistic—environments, not so much to avoid offense (there will always be a scandalous dimension to the gospel), but because the intellectual undertaking involves thoughtful negotiation with the complexity of other persons, groups, and discourses.[20]

17. See Fournier, *Episode at Lystra*.

18. Copan and Litwak, *Gospel in the Marketplace of Ideas*, is a bit more apologetic in approach; see also Rothschild, *Paul in Athens*.

19. My rephrasing of Keener, *Acts*, 3:2937.

20. For instance, Christian public intellectual discourse will need to encounter and

The public sphere is never politically, socially, or economically neutral, but these domains are always overlaid or sustained by values derived from underlying indigenous and local but also more global religious, philosophical, and wisdom traditions.[21] The work of the theologian as public intellectual thus invites sustained immersion—study, research, and experiential participation—in the intersecting worlds that constitute today's global public square.[22]

Apostolic Exchanges to Targeted Audiences

My last set of comments in this section focuses on Luke's characterization of St. Paul's three extended apologies in the book of Acts, each of which were public albeit in different respects.[23] The first (22:1–21) occurred in some respects before "all the city" of Jerusalem (21:30), even if Paul addressed himself primarily to his Jewish compatriots from the temple steps (21:40). The next two were before governmental officials: Felix the governor of the province of Judea (24:10–21) and Herod Agrippa, a Roman client-king over Judea and its surrounding territories (26:2–29).

The former seeks mostly for self-absolution from charges against Paul brought by the Jewish authorities, without minimizing the theological aspect. This includes reference to his belief in the resurrection from the dead, which is underscored as being the source of agitation between him and his accusers. The latter, Herod, is much more intensely testimonial but includes a persuasive aspect, appealing that the king consider his own personal response to the witness of the good news of the messiah sent for the world. Of course, these narratives constitute Luke's own apology for Christianity.[24] They also give us additional windows into the public nature of apostolic life and witness.

---

interact with those emerging out of East Asian traditions; e.g., Tu, *Way, Learning, and Politics*.

21. Volf, *Public Faith*, thus rightly urges Christians to embrace pluralism as political project.

22. Thus my own motivation at the beginning of my theological vocation in the task of comparative theology, wherein my focus has been on Buddhist traditions; see, e.g., Yong, *Pneumatology and the Christian-Buddhist Dialogue*; Yong, *Cosmic Breath*.

23. I skip over Luke's portrayal of Paul before the high priest Ananias and the council of Sadducees and Pharisees (22:30—23:10) because this is much less of a public environment than the others I focus on here.

24. See Mauck, *Paul on Trial*.

Personal testimony in this case can be public in at least two ways: commencing in public space or given before public officials, almost to an audience of one. Even in the latter instance, such witness has public implications and possibly effects, including the result that carves out public and private interests, such as that pronounced by Agrippa that the Pauline case did not belong in the realm of public or state adjudication (26:32).

What are some takeaways for public theologians then considering public intellectual work? First, the Acts account suggests that the testimony, while a profoundly personal matter, has the potential for public diffusion. If modernity separates the public from the religious or the common from the private, the apostolic narrative indicates that there are moments when these intersect. More important, the bearing of witness to the gospel, even for the public intellectual endeavor, cannot but be personal and testimonial in some respect. When and where this is called for or may be effective is an ongoing occasion for discernment.

Second, and just as relevant, public encounter involves knowing both one's audience, especially if these are governmental officials, and their contexts. The latter may be imbibed experientially and over time, but effective interaction with the public sphere gains from sound knowledge of historical and social dynamics and of legal and political currents. In today's climate, public theologians are made—oftentimes through prolonged research and study—not born; similarly, public intellectuals, even of the theological type, are forged through the anvil of inquiry rather than emerging overnight.[25] Putting these together means that an interesting tension emerges: on the one hand, public speech can be at its most effective when such comes from a deeply personal base; on the other hand, public relating includes the public other, whether as individuals or groups, hence the personal narrative will also have to effectually connect with these wider and broader realities.

25. It could be that theologians grow into a public intellectual vocation or gradually attain a public intellectual platform; Jürgen Moltmann, e.g., wrote two series of theological monographs before the appearance of his *God for a Secular Society*.

"I ORDER YOU IN THE NAME OF JESUS CHRIST TO COME OUT OF HER": APOSTOLIC SPEECH-ACTS IN PUBLIC (INTELLECTUAL) PERSPECTIVE

In this last section, I look at a specific type of apostolic interaction with the public sphere, namely, their speech-acts, and explore their ramifications for thinking about public theological work. The apostles do not merely speak publicly (we have already discussed some of their recorded addresses), but they also effect results with what they say, thus by definition turning speech into speech-acts. Such observations invite consideration of public theologizing not only in terms of what is verbalized, but also what might be performed or achieved through such enunciations. This suggests the exploratory thesis that there is a performative dimension to public intellectual efforts particularly when refracted through the apostolic lens.

Two examples in the book of Acts are worthy of note at this point. First, Stephen's apology was given to what seems to be a large group of people, including elders, scribes, and other witnesses (6:9–12; 7:58). But at the moment of his martyrdom, he prayed, "Lord, do not hold this sin against them" (7:60). Thus Stephen's final public utterance was one of forgiveness, at least ensuring that his own conscience was freed from begrudging his enemies, but also declaring and thereby bringing about—implicitly in this scenario—their absolution from guilt.[26] Then, on the island of Malta, when Paul was hosted by "the leading man of the island, named Publius," it is said of the apostle that the only words he spoke were those of another form of prayer, in this case a petition for Publius's father, who "lay sick in bed with fever and dysentery," with the result that he was cured (28:7–8). In this case, even if privately uttered, the apostolic words had public effect, not only in that it was a public official's father who personally benefited, but also in that such healing solidified the apostolic standing with public opinion and effected the corresponding treatment. Apostolic words, hence, do not merely convey information, but they also shape public estimation and make social reality.

Another set of such speech-acts touches on that which we have introduced above, when the apostles were imprisoned by the oppositional Jewish leadership. In the early Christian community, such public speech

26. According to the Johannine Pentecost in which it was promised: "If you forgive the sins of any, they are forgiven them; if you retain the sins of any, they are retained" (John 20:23).

was also an embodied form of what we would call civic disobedience. When challenged by the religious leadership and commanded to be silent, the apostolic response was, initially, "Whether it is right in God's sight to listen to you rather than to God, you must judge; for we cannot keep from speaking about what we have seen and heard" (4:19–20); and later, "We must obey God rather than any human authority" (5:29). These were words backed up with actions, or we could also say that they were words generated out of virtuous actions and commitments.[27] To the point, these speech-acts of resistance were born out of a stance protective of what we might today call religious freedom, but they might fit into the broader category of speaking truth to power, a familiar dynamic of public intellectual work at least historically.[28]

In response, before the same religious council, Gamaliel, a respected teacher, also spoke, concluding that "if it is of God, you will not be able to overthrow them—in that case you may even be found fighting against God!" (5:39).[29] Here, Gamaliel did not merely provide information, but he did something with his words, specifically, he warned his hearers. Thus apostolic sayings were also public actions of civic resistance even as Gamaliel's words were also a performative act of admonishment.

Perhaps the most unexpected observation in this regard concerns three instances of exorcism in the book of Acts that take place in public space. Luke tells us that the Samarian "crowds with one accord listened eagerly to what was said by Philip, hearing and seeing the signs that he did, for unclean spirits, crying with loud shrieks, came out of many who were possessed" (8:6–7); thus we know that Philip is not only proclaiming about the Messiah and the coming rule of God (see also the discussion above) but also commanding unclean spirits to depart from their hosts.

Then, on the island of Cyprus, Paul and Barnabas are interrelating with the proconsul but interrupted by Elymas the magician; in this context, Luke detailed precisely not only the exorcistic utterance but also the aftermath that occurred exactly as commanded, resulting in the proconsul's belief (13:10–12). The final occasion then concerns the slave girl

27. The voice of the public theologian resounds from out of a virtuously formed life that is in turn shaped liturgically by the gospel, so argues Smith, *Awaiting the King*.

28. On this theme, see the essays in Etzioni and Bowditch, *Public Intellectuals*, part 6.

29. These apostolic stances against the religious status quo (that historically since has been co-opted by the wider public) anticipate what Farganis calls "dissenting intellectuals" who are self-critical also about their own social and intellectual location; see her essay, "Public or Dissenting Intellectual?"

with a spirit of divination at Philippi, who attempted to make a spectacle of Paul and his colleagues. In that public space, Paul finally confronted the situation: "I order you in the name of Jesus Christ to come out of her"; this directive results in a transformed situation that Luke simply described thus: "And it came out that very hour" (16:18).

Although the Lukan point for these exorcisms has to do more with validating the apostolic ministry (of Philip and Paul in these cases),[30] our own lenses highlight the very public nature of these acts of deliverance. Apostolic public discourses include performative elements—in these cases, the casting out of unclean spirits and liberation of those held by such.

I sense that when colleagues consider the public intellectual duty, they pay little attention to the performative dimensions of such speech, beyond the rhetorical aspects designed to move the various publics being addressed in the directions commended by the speaker. But observing that apostolic public expression includes speech-acts that attempt to achieve various objectives, such as forgive or caution audiences, heal and deliver bodies in the public sphere, and resist the operative powers of the public square—all of this indicates that there is or can be a performative element to public intellectual work. Yes, public intellectual discourse attempts to influence and convince, but perhaps can also renew the common realm. It may be that there is an activist component to the public intellectual enterprise, one that not only persuades audiences but also enacts reality.[31]

If modern (Enlightenment) models of the public intellectual emphasized the cerebral character of rhetorical and persuasive argumentation, late modern transformations of this ideal type have insisted that the cognitive is interwoven with the affective and the embodied—and thus the performative—and vice versa;[32] whereas the intellectual and the activist were formerly of distinct, and even contrary, sorts, they are now understood as also being fused together. The Lukan narrative indicates apostolic speech and activities were distinct but inevitably interwoven aspects of the one call to bear witness in the power of the Holy Spirit.

30. Klutz, *Exorcism Stories in Luke-Acts*, treats only the slave girl narrative (plus three exorcisms in the Third Gospel), but his overarching assessment applies also to the other two texts I discuss here.

31. See Isasi-Díaz et al., *Theological Perspectives for Life, Liberty, and the Pursuit of Happiness*, xiv.

32. The contrast is evident not least when we consult public theological projects such as Hopkins, *Black Faith and Public Talk*.

Public theologians in the present time surely ought to be discursively articulate, but they may and perhaps should be, as led by the Spirit of Pentecost, also practically engaged. Such apostolic insights would then urge that public theological and intellectual work not only formulates an abstract vision for the common good but also seeks to socially, materially, and concretely actualize such in our midst.

Chapter 5

Where Did the Holy Spirit Go?

Ephesian Pneumatologies from the Third Apostolic Missionary Journey for a "Post-Secular Age"

As pneumatology, from the Greek *pneuma* (spirit) and *logos* (word), refers in Christian theology to the study or understanding of the work and person of the Holy Spirit, the question in the title of this essay remains relevant for many around the world, not least those in North America and Europe. The West surely has been secularizing for over the last few hundred years, and many if not most of us have been formed by this secularity. The experience of secularization and secularism in Europe is certainly different from that in North America, especially since the principle of the relationship between or separation of church and state has played out variously across the continent in contrast to Canada and the USA. Yet at the heart of secularism and the secular mindset wherever it has spread, religious matters are assumed to be privatized.[1] By contrast, the post-secular refers to the re-emergence of religiosity especially in public spaces; this means either blurring the lines between the private/religious and the public/secular or resisting the separation of the latter from the former.

Speaking especially (if not only) to ministers in the pentecostal-charismatic churches as a second-generation Pentecostal preacher,[2] I have

1. A helpful description of our secular age and time crafted in conversation with social philosopher Charles Taylor is provided by Bjørndal, *Church in a Secular Age*, part 1.

2. For Yong the pentecostal preacher, see my book of sermons, *Kerygmatic Spirit*.

long been trying to understand how we can better comprehend the person and work of the Holy Spirit in both secular and growing post-secular spheres. As Christianity has grown in the majority world, the center of gravity of Christian faith has shifted from Europe and North America to Asia, Africa, and Latin America. Yet, with migration and globalization shrinking our world, so to speak, greater connectivity, travel, and digital interaction, boosted during the years of the coronavirus pandemic, means also both that secularization is no longer only a Western phenomenon and that other cultural perspectives that hold together the religious and the public domains in a more seamless manner are increasingly to be found in the Euro-American West. So, how do we understand the person and work of the Holy Spirit amid the late modern, highly secularized and also post-secularizing climates we're all experiencing? And yet even emerging post-secular spaces do not presume we have moved beyond the modern secular/religious split but that secularity, secularization, and secularism are being questioned and navigated afresh.[3] Thus, a late-secular and even post-secular pneumatology remains important for us, and we will need the Holy Spirit to be our teacher as we engage these explorations.

POST-APOSTOLIC DISCIPLESHIP FOR AN IMPERIAL AGE? WHERE DID PENTECOST GO?

To take up these matters, I consider what I call "post-apostolic discipleship for an imperial age." I believe this will be an important methodological and hermeneutical strategy for us who have been shaped by pentecostal-charismatic spirituality, upbringing, and so on. My "post-apostolic" indicator foregrounds both our own location in the twenty-first century and the positionality of the writers and readers of the original Twelve commissioned by Jesus. While the word *apostolic* has historically referred to the New Testament authors and their experiences as we see across the pages of the Christian canon, yet there is also a sense in which the written documents emerged from the second generation—for instance the Second and Third Gospels written by those who were also disciples of the apostles chosen and commissioned by Jesus—and in that respect, provide windows into the emerging period of life after the passing of the Twelve. Post-apostolic discipleship, then, endeavors to be faithful

3. I take up some questions about secularity in dialogue with Lesslie Newbigin in my essay "Pluralism, Secularism, and Pentecost."

to the witness of Jesus whether that be in the late first century (second generation authors of New Testament writings and original readers of the apostolic writings) or at the beginnings of the third millennium (you reading this essay).

Yet, we also live today in a particular historical context, certainly long after the apostolic period, that can be further described as shaped by late modern, global, capitalist, imperial conditions. There are dominant political-economic forces to which the rest of the world continues to react if not also strain under, even as within the West, the masses continue to struggle under politics and economic pressures that favor the rich and powerful. And, we are nowadays also more keenly attuned to the fact that the first-century apostolic experiences also unfolded within an imperial horizon.[4] St. Luke, the author of the Third Gospel and its sequel, the book of Acts, frames the latter's ministry of the disciples and the work of the Holy Spirit as starting in Jerusalem and continuing through to the ends of the earth, which refers the city of Rome, the center of the Roman Empire, where the Acts 28 narrative concludes. And in the Third Gospel, Luke emphasizes that the story of Jesus unfolds against the backdrop of the rules of both Augustus and Tiberius Caesars (Luke 2:1; 3:1), so the entirety of Jesus' ministry is also carried out within the realm in which Caesar is claimed to be Lord. However, Luke gives us many more windows into how the Spirit empowers Jesus' ministry absent in the other gospel writers, and in that sense, the Lukan Jesus is prominently presented as the Messiah, the one anointed by the Spirit. Hence, the Spirit that came upon Jesus and enabled him to do his works of ministry recorded in the Gospel under the shadow of Rome is the same given and poured out upon the disciples in the book of Acts, to empower their heralding across the Pax Romana the reign of God that Jesus himself embodied and proclaimed. So, the work of the Spirit advances amid imperial contexts across the entirety of Luke's two volumes.

Knowing then that the story of Jesus and the apostles comes after the Pentecost experience—the outpouring of the Spirit to enable witness to the good news to the ends of the earth—our question today is: Where did Pentecost go?[5] This remains a significant contemporary concern for us in our secular and post-secular 2020s: How can or should we continue

4. The following condenses what I elaborate on in my *Who Is the Holy Spirit?*

5. This is a bit of a twist on the question asked elsewhere about trying to follow the Spirit's elusive paths: "You wonder where the Spirit went . . ."; see Rogers, *After the Spirit*, 17.

to experience the work of the Holy Spirit? Yet I want us to pick up this question by looking also at how the disciples and the first generations in the first century experienced—or did not experience—the Holy Spirit themselves. As I am a theologian rather than a biblical scholar, this is not an exegetical exercise. While much of the rest of this chapter will focus on biblical texts (Acts 19 to be exact), I'm conducting instead what we might call theological readings of the New Testament and of Scripture.[6] This involves bringing our horizon to meet that of the New Testament writers and readers, Luke and his audiences (e.g., Theophilus, who Luke specifically addresses at the beginning of both his texts) particularly. On the one hand, we live after Pentecost, but on the other, we wish to live in light of Pentecost, in ways that exemplify our ongoing experience of the outpouring of the Spirit (what some pentecostals would call the baptism of the Holy Spirit). So, the goal is to both check our experience against that of the apostles and also continue to be formed by these apostolic writings for discipleship today.

WHEN THE SPIRIT GOES SILENT? APOSTOLIC ANTICIPATIONS OF THE "POST-SECULAR"?

More specifically, our question here concerns our experience of secularization and of secularity. In our current contexts, many of us continuously wonder if and then why the Holy Spirit goes silent, or at least appears to do so. We who inhabit late modernity and live amid secularism often get by best on our own, without appealing to or reluctant to name the divine Spirit's presence and activity in our lives. Our apostolic hermeneutic thus prompts consideration of where if at all in the apostolic experience such or similar questions were uttered. Did the earliest generations sense the silence—or a silencing—of the Holy Spirit?

Accompany me on the following thought-exercise in the book of Acts. Note, for instance, that it is in the first half of Luke's account of the early church that the majority of the references to the Holy Spirit take place (almost 80 percent of the over fifty mentions). Thus, in the second half of the Acts, including all through Paul's missionary journeys, the Spirit is mentioned far less frequently. Similar observations have been made over millennia about these much more prominent and extensive appearances in the first part of the book, and then in the latter portions of the narrative

6. See my book *Hermeneutical Spirit*.

over the course of the first generation's experiences it seems like the Pentecost fires had subsided. When then considering where the Spirit went in our late modern and secular time, this "fact" arises to consciousness. For pentecostals presuming a this-is-that hermeneutic that believes our experiences can be found in scripture and vice-versa, it is always appropriate to return to the apostolic experiences in the book of Acts. So, what happened to the apostles, and what did they do? Why is the Spirit mentioned far less in the second half of Luke's story of the earliest Christians?

Upon closer consideration, however, we can also realize this is a misleading question. Or at least there is another way to look at this matter rather than just by counting references to the Spirit and comparing the amounts in the two halves of the book. Acts 1:8 not only provides a kind of table of contents for the book but also gives us a clue toward approaching our question otherwise: "But you will receive power when the Holy Spirit has come upon you; and you will be my witnesses in Jerusalem, in all Judea and Samaria, and to the ends of the earth." This verse tells us that the empowering work of the Holy Spirit and its gift for the apostles and disciples frames the entire narrative. From this perspective, it would be inaccurate to claim that Luke thinks the Spirit is present and active only when specifically mentioned across the chapters of his book. Rather the entire apostolic journey, starting in Jerusalem, into Judea, Samaria, and culminating at the ends of the earth, is fully enabled by the Spirit. That's why historically this book has been known not only as the Acts of the Apostles but as the Acts of the Holy Spirit.

So, this is another way to look at the last half of the Acts narrative. Whereas the Spirit's being mentioned less suggests a greater silence of the Spirit's works than in the first half of Acts, chapter 1 verse 8 clarifies otherwise: that the Spirit is present and active even when not specifically mentioned. Such a perspective has implications not only for reading the latter portion of the Acts account but also for how we might think about secularization and especially where secularism presumes a hard-and-fast ideological boundary between the public spaces where we all exist and the private spaces where we are allowed to call on the Holy Spirit all we want. Yet if the apostolic experience of the book of Acts can teach us anything, it's that the Spirit is not absent even when un-mentioned. Put alternatively, even in public spaces where we're not supposed to mention the Spirit, she remains at work.[7]

7. I long ago learned to appreciate the appropriateness of using the feminine pronoun for the Spirit, e.g., Gelpi, *Divine Mother*; Pinnock, *Flame of Love*.

I realize that the apostolic church's traversals of imperial Rome were not guided by our secular assumptions separating private religious life from public, market, and social lives, so in a strict sense, reading these ancient texts from our secular horizon is anachronistic. On the other hand, observing how the apostolic believers engaged the Pax Romana faithfully and missionally provides perspective for our own intersection with the imperial forces of late modernity, particularly but not only for navigating post-secular milieus.[8] So, rather than wondering if Pentecost has gone somewhere or disappeared, whether today or in the apostolic narrative, perhaps we should inquire instead about how we might do better at recognizing Pentecost? How might apostolic quests for the Spirit in the age of Roman imperialism connect with our own pneumatic expeditions in a secular-and-yet-post-secularizing time?

POST-PENTECOST FAITHFULNESS: APOSTOLIC (EPHESIAN) DISCIPLESHIP FOR AN IMPERIAL AGE

In and out of our secularized and even post-secular world, we will open a set of windows into the book of Acts. After Paul's third missionary journey is introduced with quick broad brushstrokes in a few sentences (Acts 18:22–23), Luke turns to the apostolic sojourn at Ephesus. Over the next few pages, our goal is to understand the person and work of the Holy Spirit both where mentioned and also when unspecified. Put otherwise: How do we recognize the Spirit's presence and activity in this "pre-secularized" and yet thoroughly imperial space that is the ancient Asian Roman city of Ephesus? While there is much to pull from across the New Testament about Ephesus,[9] our focus will be on what is detailed in Acts 19.

Ephesian Window 1: On the Way to the Lecture Hall

The chapter opens thus: "While Apollos was in Corinth, Paul passed through the interior regions and came to Ephesus, where he found some

8. I have attempted a prior reading of the Acts narrative for the purposes of constructing a post-secular and prophetic stance toward civil society; see *In the Days of Caesar*, esp. ch. 6.3.1.

9. Not only Paul's letter to the Ephesians but also the pastoral letters to Timothy (in Ephesus according to 1 Tim 1:3) and the Revelation given to St. John addressed to Ephesus among six other (west) Asian cities, etc.; on the latter, see my *Revelation*, 42–47.

disciples. He said to them, 'Did you receive the Holy Spirit when you became believers?' They replied, 'No, we have not even heard that there is a Holy Spirit'" (Acts 19:1–2). What ensues has become a classical text for pentecostal readers since it documents how Christian conversion,[10] or at least growth in Christian discipleship, involves being filled and baptized with the Holy Spirit with the manifest sign of speaking in tongues (and prophecy). Thus, 19:6 becomes an important proof-text for the classical pentecostal doctrine of Spirit-baptism as evidenced by tongues speech.[11]

Our question here is different, motivated by our secular and post-secular context. For such environments, it is not the sixth but second verse that is important: "He said to them, 'Did you receive the Holy Spirit when you became believers?' They replied, 'No, we have not even heard that there is a Holy Spirit.'" Most secularized persons, like these disciples of John, would not know anything about the Holy Spirit. What does this even refer to? In this respect, this account provides a window into the real world where the person and work of the Holy Spirit is neither understood nor even recognized. For most of us who inhabit a secular city, our colleagues, relationships, and the spaces that we navigate at our locations of employment or in our daily lives are bereft of at least mention of the Spirit. Is it then possible to consider how this text can be an encouragement? Not only was there a similar obliviousness to the Spirit in the apostolic narrative, but even in such a context, there is an opportunity for the Spirit to be made explicit. So, in any moment when awareness of the Spirit's silence or absence surfaces, such might instead be an occasion for the Spirit's person and work to be made perspicuous. Rather than the Spirit not being there at all, there is currently an opportunity to encounter the Spirit.

I also then want to focus momentarily on verses 8 to 10: "He entered the synagogue and for three months spoke out boldly, and argued persuasively about the kingdom of God. When some stubbornly refused to believe and spoke evil of the Way before the congregation, he left them, taking the disciples with him, and argued daily in the lecture hall of Tyrannus. This continued for two years, so that all the residents of Asia, both Jews and Greeks, heard the word of the Lord." Whereas the

10. This is the dominant history of interpretation, that these were John the Baptist's disciples, pointed to by John but not yet converted to Jesus; e.g., Kurz, *Acts of the Apostles*, 291–92.

11. I provide a contemporary reconsideration of this doctrine in my *Renewing Christian Theology*, ch. 3.

preceding pericope clearly names the Spirit, including her agency, this two-year period is summarized as if what occurs is mundane, the opposite of being Spirit-infused. Such might even be assumed by populist groups that have been shaped with anti-intellectualist sentiments,[12] particularly when we notice the argumentation described as occurring ho-hummingly daily in (over months) the synagogue considered as a place of (book) study and (over years) Tyrannus's lecture hall (from the Greek *schole* or school). Yet, "argued," from the Greek *dialegómenos* (19:8, 10), involves dialogical give-and-take that would occur in both locales, within rabbinic exchanges on the one hand and within a community or scholarly inquiry involving teachers and students on the other hand. Ironically, we might conclude that since Paul was unsuccessful in the synagogue, and hence less persuasive, the Holy Spirit was absent there, compared to the results experienced at the other site. But rather than drawing such pneumatological inferences and then concluding that the Spirit manifests in power only when there are numerical results and is otherwise dormant (or that hearts are hard, which in the case of the synagogue is stated as such, consistent with how Jews in Acts are portrayed as opposing the expansion of the Christian way),[13] why not conclude instead that all of this happens by the enablement of the Spirit and that this is where we should find encouragement, not only in mass conversions. Put another way: The Spirit is at work through any periods of struggle and stubborn disbelief (like in the Ephesian synagogue) even as the Spirit is present also when it seems there is greater receptivity to proclamation of the gospel. If our capacity to persist in faithfulness despite opposition and challenge (even for only two months) is enabled by the Spirit, then the lack of signs and wonders should not be understood as the absence of the Spirit.

What happens after verse 10 may, if we are not careful, perpetuate some of the assumptions we have been attempting to overturn so far. While "*all* the residents of Asia, both Jews and Greeks, heard the word of the Lord" (italics added) is surely hyperbolic, it is also suggestive that whatever positive results may have emanated from the Pauline efforts impacted less Ephesus than the wider Asian region. But even granting the latter for the moment, there are other indications—for instance the Pauline complaint later that "all who are in Asia have turned away from me" (2 Tim 1:15)—that the fruits of these endeavors did not last.[14] In

12. Well described of classical pentecostals by Nañez, *Full Gospel, Fractured Minds*.

13. E.g., Smith, *Literary Construction of the Other in the Acts of the Apostles*, ch. 2.

14. See Strelan, *Paul, Artemis, and the Jews in Ephesus*, 254, 297.

short, such a declaration of missional accomplishments cautions us to not presume we can always know how deep the work of the Spirit lands in our communities, contexts, and environments. The rest of Acts 19 suggests there were some phenomenological signs and manifestations even as there was also hostility and melee. Yet the Spirit's work in 19:9–10, except as intimated in the final clause, seems relatively subdued, even if no less real, precisely in the casual dialogical efforts extended over a significant stretch of time. The point is that it is this daily less than spectacular conversation Paul perseveres with that forms the backdrop of the gospel's proclamation—whatever its reception—in Ephesus and across its wider Asian region.[15] We must keep this in mind as we explore what happens next at Ephesus.

Ephesian Window 2: Out of the House and to Bonfires

Amid his ongoing teaching and conversational endeavors, "God did extraordinary miracles through Paul, so that when the handkerchiefs or aprons that had touched his skin were brought to the sick, their diseases left them, and the evil spirits came out of them" (Acts 19:11–12).[16] This latter reference opens up to what happened with the sons of Sceva:

> Then some itinerant Jewish exorcists tried to use the name of the Lord Jesus over those who had evil spirits, saying, "I adjure you by the Jesus whom Paul proclaims." Seven sons of a Jewish high priest named Sceva were doing this. But the evil spirit said to them in reply, "Jesus I know, and Paul I know; but who are you?" Then the man with the evil spirit leapt on them, mastered them all, and so overpowered them that they fled out of the house naked and wounded. When this became known to all residents of Ephesus, both Jews and Greeks, everyone was awestruck; and the name of the Lord Jesus was praised. (19:13–17)

Important to note in this description is the appearance of other spirits but no specific reference to the Holy Spirit. Of course, we have

15. That is the point about Luke's Tyrannus lecture hall report, notes Penna, *St. Paul the Apostle*, 208–9.

16. God is the primary agent here, although Paul's ministry is also vindicated, surely against the magicians of the Ephesian world; this point is made thoroughly in the one full-length study of Acts 19 which argues that the narrative presents Ephesus as the climax of Paul's missionary successes—see Schauf, *Theology as History*, 170–72 and passim.

been accustomed to see the Spirit's work in these kinds of "extraordinary" occurrences, although for our present purposes, I commend it is also appropriate then to see the Spirit in the "ordinariness" of the Acts narrative's daily, and unremarkable, business. Whether the Spirit is named or not, the entirety of the apostolic witness across the book occurs by the Spirit.

Yet this passage also features what might be incomprehensible to most secular folk: pervasiveness of evil spirits. In this Ephesian context, evil spirits are those that prompt resistance to the Christian Way (19:9) or are practitioners of the magic arts or aligned with Artemis worship.[17] On the one hand, it might be argued that our emerging post-secular (or post-modern) experience is increasingly spiritualized, albeit now by all kinds of other spirits.[18] In such a pluralistic cosmos all kinds of other pneumatological questions arise: How can we discern the work of the Holy Spirit vis-à-vis these other spirits? How might we compare and contrast these many spirits? How to contest, resist, and overcome specifically evil spirits? A post-secular world actually opens up to, if not enables naming of, a world teeming with spirits. What are the pros and cons of trekking amid such a plethora of spirits? This would be quite different from the modern and secular mentality that rejected as incoherent all talk of, much less action presuming to engage, spiritual realities. Post-secularity instead says, the more spirits the merrier![19]

In our post-secular context, the opportunities and challenges related to discernment of spirits become much more important, and, if the latter results in judgments that evil spirits are present and active, then exorcisms and their competencies would become paramount. That this text itself compares Jewish exorcists who operated in the name of Paul with the latter's approach in Jesus' name suggests the continuation of a long-running theme in the first century contrasting the way of Jesus with the ways of ancient Israel. As already noted above (albeit in passing then), much of the Acts narrative is taken up with justifying the emergence of the Christian path over and against that of the Jews, thus exposing the deep and complex issues percolating in the relationship between Jews and the early gentile followers of Jesus in the apostolic context. The spiritual issues are thus complicated by the divergences between Jewish and emerging messianic/Christian communities. What may be an otherwise

17. See Walton, "Evil in Ephesus."

18. E.g., Partridge, *Re-Enchantment of the West*.

19. I explore the possibility of a pluralistic cosmology in my *Spirit of Creation*, esp. ch. 6.

straightforward question about who has the Holy Spirit and thus is empowered to engage with and ward off evil spirits is overlain by whether Jews had access to the divine spirit or operated on their own and even perhaps, more problematically, in ways that served the forces of evil.

Yet because the sons of Sceva are identified as Jewish in this account,[20] we could conclude not just that they are impotent against real evil (since the spirit dismisses their exorcistic efforts) but the humiliating manner of their failure is but a short step away from catalyzing even more problematic associations. Their fleeing naked and wounded suggests not only that the evil spirits were hot on their trails but these associated images did nothing to forestall the anti-Semitic tendencies that festered over time. The sons of Sceva are no longer pitied but instead demonized just like the practitioners of magic that are a part of this moment of the "triumph" of the Pauline mission at Ephesus: both are the "bad guys" in contrast to apostolically empowered witnesses.[21] In the process, those who were rescued from evil spirits are lost, and while we might celebrate their deliverance, difficult questions about spiritual discernment in multi-religious contexts, or about mental health and illness matters vis-à-vis historic associations with demonization, or about successfully documented exorcisms by Jews or those in other faith[22]—all relevant to Christian life and work in a post-secular world—are marginalized or effectively shelved. These matters, especially but not only how biblical texts inspire the imaginative postures and practices of those of us who live in religiously pluralistic societies (like most post-secular states are) in relationship to those of other faith commitments, are doubly pronounced even before we get into the next section regarding the dominant Artemis religiosity at Ephesus.

I want to return to this important matter about not only Jews but also those in other faiths, but before doing so, note Luke transitions from

20. There has always been some discussion to associate these sons with imperial cults instead, although the Jewish designation persists almost uniformly in the manuscript evidence; see Fitzmyer, *To Advance the Gospel*, 332–38.

21. All difficult matters that do not exhaust tributaries of implications unleashed by the textual images; I have taken up the question of anti-Semitism as part of my discussion of the doctrine of the church—reconsidering its relationship to Israel of old and especially in our time against the long history of ecclesial anti-Jewishness in the background—in my *Renewing Christian Theology*, ch. 6.

22. I have addressed some of these matters in, e.g., *Discerning the Spirit(s)*; on the question of exorcisms in interreligious contexts, see my "Demonic in Pentecostal-Charismatic Christianity."

the sons of Sceva: "Also many of those who became believers confessed and disclosed their practices. A number of those who practiced magic collected their books and burned them publicly; when the value of these books was calculated, it was found to come to fifty thousand silver coins. So the word of the Lord grew mightily and prevailed" (19:18–20). Exorcistic formulas in the foregoing sons of Sceva report give way to everyday diviner prescriptions and spell-incantations cast into bonfires. The Christian Way thus contrasts with magical approaches, with the latter, as one scholar puts it, going "up in flames."[23] The burning of books worth fifty thousand days of wages—the value then of drachmas or silver coins[24]—highlights the intertwining of our economic and spiritual lives.

Ephesian Window 3: Into and Around the Theater

We who abide in late modern times realize in more ways than one how money makes the world go round. People vote according to what makes the most difference in their pocketbooks, for instance, and we recognize the economic domain cannot be divorced from our religious lives. Post-secularity means also, or at least, that our public lives and private religious engagements are interconnected by monetary configurations, motivations, and related matters. Turns out this economic bridge between religiosity and society existed then in the apostolic period also. This next portion of Acts 19 helps us see even more starkly how economic and political registers are interwoven with our religious and spiritual efforts so that our discernment should unfold with multi-layered and multi-dimensional capacities.[25]

The scene is set up by Luke's describing Paul's resolution to leave Ephesus for Macedonia, then Achaia, and from there to Jerusalem and even Rome (lots of travel anticipated ahead!), yet this resolve "in the spirit" (Acts 19:21) can also be understood grammatically at least as implying if not also clearly appealing to, the leading of the Holy Spirit. Whereas earlier in the Acts narrative Paul was guided away from Ephesus by the Spirit (16:6–10), now his lingering in Ephesus can be understood deriving from his own discernment and his attempts to be obedient to

23. See Rowe, *World Upside Down*, 42.

24. Kurz, *Acts of the Apostles*, 295n2.

25. Elsewhere, e.g., "Glocalization and the Gift-Giving Spirit," I elaborate more on the economics of the book of Acts.

the Spirit's leading.[26] The text thus suggests not only that it is not always clear when our own decisions are demarcate-able from the Spirit's directives but also that there are instances when we may be in sync with the Spirit, even when not specifically realized or articulated. And, back to Paul: Perhaps in his attempts to be Spirit-led, in time, the divine breath arranges for his presence at, even if perhaps fortunately on the sidelines of, the upheaval that breaks out:

> About that time no little disturbance broke out concerning the Way. A man named Demetrius, a silversmith who made silver shrines of Artemis, brought no little business to the artisans. These he gathered together, with the workers of the same trade, and said, "Men, you know that we get our wealth from this business. You also see and hear that not only in Ephesus but in almost the whole of Asia this Paul has persuaded and drawn away a considerable number of people by saying that gods made with hands are not gods. And there is danger not only that this trade of ours may come into disrepute but also that the temple of the great goddess Artemis will be scorned, and she will be deprived of her majesty that brought all Asia and the world to worship her." When they heard this, they were enraged and shouted, "Great is Artemis of the Ephesians!" (19:23–28)

Ephesus was not only a major Roman city in the first century but also where the worship of Artemis had taken hold.[27] Demetrius the silversmith is recorded as repeating what Luke indicated Paul had heralded earlier: "The God who made the world and everything in it, he who is Lord of heaven and earth, does not live in shrines made by human hands, nor is he served by human hands, as though he needed anything, since he himself gives to all mortals life and breath and all things" (17:24–25; also 17:29). Demetrius's logic, arguably, is that Paul's message directly undercuts Ephesian religiosity to the degree the latter includes shrine devotion and piety, and as a further extension, also threatens the Ephesian religious economy, especially Artemis artisanship.

26. The NRSV translates "in his spirit," meaning Paul's, although "by the Spirit," meaning the Holy Spirit, is also possible. "Grammar cannot settle the question either way, but Luke's theology and usage strongly favor the latter interpretation, which most scholars consequently prefer," says Keener, *Acts*, 3:2861.

27. English-language research on the religion of Artemis in Ephesus was initiated by Strelan, *Paul, Artemis, and the Jews in Ephesus*, but recently extended vis-à-vis the book of Ephesians by Immendörfer, *Ephesians and Artemis*, and then in relationship to 1 Timothy by Glahn, *Nobody's Mother*.

As Demetrius whipped up the crowd, Luke reports that the "people rushed together to the theater, dragging with them Gaius and Aristarchus, Macedonians who were Paul's traveling-companions" (19:29). What about Paul? Luke continues: "Paul wished to go into the crowd, but the disciples would not let him; even some officials of the province of Asia, who were friendly to him, sent him a message urging him not to venture into the theater" (19:30–31). Two years was more than enough time for Paul to have developed some Ephesian friends in "high places," so to speak,[28] and he is thus spared through their intervention from direct confrontation with the mob. Other efforts to quiet the multitude were not only unsuccessful but generated further furor: "For about two hours all of them shouted in unison, 'Great is Artemis of the Ephesians!'" (19:34b).

At some point, the town clerk (otherwise unnamed) appears to calm the throng, and does so by admonishing the citizenry of the dangers to them of further out-of-control rioting. Part of his strategy, however, was articulated thus: "Citizens of Ephesus, who is there that does not know that the city of the Ephesians is the temple-keeper of the great Artemis and of the statue that fell from heaven? Since these things cannot be denied, you ought to be quiet and do nothing rash. You have brought these men here who are neither temple-robbers nor blasphemers of our goddess" (19:35b–37). Retrieving the heavenly origins of the goddess myth may have been an intentional distanciation of Artemis from what Paul otherwise named as idols of human construction, even while there is a direct refutation of Christian action against the Artemesian religious economy. The other claim about the apostolic proclamation not being blasphemous about the Ephesian deity, however, is also a bit unclear, not only given Demetrius's statements against the backdrop of Paul's Areopagus speech noted above. Perhaps the town clerk was referring to those of Paul's mission *in* the theater (Gaius and Aristarchus),[29] and relieving only them of repercussions due to anti-Artemis evangelistic rhetoric. But read more charitably, the clerk's disclaimer also absolves the Pauline proclamation from direct disrespecting of Artemis.

What we see in this Ephesian public square, so to speak, is an interreligious encounter driven by religio-economic dynamics. The Ephesian political economy is the site where the God of Israel and of Jesus meets the goddess Artemis. Demetrius may have been the better theologian

28. The conclusion of Witetschek, "Artemis and Asiarchs," esp. 347–48.

29. As noted by Price, *Widow Traditions in Luke-Acts*, 244–45.

than the town clerk since the former recognizes that there is a religious confrontation even if his motivations had been primarily economic, while the latter may have downplayed the religious dimensions of the encounter even if he proved to be the effective and needed politician in a tenuous situation.[30] More precisely, two years of kerygmatic dialogue, argument, and proclamation did have political and economic ramifications. The surfacing of this opposition was predictable as "all the residents of Asia, both Jews and Greeks, heard the word of the Lord" (19:10), since before, the allegiances of these same peoples were to "the great goddess Artemis . . . and . . . her majesty that brought all Asia and the world to worship her" (19:27b).[31]

Where is the work of the Spirit in all of this? The theater incident is one moment across Paul's multi-year Ephesian ministry. Over two years, the Spirit was at work whether some believed or others did not, whether people were engaged with what occurred in the lecture hall or when others felt economic repercussions of the mission. Similarly, we can also hold that the Spirit remained at work for the few hours of Artemesian uproar, indeed, even seeing the Spirit's interventions in the ebb and flow of Artemis religiosity in this city, whether in preserving Paul from harm, or in protecting his compatriots, or in inspiring the town clerk, or otherwise keeping more destruction and harm from evolving. In all of this, we might also conclude that a Spirit-ed engagement with those in other faiths can proceed along multiple pathways, from dialogical discussion to public exorcisms along one track, to apologetic preaching and yet respectful interaction along another. As our apostolic exemplars were able to bear authentic but yet non-derogatory public witness within a multi-religious imperial context, we would do well to not demonize those in other faiths in a post-secular world.[32] Ministry in the power of the Spirit need not be religiously disparaging in a post-secular world of many faiths, even and perhaps especially where we might have historically had Christian majorities. Acts 19 give us windows into Spirit-inspired apostolic ministry in an imperial and pluralistic public square.

30. I get this from Rowe, *World Upside Down*, 49.

31. See Brinks, "Great Is Artemis of the Ephesians," esp. 792–93.

32. See my "From Demonization to Kin-domization," 157–74.

POST-APOSTOLIC DISCIPLESHIP FOR A NEO-IMPERIAL AND POST-SECULAR AGE

Acts 19 refracts the interfacing of various spiritual realities with the imperial Roman regime, and this highlights how, even in our own secular and post-secular contexts, there are multiple overlapping spiritual dimensions cutting across our social, political, and economic lives. Being of and even amid the secular does not mean the spiritual is absent. It simply means we have less capacity to name it. But our presently evolving post-secular situation also means we have at our disposal apostolic languages about the Spirit from the biblical narrative to enable the urgent discernment of and imperative engagement with many spirits. The public square is not bereft but replete with spiritual realities, and there is greater capacity for what modern secularism names as only economic, political, social, or cultural to be recognizably spiritual as well.

The Pentecost narrative (Acts 2) already invites us to think about many forms of witness in and through the many languages of those "from every nation under heaven" (Acts 2:5). This suggests also that there are many perspectives to be engaged in the various public squares of our secular and post-secular world.[33] Whereas town clerks may not even have heard about whether there is a Holy Spirit, she can and does bear witness to the Spirit's work for those of us with eyes to see and ears to hear. And even if specific Jews, as in the case of these sons of Sceva, may not be exemplary exorcists, that does not mean that all Jews are to be eschewed as possible partners in our battle against evil, especially since "our struggle is not against enemies of blood and flesh, but against the rulers, against the authorities, against the cosmic powers of this present darkness, against the spiritual forces of evil in the heavenly places" (Eph 6:12). How do we recognize friends from foes? How do we witness further to the impending reign of God in the public squares of our post-secular spaces? Perhaps ongoing return to the apostolic narrative can guide our partnership and collaboration with others in our missional efforts for the common good?[34]

33. E.g., Yong, "Pentecostal Christianities and Their Political Lives."

34. This essay emerged out of transcription of a talk I was asked to give (via Zoom) at the "Church with Spirit, in Our Secular Age" pastor's conference hosted by the Danish StudieCenter Menighedsbaseret Teology (Study Centre for Church-Based Theology), on May 11, 2023. Thanks to Dr. Silje Kvamme Bjørndal for the initial invitation and to SCMT staff who recorded the session to make this possible. Although the published version has been edited, the oral presentation flavor has not been totally eliminated. Numerous clarifications have been added all throughout the text, and all of the notes.

Chapter 6

Community Engagement After Pentecost

Apostolic Forays Then and Now

I BEGIN WITH A few introductory comments about the title of this chapter.[1] The *community engagement* at the beginning relates to what I understand to be central to the Whitelands seminar initiative. The notion of "after Pentecost" has been foregrounded especially in my more recent work, as those familiar with such will recognize.[2] While it is known I've been doing work as a theologian in the pentecostal tradition or movement for most of my theological career,[3] in the last decade or so, this "after Pentecost" theme has emerged to the forefront. As should be clear to theological students, especially, Pentecost belongs not to any particular group or movement, not even those who are part of the pentecostal

1. Thanks for how this essay emerged is due in three directions: first, to the volume editors for extending the invitation to include my work in the volume where this chapter was first published; second, to Caroline Polly Ueriraisa Tjihenuna, the Dean's Fellow for the College of Theology and Ministry at Oral Roberts University, for help with transcription of the audio recording of a Zoom-mediated lecture I prepared for the Whitelands Centre for Pentecostalism and Community Engagement at the University of Roehampton, presented June 5, 2023; and third to Prof. Richard Burgess at the Whitelands Centre for inviting my talk and to Prof. David Clark for facilitating the recording. I have further edited the transcribed version, retained some (not all) of the oral elements, and added especially notes and references (with a bit of an embarrassed forewarning needed here about the many self-references included). I take responsibility, however, for all errors of fact or interpretation.

2. E.g., Yong, *Mission After Pentecost*; Yong, *Renewing the Church by the Spirit*.

3. Here, as elsewhere in my writings, I do not capitalize *pentecostal* when used adjectivally, only when in titles or with reference to proper nouns.

community. Rather, it is a New Testament event, recorded in Luke's book of Acts and, in that respect, belongs to the entire Christian *oecumene*. So, even as I do not apologize for my reflections as a pentecostal theologian, I bid all of us, those within pentecostal communities and churches, or otherwise included in the wider body of Jesus Christ, to consider how Pentecost—or the Pentecost narrative, or the arc of the Pentecost event and its aftermath—may have implications for all Christian practice, discipleship, and theologizing. In that sense, our focus here is to consider community engagement in this "after Pentecost" mode.

And that also leads us to the subtitle of this essay. As we know, the Pentecost event in the book of Acts is at the beginning of Luke's account of the apostolic experience and the early Christian and messianic movement. Hence, we look at this notion of community engagement through this apostolic lens in the Third Evangelist's sequel to his Gospel account and then explore and inquire about the implications of specific readings of this narrative after (the Day of) Pentecost for this task, both in terms of the apostolic experience of such and then also in terms of our own engagements with our communities today.[4]

Before we begin, however, let me add a paragraph that connects the original form of this presentation to the purposes of this Festschrift by recognizing the achievements of its honoree, Rev. Dr. Younghoon Lee. It is indeed remarkable that here we have a leading pentecostal scholar-practitioner, one who has emerged at the vanguard of a maturing Korean pentecostal academy on the one hand,[5] and yet also who has had the responsibility of being the chief shepherd of both Yoido Full Gospel Church and of the Assemblies of God of South Korea on the other hand. And with regard to the thematic focus of this essay, it is particularly important to recognize how Yoido Full Gospel Church, beginning with Lee's predecessor but continued since under Lee's guidance, has also been exemplary as a pentecostal ecclesial community in engaging with the broader society, impacting its local communities, and having a public

4. As we shall see, my own approach is less on apostolicity as understood in its traditional historical and ecclesiological senses than a hermeneutical one wherein the adjectival *apostolic* points to attempts to retrieve the New Testament more generally and the book of Acts more specifically for contemporary theological purposes; see, for instance, other essays of mine adopting similar interpretive strategies for present endeavors such as Yong, "Jubilee, Liberation, and Pentecost"; Yong, "Understanding and Living the Apostolic Way."

5. I know only of Dr. Lee's English-language works, e.g., Lee, *Holy Spirit Movement in Korea*; Lee et al., *Pentecostal Mission and Global Christianity*.

witness and impact.[6] In these various respects, consider the following reflections inspired in part by Yoido's role in inviting and urging pentecostal churches around the world to open up to their communities, and perhaps also in the process, our discussion might further inspire such efforts both theologically and on the ground wherever pentecostal disciples and churches meet and serve with others.

FROM FAITH-ROOTED COMMUNITY ORGANIZING TO FAITH-ROOTED COMMUNITY ENGAGEMENT

I'll start by introducing us to a work that needs to get more attention globally, which is a book by two colleagues: Alexia Salvatierra, who is professor of Global Transformation and Missional Engagement at Fuller Seminary, and a mutual friend, Dr. Peter Heltzel. I'd like to highlight a few elements that I have gleaned from my reading of their *Faith Rooted Organizing: Mobilizing the Church in Service of the World*, especially how they commend faith-rooted community organizing. Salvatierra has spent many decades working as a practical theologian and community organizer, and Heltzel has long been a theological advocate for marginalized communities.[7] Here are some basic interlocking and interrelated principles they present that those wanting to engage in/with and organize community from a faith-rooted perspective should consider.

They urge us to first ask, What kind of goals are we looking for on the other side of whatever community organizing we might be envisioning. Then we need to take assessment of the initiative in light of those objectives, for instance, Where do we start? What are the obstacles? What are the resources at our disposal? These considerations involve the situation of the community that we want to organize, mobilize, or engage with, as well as our own situatedness vis-à-vis that community. Third, then, includes developing some strategic pathways into and within that community. How do we get from "here" to "there," particularly in light of our goals, the present situation, and the existing set of circumstances? Fourth: recruitment. How do we galvanize the body of Christ in particular, but maybe also adjacent groups of/or persons, to achieve whatever community organizational goals we might be committed to?

6. I discuss some of these developments and contributions in my articles "Glocalization and the Gift-Giving Spirit"; and "Salvation, Society, and the Spirit."

7. I write about and reflect on my personal experiences with the advocacy dimension of Peter's work in my article "Liberating and Diversifying Theological Education."

But the focus of Salvatierra and Heltzel is on the body of Christ in any particular community. How do we motivate, recruit, and then empower disciples of Jesus to serve their community and to achieve what strategic purposes? And any notion of empowering the body of Christ involves developing and orienting leaders, equipping and enabling the analysis, implementation, and adjustment of the strategy toward those goals, and mobilizing resources. So, the process at some time includes a launching of the organizational endeavor and then reiterative assessment-interaction that may require adjustments in all kinds of respects, maybe even adjustments of some of the goals. In being attentive to the process of community organization itself, we need to be flexible rather than rigid with our aspirations, since some challenges that might come up in the meanwhile may be of the sort that call for and even require redirection.[8]

Finally, Salvatierra and Heltzel name the sustainability indices of this community organizational initiative, particularly as they relate to the specifics of the set or types of interfaces anticipated. How are leaders flourishing or thriving—being sustained—through this process? Then and also, how are "followers," those doing the work of community organization, doing? How is the community collectively and in its various parts responding to the witness of the body of Christ, and how are the ecclesial community and the wider social and public community thriving in the short, mid-, and longer term? So again, depending on the community organizational goals, its time frames—e.g., is this a one-year, two-year, or three-year project?—and as we are being attentive to the developments, resourcing the leaders, and empowering the members, how do we ensure the initiative is flourishing and thriving? Is what is envisioned sustainable? This should be an ongoing question, in the shorter, mid-, and longer terms. As such, any community organizational strategy has to be reiterative.[9] Some of the goals may be revised as we go forward. That leads to differentiated ongoing assessment, and then maybe further adjustments of strategies. As we know, the vagaries of life intrude, e.g., members of the community come and go, and others join into the initiative. But how do we maintain a certain degree of stability from a leadership perspective

8. I expect that some if not most of these principles will be manifest and further exemplified in Salvatierra's more recent (collaborative) work, e.g., with Christerson et al., *God's Resistance*.

9. In his earlier book devoted to articulating a practical theology addressing racism and poverty, Heltzel proposes an improvisational methodology that reappears as this flexible and dynamic praxis for *Faith Rooted Organizing*; see Heltzel, *Resurrection City*.

and advance this vision and strategy in a sustainable and more rather than less coherent manner?

Salvatierra and Heltzel invite us to consider, and then participate in and contribute to, community organizing initiatives from a Christian or a faith-rooted perspective. Our focus on community engagement maps onto their community organizing proposals and both parallels and also grows out of the latter. In other words, any community engagement enterprise seeks to accomplish some or other set of objectives in relationship to that community, and in that respect, presumes and, at some point, has to enact, the sort of community organizing practices presented by our colleagues. Both community organization and community engagement ultimately, in the broadest sense, are intended to foster Christian service in and to the wider world. Perhaps not every point I have summarized from their contribution will be relevant to diverse global and local contexts, and surely every one will need to be adapted also when implemented in various sites. Nevertheless, as an orientation to our search for a relevant theological praxis for community engagement, I begin with this helpful resource.

WHAT DID/WOULD THE APOSTLES DO?

Now, then, *What did or what would the apostles do?* That is our play on the popular slogan WWJD? (*What would Jesus do?*). I take us on a hermeneutical detour now from what we've just discussed before diving into the heart of the matter. I'm keenly attuned to the possibility that some among us may presume a sharp contrast between what we might call *exegesis* and what we might call *eisegesis*. The former might be understood generally as how we hermeneutically and appropriately retrieve what the biblical text says, while the latter, less prominently in use but still present in at least in some theological circles as a pejorative practice, involves in that set of estimations less appropriate impositions brought by readers on the scriptural text. So, plainly said, for some of our hermeneutic seminars or hermeneutical schools, what is good *exegesis* is presumed to be readings controlled by the biblical authors, and what is not so good *eisegesis* is when we bring too many of our presuppositions and read them into the Bible.[10] Although I recognize these perspectives, I also think it is impos-

10. Some of the arguments in these directions are in Carson, *Exegetical Fallacies*; attentive readers of Carson's text will discern I would not agree with all of his presuppositions.

sible to insist on too hard and fast of a distinction between the horizon of the biblical authors on the one hand and that of any contemporary generation of readers on the other hand.[11] Without saying, therefore, that we want to neglect completely what the text says, I also believe that any interpreter of scripture involves various dynamic commitments. So, as a theologian, I approach scripture with a set of emergent and provisional theological perspectives, one that presumes, in this two-horizons sense, that our present world and experiences of such and the past worlds of Scripture meet unpredictably in any act of reading. Hence, we cannot avoid bringing our assumptions, experiences, and present realities to the scripture. Yet also, as we read scripture, we wait on the Holy Spirit to bring that scriptural message to challenge and interrogate our present experiences and assumptions as well. There is the *then* horizon and the *now* horizon, and we always want to be careful both that we are presuming too much about how our present horizon might construe the past horizon of Scripture, and yet, at the same time, we also realize that as embodied, situated, and historically informed creatures, none of us ever approaches the scriptural (or any other textual) horizon only and absolutely on its terms. What is at stake, then, is an ongoing navigation of these two horizons.[12]

And in that respect, what I'd like to provide in the following is a pentecostal response or an after-Pentecost perspective where we revisit the apostolic witness in part, although not necessarily only, for understanding of the goals, assessment strategies, recruitment, leadership development, and sustainability elements that Salvatierra and Heltzel have asked us to consider. So, I want us to go back to the book of Acts and look at some of the passages there and ask ourselves whether or not some of these contemporary faith-rooted organizational notions that have been introduced for community engagement purposes may or may not be applicable or illuminative of our reading and understanding the apostolic experience. What we're doing, then, is traversing the terrain between normative sets of theological and theoretical commitments—theologically as understood in the apostolic legacy and theoretically as informed by our community-organizational colleagues—and the ecclesial practices of actual community engagement. And to navigate these two horizons,

11. I go back here a generation ago to Thiselton, *Two Horizons*.

12. My summary statement here is more elaborately articulated in chapter 1 of *Learning Theology*: "Scripture: The Word and Breath of God," where I discuss the world behind the text, the world of the text, and the world in front of the text.

I want to look through five windows into the apostolic community organizing and engagement world. I realize mine is the perspective of a non-community organizer, meaning I haven't had decades of experience in participating in community organization as my colleagues. Yet, what I'd like to do is conduct a thought experiment in which we revisit the apostolic narrative, or at least five snapshots of that account, from this community engagement posture, and then observe how the readings might unfold.[13]

WINDOW 1: COMMUNITY ENGAGEMENT AFTER PENTECOST (ACTS 2:42–47)

Here we go. The first apostolic community emerges on the Day of Pentecost. In a familiar passage, Acts 2:42–47, we observe the first interactions of these messianists with their community:

> They devoted themselves to the apostles' teaching and fellowship, to the breaking of bread and the prayers. Awe came upon everyone, because many wonders and signs were being done by the apostles. All who believed were together and had all things in common; they would sell their possessions and goods and distribute the proceeds to all, as any had need. Day by day, as they spent much time together in the temple, they broke bread at home and ate their food with glad and generous hearts, praising God and having the goodwill of all the people. And day by day the Lord added to their number those who were being saved.[14]

A few things to highlight here from some of the community engagement tools we have been provided with. First, what was the nature of the community engagement? A number of the previously mentioned elements are at least phenomenologically observable, including, on the one hand, the selling of possessions and goods and then a redistribution

13. Elsewhere I have attempted an identical hermeneutical strategy for constructive missiological and theological (respectively vis-à-vis the next two references) purposes, e.g., Yong, "Apostolic Evangelism in the Postcolony"; Yong, "Spirit, the Common Good, and the Public Sphere" (also chapter 4 in this volume). Those interested can consult and compare how this overall method might be performing when applied across various realms of theological praxis.

14. These (and all later) scriptural passages are simply the transcriptions of the audio recording (even as my scriptural recitations relied on the New Revised Standard Version); I have not gone back to correct any misreadings and have retained instead the transcribed renditions.

of the proceeds to all. Now the *all* refers to probably the community of three thousand or so recorded as responding to Peter's Day of Pentecost sermon (Acts 2:41). But the selling of possessions and goods would involve interfaces with the broader Jerusalem community, and it is within that wider geopolitical community that this fledgling apostolic group bubbled up.

Then in verse 47, there's another intimation of sort of the blurring of the lines between this apostolic band and its surrounding community, where it says that "they spend much time together in the temple breaking bread at home, eating the food with glad and generous hearts," thus trafficking (maybe not the best word) and traveling between home and temple. Amid this movement, members of this embryonic apostolic community were also "praising God and having the goodwill of all the people." The "goodwill of all the people" includes those of the surrounding community. So, it's this apostolic community of three thousand, living in these various homes around the temple community, that gains "the goodwill" and estimation of those in the wider public space. And the result Luke narrates is that: "day by day, the Lord added to the number of those who were being saved."[15]

So, goodwill was being fostered by the apostolic band, and that goodwill also produced additions to the community. Hence, we are not surprised when, between Acts chapter 2 and chapter 4, the number of three thousand initially baptized had increased to about five thousand (4:4). This window thus invites observation of a variety of community engagement forms "after Pentecost." Neither individually nor cumulatively does what we see in these early chapters of the book of Acts fit completely the criteria for understanding community organizing and engagement that we saw in the Salvatierra and Heltzel volume. However, as we bring those insights into these passages, we can hopefully appreciate more deeply Luke's sketched account.

So, this is a case in which there are communal relationships, there is goodwill being generated, and there is movement—literal, economic, ideological, etc.—in multiple directions. There is addition to and growth of the apostolic community. More importantly for our purposes, there is an openness of exchange, in terms both of the selling and buying of possessions and of the interactive space sharing between homes and temple,

15. Biblical scholarship might be more focused on attempting to assess the historicity of the Lukan narrative, but ours is first and foremost a theologically informed hermeneutical approach; see also the introductory chapter to Yong, *Hermeneutical Spirit*.

that facilitates the interpersonal give-and-take of apostolic disciples and those in the wider community.[16]

WINDOW 2: SIGNS AND WONDERS IN COMMUNITY ENGAGEMENT (ACTS 3–4)

Another window, an extension of the first, comes in Acts 3 and 4 that begins with the day Peter and John were going up to the temple at the hour of prayer at three o'clock in the afternoon. For healing the lame man on the Sabbath, they were arrested and put in custody until the next day. Then, Luke records further encounters with the religious leaders and community leaders.

We read about one form of the early apostolic posture and approach to the wider community at the end of Acts 4: "They went to their friends and reported what the chief priest and elders had said to them [and] when they heard it, they raised their voices together to God. . . . And when they had prayed, the place in which they had gathered together was shaken, and they all filled with Holy Spirit and spoke the word of God with boldness" (4:24–25, 31).[17] The rest of the passage also records Peter and John saying to the religious leaders that if it was between being submissive to God and listening to the authorities, they would be obedient to God instead (4:19–20). Their convictions were predicated in part on their allegiances: "For there's no other name under heaven by which human beings would be saved" (4:12).

It is in this context that I want us to consider the manifestation of healings, signs, and wonders (4:30) as part of this early apostolic community engagement experience.[18] This is replicated in Acts 5, when Peter's shadow was healing people and people from the countryside were joining the apostolic community (5:12–16), and also in Samaria in the story of Simon Magus and his dealings with Phillip and his ministry (8:4–25). We see thereby different forms of community engagement with various

16. For more on especially the economic aspects of this nascent apostolic group's engagement with the broader community, see part 3 of Yong, "Pentecostal Health and Wealth," which is a reprint from my *In the Days of Caesar*, 295–303.

17. I once preached on this Acts 4:23–31 prayer passage; see my "Praying with the Apostles: Then and Tomorrow," ch. 8 in my *Kerygmatic Spirit*, 107–19.

18. This is not an essay on signs and wonders, so I do not want to be detracted on the plausibility or veracity of this Lukan account; yet those interested to hear more from me about signs, wonders, and miracles can consult Yong, "Theological and Scientific Perspectives on Signs, Wonders, and Miracles.'

experiences of prayer, of worship, and of signs and wonders that prompt, catalyze, and present opportunities for interacting with the broader community. We see the disciples in their prayer time at the end of chapter 4 include an assessment of their situation and of next steps in their engagement. Prayer and worship are thus part and parcel of their process of discernment. In that respect, community engagement assessments can involve a variety of ecclesial practices, not least that of prayer and of worship.[19]

And now on the sustainability front, obviously getting incarcerated isn't at the top of the list of anyone's community engagement strategy. And, again, it wasn't necessarily the case that as Peter and John were going up to the temple and then healing this man, they expected landing in the local jail. But there were indications in the Gospel of Luke of similar actions of Jesus leading to his apprehension and final execution. In that respect, the disciples might have anticipated that healing acts on the Sabbath might be incendiary. This window thus urges our seeing apostolic engagements with the early Judean community in their broader context and how those might have evolved over time as well.

WINDOW 3: COMMUNITY ENGAGEMENT CHALLENGES (ACTS 6:1–7)

A third window I want to open is Acts chapter 6, "During those days when the disciples were increasing the number, Hellenists complained against the Hebrews because their widows were being neglected in the daily distribution of food" (6:1).[20] This is an ongoing unfolding of the very dynamic early messianic community that included Judean and Jerusalemite locals as well as those gathered from every nation under heaven (2:5), and all those visiting back and forth, maybe with their families. And we can see that the three thousand who were baptized included Hellenists as well, and both party segments continued to grow. This fluid dual-language community had to respond to the needs of locals as well as those who may have had some broader Mediterranean cultural roots and other kinds of backgrounds, and both groups were now called to

19. I have some short articles on worship that are suggestive, in light of our focus here, on how what is otherwise an intra-Christian practice can have wider (public and social) implications; see Yong, "Worship in Many Tongues"; Yong, "Power of Language," both reprinted in ch. 2 of my *Heteroglossic Spirit*.

20. For more on the contexts surrounding this passage, see parts 2–3 of my book *Who Is the Holy Spirit?*

grow community in and between their homes and the temple, including intermingling with other locals. Exceeding five thousand and growing, centered loosely around the temple, and also with ongoing exchanges with the wider community, the question intensified over time: How is the daily distribution of food to be managed in light of the fact that apostolic believers were already involved in a great deal of buying and selling to meet its communal needs?

The Twelve called together the whole group of disciples and said, "It's not right that we should neglect the word of God in order to wait tables. Therefore, friends select from among yourselves seven men of God, good standing full of the spirit and wisdom, whom we may appoint to this task" (6:2–3). Here we see not only the mobilization of the community that we saw in Salvatierra and Heltzel, but also the appointment of leadership. "'While we, for our part, will devote ourselves to prayer and to serving the word.' What they said pleased the whole community, and they chose Stephen, a man full of faith and the Holy Spirit, together with Philip, Prochorus, Nicanor, Timon, Parmenas, and Nicolaus, a proselyte of Antioch. They had these men stand before the apostles, who prayed and laid their hands on them. The word of God continued to spread; the number of the disciples increased greatly in Jerusalem, and a great many of the priests became obedient to the faith" (6:4–7).[21]

In this passage, the goals were in part to continue to meet the needs of those within the community. There's ongoing recruitment and there's leadership development, and in many respects, this enlargement of the circle of community leadership comes about precisely as a result of growing sustainability capacities in and for the community. In doing so, the apostolic leadership community drew from those with broader "global" (wider Mediterranean) experiences and ties. So, in this instance, we see the apostolic community continue to engage with the broader community in differentiated respects.

WINDOW 4: COMMUNAL DIALOGUE AND DISPUTATION (ACTS 17–19)

I want to fast forward now to Acts 17–19 for a different window, with multiple frames even, into community engagement.[22] "While Paul was

21. For more on this passage, see Hertig, "Cross-Cultural Mediation."

22. My reflections in "From Demonization to Kin-domization" provide further

waiting for them in Athens, he was deeply distressed to see the city was full of idols. So he argued in the synagogue with the Jews and the devout persons, and also in the marketplace every day with those who happen to be there" (17:16–17). There is so much to unpack in every one of these passages, but I want to look through these windows into how the apostle engaged with the broader community. We see here certainly a sense in which St. Paul was discerning, assessing the local situation. And his response was to engage first in the synagogue, and then that engagement with the synagogue opened up to engagement in and with the marketplace. And we can well imagine how these marketplace exchanges extended and stimulated further dimensions of community engagement as he was assessing and responding to the developments, next landing him in the Areopagus (17:22). Now obviously in these instances, community engagements came out of his own apostolic mandate or were derived from his apostolic commitments to be a purveyor of the good news of Jesus Christ and to establish local bodies of messianic believers. Community engagement was hence central to this apostolic vocation.

In Corinth: Paul "left the synagogue and went to the house of a man named Titius Justus, a worshiper of God; his house was next door to the synagogue. Crispus, the official of the synagogue, became a believer in the Lord, together with all his household; and many of the Corinthians who heard Paul became believers and were baptized" (18:7–8). Here we can see some of the dynamics of how the local synagogue might have been considered to be a center of the believing community, and the house next door, belonging to Titius Justus, again, replicated the early apostolic experience in Acts 2–4 where we saw the believing community navigating the spaces of the broader community between homes and temple. And now, at Corinth, the synagogue was a site that had both some insider status to Paul and his ministry, but also some outsider dimensions as well, as the space wherein Paul the apostle engaged with other Corinthians. For apostolic and evangelistic purposes, Paul's community engagement modality deployed dialogical and disputational forms: "Every sabbath he would argue in the synagogue and would try to convince Jews and Greeks" (18:4).[23]

Lastly, refracting Acts 17–19 as a kind of rotating or multi-lensed/framed window (to extend our window metaphor), Paul "entered the

discussion of a number of the "windows" of chapters discussed here, including Acts 6, what we now turn to here at the Areopagus, and what we discuss later at Ephesus and Malta.

23. For more on my dialogical method and approach, see Yong, *Dialogical Spirit*.

synagogue and for three months spoke out boldly, and argued persuasively about the kingdom of God. When some stubbornly refused to believe and spoke evil of the Way before the congregation, he left them, taking the disciples with him, and argued daily in the lecture hall of Tyrannus. This continued for two years, so that all the residents of Asia, both Jews and Greeks, heard the word of the Lord" (19:8–10). Note the ongoing navigation of Paul between the synagogue and the lecture hall, particularly the latter as a site and locus of community engagement. This was a space of community discussion, dialogue, and disputation, so to speak. As Luke tells us these engagements transpired over two years and even longer, what we have is a more extended set of apostolic contacts with the surrounding community, and, in that sense, we can appreciate many aspects and dimensions of what Salvatierra and Heltzel shared with us, especially if we had more time to read between the lines of the text and explore the world behind these texts. We might be able to name better the goals, assessments, recruitment, pathways, resourcings, and sustainability elements in Athens (the Areopagus), Corinth (note Priscilla and Aquila, and the adding of Apollo as part of the mobilized group of both members and leaders to engage in the Corinthian community), and Ephesus. In the latter context, to stay on this point for a moment, there is a lot happening, including the seven sons of Sceva, the ensuing (after some time) riot, the communications with the town clerk and how the town clerk attempted to calm down those who felt that the spirit of the gospel threatened the worship of Artemis, the sales of the Artemesian artifacts in the Ephesian community, etc.[24] Unpacking further Paul's efforts in Athens, Corinth, and Ephesus (really everywhere throughout Paul's travels) from our community organizing perspective will shed further light on contemporary community engagement after Pentecost.

WINDOW 5: INDIGENOUS COMMUNITY ENGAGEMENT (ACTS 28:1–10)

I want to close briefly with looking at Malta, in which the natives—the Greek refers to *barbaroi*, transliterated *barbarians*, so to speak (28:2)—and

24. My Zoom-mediated lecture "Where Did the Holy Spirit Go? Pneumatology for a Post-Secular Age," presented to the "Church with Spirit, in Our Secular Age" conference organized by the Danish StudieCenter Menighedsbaseret Teology (Study Centre for Church Based Theology), May 11, 2023 (included as ch. 5 of the present volume), focuses on Acts 19 and elaborates further some of the themes I have introduced here.

indigenous population of the island showed unusual kindness to Paul and his companions. This is after the shipwreck of Acts 27 in which Paul and Luke and others find themselves as castaways. Later in the account we read: "Now in the neighborhood of that place were lands belonging to the leading man of the island, named Publius, who received us and entertained us hospitably for three days" (28:7). Here we find community engagement simply to be no more or less than the receiving of hospitality from others. Then we discover: "It so happened that the father of Publius lay sick in bed with fever and dysentery. Paul visited him and cured him by praying and putting his hands on him. After this happened, the rest of the people on the island who had diseases also came and were cured" (28:8–9). Here we see indigenous community engagement as it happens, not planned, through developing circumstances that were beyond apostolic control, the aftermath of "acts of God," so to speak, in which the community engagement on the island comes through faithful dependence upon God, prayer, with the ministry of prayer to those who are sick extended beyond any arbitrary border that might be erected between "us" and "them."

But attend carefully to the fact that the apostolic reception of hospitality is given by those like "barbarians" who historically we (as Jesus-followers) have not considered to be communities worthy of engagement, even. "They bestowed many honors on us, and when we were about to sail, they put on board all the provisions we needed" (28:10). This window reflects a bright and even burning set of rays inviting our willingness to receive from otherwise dismissed communities for our benefit and even salvation (Paul and his companions literally saved out of the storm). So here is a mode of community engagement that we stumble upon and wherein we realize that it is not so much what we might bring to the community, but how we can and must receive from those in places we find ourselves who are in a position to bless us.[25]

RECONSIDERATION: COMMUNITY ENGAGEMENT AFTER PENTECOST

Goals: A few summary remarks, gleaned from the above, of apostolic engagement after Pentecost goals. Primarily, we see heralding the reign of God as a priority, and doing so through many tongues. Again, many

25. The final chapter of my *Who Is the Holy Spirit?* is titled "Barbarians, Believers, and the Spirit of Hospitality" (185–88); see further Yong, "Guests, Hosts, and the Holy Ghost," 172–74.

opportunities, many locations, many cultures, many ethnicities, many nationalities (usually the form *ethnos* in the New Testament) occur all throughout the book of Acts. So, in that respect, the many tongues of Pentecost are the many languages and peoples through whom the gospel is resounded and to whom also the gospel is declared.[26]

Assessment: Assessment involves understanding the present state of the local ecclesial community, that of its wider community, and the community resources and needs. In fact, the windows we have peered through indicate that there were many needs even within the early apostolic community. So, the community engagements of the apostolic narrative involve engagements of those wider communities but sometimes for the benefit of the body of Christ, as we've seen in Acts 2, Acts 4, Acts 6, and then in Acts 28. Thus, the apostolic brothers and sisters were beneficiaries of that broader community engagement. So, the assessment goes both ways: both of who we are as a malleable body of Christ, but also of the wider communities within which we are situated and find ourselves. Sometimes, we should acknowledge being at the mercy of others, like for instance in the Maltese example.

Strategies: The many tongues of Pentecost, I suggest, is an effective metaphorical pointer that directs our attentiveness to the many modalities through which we collaborate toward the common good, including the good of the apostolic community. The modalities of engagement could involve, as we have seen, signs and wonders, dialogue and disputation, and the giving and receiving of hospitality. So, we could say many tongues and many forms of community engagement practices.[27]

Recruitment: The Holy Spirit enlarges our relational capacity and even our relational capital by bringing us into the broader community. The Spirit empowers and equips us who are on the margins of society, if you will, and in that respect also privileges others who are marginalized communities in other respects, like Hellenists in the first-century Mediterranean world. The Spirt also brings us into even some adversarial relationships with the broader community, although even in and through such adversarial relationships—like between the apostolic believers and the religious leaders of Acts 3–5—further community engagement opportunities evolve. Again, Paul's public appearances are at times conversational and at times disputational and argumentative; not merely

26. See Yong, "Many Tongues, Many Practices."

27. Consistent with what I articulate elsewhere for other purposes: Yong, "Pentecostal Christianities and Their Political Lives."

dialogical but also apologetically combative. Yet these diverse modalities of rhetorical persuasiveness open up into a variety of relational dimensions that not only grow the body of Christ, but also recruit, empower, equip, and transform the ecclesial community as new members get added.

Leadership: Leadership development includes discipleship across many cultures, as we see throughout the Acts narrative beginning in Jerusalem, expanding into Judea and Samaria, and arriving to the ends of the earth as we see in Acts 28.[28]

Sustainability: This final element involves the many practices of giving, of sharing, and of embracing all things in common as we see laid out in the apostolic narrative.

Time constraints prevent more from being said, even as every one of these passages we peered into and through could have been read in much more depth. We might also have spent a lot more time unpacking and critically applying the Salvatierrean/Heltzelian categories in light of the apostolic experience. But I hope there is enough here to at least prompt further consideration and conversation regarding not just the apostolic experience, but also our best theological frames for and practical approaches to community engagement in the present time.

28. Yong, "Missional Renewal."

PART III

Catholic Letters

Toward a Diasporic Hermeneutic

Chapter 7

From the Jewish Diaspora to the Indian (Christian) Diaspora

An Autobiographical Look at 1 Peter's Message to West Asia

I WANT TO ENCOURAGE you this afternoon in your specific call or your specific vocation and your specific opportunities and challenges that you face as Indian believers in the United States.[1] For the message today, I am going to read out from the book of First Peter, chapter 1, the first two verses: "Peter, an apostle of Jesus Christ, To the exiles of the dispersion in Pontus, Galatia, Cappadocia, Asia, and Bithynia, who have been chosen and destined by God the Father and sanctified by the Spirit to be obedient to Jesus Christ and to be sprinkled with his blood: May grace and peace be yours in abundance."

1. This message was preached at India Christian Assembly in Ontario, California, on May 19, 2019. I am grateful to Rev. Dr. Valson Abraham for the invitation to minister on this occasion. Thanks to Sam George, editor of *New Life Theological Journal*, for wishing to publish the sermon and for arranging for its transcription from the video recording. I appreciate also John Alex for the editorial work on the transcription and for helping me frame the published version with a new subtitle (the message subtitle was "Grace, Peace, and Abundance," which is from the text of 1 Pet 1:2), and also wish to express my gratitude to Jeremy Bone, my graduate assistant, for proofreading the transcribed and edited version. We have attempted to keep the oral flavor of the homily—with bracketed material inserted to clarify when needed, although these have been kept to a minimum—and the footnotes have been added to provide further connections for scholars interested in pursuing these matters. I alone am responsible for any errors of transcription, fact, or interpretation.

Father may the words of my mouth and meditation be acceptable in your sight, O God, and all God's people say, Amen!

I have entitled my brief time with you this afternoon "From the Jewish Diaspora to the Indian Diaspora"—that's the main title; the subtitle is: "Grace, Peace, and Abundance."

DIASPORA AND PERPETUAL FOREIGNER: AN AUTOBIOGRAPHICAL APPROACH

Over the last few years as I have been making my way through the New Testament, I have begun to observe one word that has stuck out more and more to me as I have become older, and we see this word here in these first two verses of Peter's letter: "an Apostle of Jesus Christ to the exiles of the dispersion in Pontus, Galatia, Cappadocia," and then it says *Asia*! That word *Asia* has become more and more important to me as I have grown older.

I was ten years old when my parents moved me and my two younger brothers from Malaysia to California in 1976.[2] At that time, I thought that I was Malaysian, and I did not know I was Asian. At that time, I thought I was Malaysian or Chinese. As I began to go to school [here in the USA] I was confused about my nationality. I asked my dad at one point when I was in junior high school, "Dad, am I Malaysian or Chinese or American?" By the way during those days I didn't know I was Asian. I thought I was Malaysian or Chinese or American. My dad said, "Don't worry about it, son, you're a Christian." And that is the right answer theologically, which we will talk about this afternoon for a few moments.

As I began to grow older, I realized that I am of Malaysian nationality and of Chinese descent. [My parents are Chinese, but after living in the United States for five years, they became American citizens.] As an American, I also began to figure out I was Asian. Now how did I begin to figure out that I was Asian? Well, as you may know, *Asian American* is a category that began to emerge in the 1970s.[3] Why? Because the number of immigrants from across the continent of Asia is relatively small compared to the population in United States, so Asians have emerged as a census category during those days. If you ever filled out a form here in

2. For more autobiographical details, see my essays "Between the Local and the Global"; and "Spirit, Vocation, and the Life of the Mind."

3. Which I discuss briefly in my book *Future of Evangelical Theology*, ch. 2.

the United States over the last fifteen to twenty years, one of the boxes that you probably get to check is Asian of some sort, and it began to dawn on me that, while I have Malaysian roots and I am Chinese, I am American, and that I am also Asian [in this broader sense]. And then verses like these in First Peter began to stick out to me. Peter was writing to Galatians and Cappadocians, but I got more excited because he was also writing to Asians. Now he's writing to Asians that come from very different part of Asia than where I came from. And, of course, he's also writing to Asians who are very different than most of you.

I come from Southeast Asia, at least that is what my geography teacher told me, and you, as Indians, come from South Asia. I hope that you realize that Peter was writing to Asians in the west, way out in the west. Today we call that part of Asia Turkey, but most of us do not think of the Turkish as Asians. We think of Asia farther west from South Asia that Pakistanis are included. If you look at South Asia alone, I don't know how to calculate the languages [used regularly in that sub-continent]. Isn't it amazing that Asia can mean so many different things? *Asian* includes different ethnic groups and different languages.[4]

One of the things that I have begun to register down in my spirit is that Peter was writing not only to Asians (in the west), Galatians, Cappadocians, Bithynians, but also he was writing to "exiles of the dispersion."[5] And as I began to understand more about Peter and these West Asian and Galatian, Cappadocian, and Bithynian believers in Jesus, I actually began to see that my own experience as somebody who is an immigrant is actually very close to the people Peter was writing to. Peter comes from Palestine, the homeland of the original Jews,[6] but over the last five hundred, four hundred, three hundred, or two hundred years [before this letter was written], the Jews had been carried or deported into different parts of the world by those that conquered the Palestinian region. In the last two hundred to three hundred years before Peter actually wrote, the Romans had conquered all of those territories, and one of the things that Romans did was that they built a lot of roads that allowed Roman citizens

4. On Asian diversity, multiplicity, and pluralism, see Yong, "Many Tongues of Asian and Oceanian Pentecostalisms."

5. For exegetical elements related to this text, especially its wider socio-historical context, see my article "Diasporic Discipleship from West Asia Through Southeast Asia and Beyond" (also chapter 8 of this volume).

6. Assuming he is one of Jesus' original disciples and apostles, that is.

to travel, move, and migrate, many times and in many instances for economic reasons.

I can say that my parents were economic migrants [of a sort] and they came to California because a missionary, under whose ministry my mother came to know Lord Jesus. [This missionary woman] loved Chinese people and so she wanted to go to the Middle Kingdom (China), but it was closed at that time in the 1950s when she was called to ministry and mission, so she went to the next closest place where there were lots of Chinese, i.e., Malaysia, and my mother came to know Jesus through her ministry. Our missionary protagonist came back to Northern California in the late 1960s and began to plant churches for Chinese immigrants.

Why then? Because in 1965, the United States changed its laws to reopen migration from Asia to the United States, and now the United States began to see many Koreans, Chinese, and Southeast Asians coming to North America. This missionary who was a minister with the Assemblies of God came back to North America and began to plant churches for Chinese speaking migrants in Sacramento, Stockton, San Jose, San Francisco, and neighboring places.

The situation aroused the need for Chinese-speaking pastors in California, so she contacted a half dozen pastors from Malaysia, including my parents. My father didn't come to go to medical school or to work in Silicon Valley [which did not yet exist as such at that time]. My parents didn't come because they were professionals. They came to work among the Chinese speaking immigrants to share the gospel of Jesus Christ with them. That is why I grew up as a Malaysian Chinese diaspora immigrant.

Now we shall look at these two verses in First Peter to attempt to understand what might be the word of the Lord to you and to me as members of the South and Southeast Asian diaspora to America. What has Peter told these West Asian diasporic immigrants that might be of value, might be edifying, might be challenging, and might be empowering to you and I living a migrant life, as you and I live sometimes a challenging and difficult migrant life? As for the Indian or South Asian diaspora in America, most of them (you) are qualified students or professionals. Whereas for the Southeast Asian diaspora in America, though there are professionals coming up, a greater number of very, very lower-class migrants have come, including my parents.

The lower-class migrants coming into a diaspora situation have a different experience than professional class migrants, but nevertheless when I read this passage in First Peter, here is a passage that speaks about diasporic groups that now have had multiple generations as well, in which case you are going to see a broad spectrum of migration backgrounds, histories, and experiences. Some of these are very new, like "fresh out of the boat." And diasporic life can be challenging—to get situated, to find community, to find food that you recognize, and to get connected. And if you're a 1.5 generation like me, this means you are born somewhere else but basically grew up in America. I did my studies in America. In many ways I am American. When I go home [to my parents' house] my wife says my [Malaysian-Chinese] accent comes back out when I talk to my parents, and she says she's not quite sure if she recognizes my language, so that is a part of the 1.5 generation experience.

There were new migrants but there was also in this Petrine community multiple generations of Jews who lived in Galatia, Cappadocia, Phrygia, Bithynia, and Asia, and this is who Peter is writing to. He's writing to exiles of the dispersion, those who had found themselves exiled from their homeland somehow, distanced from their homes. My parents came in 1976, and it took them twelve years to make their first trip back to Malaysia after they came. We were a poor family, serving the Lord. We were kind of stuck in California for twelve years, which is not exactly a [great] place to get stuck in.

I did not visit Malaysia again until twenty-five years after my parents brought me from there. In 2001, after twenty-five years of being in America, I was blessed to go back to Malaysia and meet all of my cousins I never knew because I was the oldest grandchild of my family and so most of the cousins I had in Malaysia were born after I left from there. So, I got a chance to meet all these cousins whom I only knew by name, but had never met before. So, we have this broad range of migrant experiences in many respects.

I had become exiled from my homeland, but going back to Malaysia again in 2001 was a very powerful experience because I was reminded that this was the very place of my birth. This is part of my background, my language, my history, my culture, and it is easy to forget that when you are [part of] a 1.5 generation. But praise the Lord . . . there is a real sense that the reason why I felt exiled from my land of birth was mainly due to circumstances more than anything else, but since then I have tried to make efforts to go back, twice,[7] and I will continue to as I can and get the

7. For some reflections of my third visit to Malaysia, in 2013, see "Missional Renewal," esp. 149–51.

opportunity to do that. So, to be exiled in diaspora could mean a lot of different things depending on circumstances and experiences and so forth.

CHOSEN AND DESTINED BY GOD THE FATHER

But here is the word of the Lord to these members of the diaspora in West Asia that Peter is speaking, and three words that he gives to them I want to tell you about. Verse 1 explains to those of us who are of the diaspora: Peter says we "have been chosen and destined by God the Father."

I want to encourage you about our being chosen before God. As a ten-year-old boy when I first landed in America I was excited. I see in your bulletin this afternoon that one of your members is praying to get a [travel] visa, we pray for that right!? And even to get a visa we pray for divine intervention that God would make a way because, without that visa, you cannot legally [enter the country and] live here. Many are called but few are chosen and, of course, we can think about being chosen and destined in that very mundane political sense, but we do pray for it. There is a sense in which when we get that visa, God is confirming a call, God is confirming a certain destiny: You're getting on that flight. Maybe your sister might come after you later, after you have landed, maybe your cousin. So, that is how it goes! God allows us to get here (there), and maybe we can then sponsor our family members. We envision perhaps that this is what I was chosen and destined for, and now I can facilitate others to have certain hopes and aspirations to be chosen and destined by God. It encourages us to think about our chosenness before God.

But what else has God chosen for you in settling in the USA? What else has God chosen and destined you for here in the United States? What else has God chosen for you to accomplish in this space and time in history?

God has chosen and called each one of you—and Pastor Valson in particular—to be rooted in Southern California but to continue to maintain a powerful ministry in India, with the church in India and with the schools in India. Now being located here has given him the opportunity to facilitate doing ministry in India, going back and forth! Many of you are blessed in this particular community and church. God has chosen, called, and destined you and your family to be ministers in this space.

But God has chosen and destined everyone of you who are here for God's own purposes, whether it's being a part of this congregation, whether God wants you to be a light of love in your workplaces, whether it is because God wants to use you on your campus among students, whether it is because God wants to use you to reach out to other migrants or diaspora people in your neighborhood. God has chosen and destined every one of us as individuals of the diaspora.

What that calling is, what that destination is, will always be exciting. Why? The Indian diaspora community here has always been flexible, shifting locations, and many of you are perhaps very movable. That's the world we live in. Many of you are going to have opportunities that even if you are located in one space in California, God could open doors for you to go from here and there to other places. The fact that you have been given opportunity, whether to have education or experiences or whatever the case might be, the current destination is simply a midway point to another destination. Who knows how opportunities God has given you in this time and in this season will open up to for the next one? That's what diaspora actually means. Diaspora means movement and migration: it means being open to the leading of the Spirit of the God; it means being open to being chosen and destined by God. The only sure and fixed target and goal of our destination is God. God is our home.

God can unfold his chosenness in our journey of migration. I spent ten years in Northern California [when we first moved there in 1976], and since then I have lived all across the US in a lot of different places. Maybe Southern California might be the last place, but you can really never predict with God, can you? We have been chosen and destined by God. Where God might take us next, we don't know! All I know right now is that I can say and I believe by July 1 I will begin my new role [as dean of two schools] at Fuller Theological Seminary. But then that's what it means to be chosen and destined by God. Our destination is God and anywhere God sends us is our home—AMEN! So, brothers and sisters, you have been chosen and destined by God the Father.

SANCTIFIED BY THE SPIRIT

Now let us look at the next thing Peter exhorts here in verse 2: "sanctified by the Spirit." I grew up in a Pentecostal church, and one of the definitions of "sanctified" means to be holy and pure. Now my wife grew up in the Spanish speaking Assemblies of God Church; they also have an understanding of what it means to be holy and pure, and she shared with me that women had to wear dresses to church—that's how you exhibited your holiness and purity, right!? I mean to different church traditions, being sanctified means different things.

But I think there's another equally important understanding of sanctification, which is that to be holy and pure means also to be *set apart*.[8] This is what it means to be set apart: God has set you and I apart. [How do we] think about that as Asian Americans? There is an irony here that I wonder if Peter and his readers also understood. I think you and I know very, very well that you and I that look like South and Southeast Asians here in America are definitely set apart [by our looks]—Amen!? Especially if you dress as beautifully as our sister here with her sari, and we know that when she walks on the streets of United States, people know that she comes from some other part of the world. That dress sets her apart. My looks set me apart as well, and in the Asian-American community we have a saying that many of you South Asians might be familiar with: We are called as *perpetual foreigners*.

Have you ever heard that in your context? The perpetual foreigner means no matter where I go in United States somebody always asks me, *Hi, where are you from?* Even if I am say, *I am from California*, they will respond: *No, where are you really from?* I finally say I was born in Malaysia: *Are you happy now?!* And again, when I go to Malaysia and I open my mouth and speak, they ask, *Where are you from?* Perpetual foreigner: even though I am an American, I am a foreigner! I look different than the "Americans." And then when I go to Malaysia, I am the foreigner and I feel this paradox: both are home but yet not home.[9] Home is where my wife is.

So, there's a certain sense that you and I and all South and East Asians feel set apart ethnically at least in terms of our racial and ethnic identities. It is a beautiful thing, and this is part of what my dad meant as he told me when I was a teenager [that our identities are fundamentally Christian]: that you and I are not set apart only because of our looks, or dress, or because our food smells wonderful and delicious. And you and I are not only set apart because of our accent. But you and I are set apart because of the Holy Ghost. You and I are set apart by the Holy Spirit to glorify God. You and I are set apart to be the fragrance of God in our communities and guess what? God can use the beautiful smells of Indian food to be a part of that fragrance. God can use the peculiarities

8. I interpret this *set apart* in 1 Peter missiologically and pneumatologically in my book *Mission After Pentecost*, §7.3.

9. See also my essay "American Political Theology in a Post-al Age."

of your culture, your language, and your experience and mine as part of that fragrance. God can draw people to himself through the language, through the access, through the unique testimonies and stories that you and I have as migrants. Amen!

As migrants you and I now have multiple resources.[10] How many languages are represented in the Indian Christian community in one particular locality? Numerous! That's a Day of Pentecost all over again. Amen! Just imagine the power that God can unleash by his Spirit through the different languages in this congregation, the tongues and testimonies that you can give because you have had the Indian South Asian experience and the Southern Californian experience, and who knows, you might have spent a year or two in Dubai or wherever you have come from because you Indians are all over the world now. Amen! Southern California may be your fourth stop—who knows because every single stop that you made has given you experiences; every single stop that you made has given you a set of new perspectives; every single stop that you made God has been able to stretch your life. God has been able to enrich your experiences. God has been able to give you a testimony. God has been able to bring you into newer relationships. God has been able to choose you and destine you in more and more ways. Amen!

Only you have had those experiences, and so only you can be set apart to bear witness to those experiences.[11] Don't underestimate the education that God has blessed you with; don't underestimate the small town and the language you learned while growing up. Malaysia, you may know, was like a British colony, so when I was born in 1965, I was taught English in school. My grandmother didn't know any English, so I learned Cantonese when she came to visit. Then when I was ten years old, my parents moved but they didn't bring my grandmother along, so my Cantonese teacher stayed home and so now my Cantonese has gotten really, really bad. But when I am around Cantonese speaking people, my memory brings back the recollection. And many of you might be speaking multiple languages because of the city, or state, or country you grew up in. Don't underestimate God's capacity to use all of that history, all of that experience, which only you in that context and life journey have. You're uniquely set apart. You're uniquely endowed, and you're uniquely

10. See my essay "From Every Tribe."

11. This missiological argument is developed in my book *Missiological Spirit*.

gifted for your calling in this space. God has chosen and destined and set you apart in this space.[12]

BE OBEDIENT TO JESUS CHRIST

You have been chosen and destined by God the Father, and you have been sanctified and set apart by the Spirit, "to be obedient to Jesus Christ."

You are uniquely qualified for the mission that God has for your life, for the blessings that God wants you to be, and only you can be that blessing because only you have the gifts, and are chosen and destined by the Father and sanctified by the Spirit to be obedient to Jesus Christ here. I have been so in awe as I have paid more and more attention to this diaspora message, as this verse opens a window into the New Testament. The New Testament is all about people traveling around the world, the known world of that day, the Roman Empire, the Mediterranean world. We have got letters written across the world in the New Testament. The New Testament is about global citizenship in the first-century world, and that's what unites our experience today as diaspora South and Southeast Asians, all global Christians.

The thing that I have just been in awe about as I reflect more deeply on this migrant reality—this diaspora reality that's deeply a part of my and your story—is that this obedience to Jesus Christ is an obedience to one, I would say, exemplary migrant. Jesus is the exemplary migrant. Jesus is the paradigmatic diaspora migrant. Jesus is the one who has crossed more than oceans. Jesus Christ is the one who has crossed more than national boundaries. Jesus is the one who has crossed more than state, regional, and ethnic and linguistic boundaries. In the beginning was the Word, and the Word was with God and Word became flesh. The Word became flesh in Mary. Now there is no more vulnerable migration than in the womb. Amen!

Think about the vulnerability that we as migrants face in planning, in undertaking, in moving, in landing, in navigating a new culture, a new language, and everything as diaspora minorities and as perpetual foreigners who have everything against us; if it wasn't for communities like this one, that's a very vulnerable journey. And guess what? Jesus, who had been chosen and destined and set apart to be obedient, already undertook that journey. As a perpetual foreigner himself, he already stepped out of

12. See also Yong, *Dialogical Spirit*.

the boat, he already stepped across the oceans, he already moved from his place in the presence of the Father, at the right hand of the heavenly throne, and became a migrant, a marginalized migrant. He wasn't born to a king of Palestine, wasn't born in the Roman imperial household; he wasn't born into a professional class of doctors. Amen! Jesus did not have the visa handed to him, Amen! In fact, as we know, Jesus didn't have a visa; that's why he had to escape from Egypt without one (visa) looking for documentation. But Jesus to whom you and I have been chosen and set apart to be obedient already has experienced your hopes, my hopes; he has experienced your anxieties, my anxieties; he has experienced your worries and my worries.

When I think of my parents as forty some years old coming to the USA, I was only ten years old then, but now that I am past my forties and have now in the last two decades been able to more deeply appreciate how severely challenging it had been for my parents as forty-year-olds.[13] They were not trained in the medical field or in the IT field or as educators. My dad barely had a Bible college certificate to come to United States to be pastors among migrants. What an amazing calling: what a scary thing to leave eight hundred members in Malaysia where he was a pastor in a large Assembly of God church, to come to a small migrant community church. I grew up in a migrant church with less than a hundred members. We were adopted by a Caucasian church, quite a large congregation. Every Christmas I got new clothes: they were somebody else's old clothes but my new clothes [handed down to me from the adopting congregation]. That was my migrant experience.

As a teenager I did not realize what it cost my parents. I can now more deeply appreciate the worries, the challenges, of what it would have meant to my parents as forty some years old already set in their ways as adults, now having to navigate a new culture, new land, new politics, new economics. That's the call of obedience to Jesus Christ. And that's a Jesus who has already been there and done that, who calls us into his footsteps, a Jesus who has already stepped out into this other's space to embrace fully the challenges and the opportunities afforded to him in that space, who took on what it meant to become flesh and become like us in every way [sin excepted]. Wow! That's the call of obedience to that kind of Jesus Christ.

What does it mean for you and I to be obedient to Jesus Christ in Southern California? What does it mean for you and I to be obedient to

13. Scholarly work on Asian American migration is extensive; here is my own summary of some of the literature almost fifteen years ago: "Asian American Religion."

Jesus Christ in the United States? What does it mean for you and I to be obedient to Jesus Christ in the specific places that you live in, the communities you live in and work in? What does it mean for you to embrace for this day, this moment, who call this community and this people as your own in order to love them as God so loved the world that he sent his Son? That's the call of obedience to Jesus Christ that God has placed on you at this moment. Obedience to Jesus Christ is opening your hearts and embracing [others in this space and time], and they [these others] are not always going to want to welcome my smells and your smells; they are not always going to want to welcome my language and your language, my accent and your accent; they are not always going to want to welcome us.[14] But obedience to Jesus Christ is to still love and follow in his footsteps.

GRACE, PEACE, AND ABUNDANCE

I want to close this with the subtitle of my message, which I am shamelessly stealing from Peter because he ends this introduction by saying that "may grace and peace be yours in abundance." Amen!? That was Peter's word to a migrant community that I am sure had a range of ages, had a range of generations, had a range of experiences, had a range of issues, worries, anxieties, hopes, and fears. May grace and peace be yours in abundance!

How many of you know that it takes lots and lots of grace to love those who think that we are perpetual foreigners? How many of you know that it takes lots and lots of grace for you and I to be persistent and faithful in a land that oftentimes does not welcome migrants? I hear a lot about migrants today in the news. As a migrant myself I am confused. Did not America welcome me? What does it mean to be faithful to Jesus Christ now, in this time and in this space, in this world?[15] Boy do I need grace to be in this time and in this space, Amen? To be that light, to be that love, to be that witness to the gospel in whatever circumstances, whatever environments, whatever contexts, whatever occasions, meetings, relationships—whatever God makes possible for you and I to step into, may grace be yours and mine.

14. Much of this has to do with the Euro-American (white) dominance of the USA; see also Yong, "Race and Racialization in a Post-Racist Evangelicalism."

15. Migration is a difficult topic to have in the church during the administration of Donald Trump; see my own more theological and pentecostal reflections on migration written before this period: "Im/Migrant Spirit."

We are going to need grace to represent Jesus because whenever we have felt rejected as migrants, our first instinct is to defend ourselves. Now Americans think Asians are very deferential. Asians are almost more quiet and will let the dominant culture get their way. And there is a time and a place to be deferential, but every moment and every place is a time and place to be obedient to Jesus Christ. Sometime, that takes the form of being deferential, but other times, we might have to say something that our shy and unassuming cultural self might not want to. Other times we might have to stand up for others who are less fortunate than us, who don't have the position and privilege that you and I in IT or whatever have. If you are educated, you are at a different class standing in this migrant place. And maybe you are working alongside someone else that does not have that same standing, and they don't have the capacity to speak up for what is right. Maybe it's your job at that point to do that. May grace be yours and mine. May we know how to appropriately bear witness to the gospel in whatever context we find ourselves, and if we have to speak up in the name of Jesus, may grace be ours and may grace be yours.

And may *peace* be yours and mine as we navigate life in a strange land. Let's not get too comfortable, Amen? I mean, we are all going to get comfortable at a certain level in order for us as human beings to flourish and thrive. But we can accommodate ourselves to our comforts too much and not realize that our citizenship is with God, our destiny is God. And so, may peace be ours in the sense that whatever our circumstances are, may peace be ours. May peace be ours in the sense that no matter what headlines we hear about our country (or our hybrid country)—for Peter and his group, it was West Asia, along with Cappadocia, Bithynia, Galatia, Pontus, Phyrgia, Pamphilia (that is all from the book of Acts, chapter 2).[16] For us here in North America, may peace be ours when we hear the news about whatever our president thinks he may be doing with regard to North Korea, or with regard to Iran and Iraq, or whatever.

And certainly, you as South Asians in North America, we are always praying for the church in India, because we hear about the lack of peace, the threats, and persecution. There is always the possibility of persecution breaking out; there is always the possibility of unrest and violence. So, as we hear, and as we pray, and as we hope, may peace nevertheless be yours and mine. As we worry about our loved ones back home, as you worry about and pray for your loved ones back home, may God's peace

16. I usually preach from the book of Acts; see my collection of sermons, *Kerygmatic Spirit*.

be yours. That's Peter's word to a migrant congregation: May peace be yours. You are going to hear about what Rome is doing; you are going to hear about what Jerusalem is doing; you are going to hear about here and there: may peace be yours. May grace and peace be yours no matter what we hear, no matter what we feel, no matter how we worry—worrying leads us to pray so worrying is good for that reason. But in our prayers, may peace be yours.

And may grace and peace be yours in abundance. And that abundance I pray may be manifest abundantly and multiply. May that abundance I pray be manifest in the children that you have; may that abundance be manifest in your prosperity;[17] may that abundance be multiplied in your health, in your blessing, in the honor that will be given you because you are obedient followers of Jesus Christ; in the respect that will be given you because you are set apart to be different, and set apart to be different in a graceful and peaceful way that makes people want to be with you, that makes people want you to pray for them, that makes people want to hang out with you. May blessing and grace and peace be yours in abundance, in the name of Jesus.

17. See also my discussion of prosperity theology within pentecostal circles: "Typology of Prosperity Theology."

Chapter 8

Diasporic Discipleship from West Asia Through Southeast Asia and Beyond

A Dialogue with 1 Peter

How does faithful Christian discipleship look like for Asian and Asian diaspora Protestants in the present time?[1] For our purposes, I wish to begin and engage dialogically with the first letter of St. Peter in the New Testament. This is suitable, I suggest, on two fronts: first given the Reformation's theological commitment to *sola scriptura* or the primacy of scripture, and second, given that this Petrine correspondence was addressed directly to the Christian diaspora in Asia, among other nearby locales (1 Pet 1:1). Of course, we will need to extrapolate from 1 Peter's first-century Mediterranean context since the *Asia* of that letter is specifically West Asia (what is today the Turkish peninsula), to the contemporary world of Southeast Asia and its American diaspora, but that is precisely the purpose of this essay.

1. The essay was originally presented as one of the plenary lectures at Union University of California's Annual Theological Conference on October 24, 2017, this year devoted to the theme of "Doing Theology in the Vietnamese Context," as well receiving the legacy of the Protestant Reformation in its five hundredth year. I am grateful for this invitation to President Linh Doan and Dr. Philip Khanh Trinh of Union University. Questions and comments from the audience helped me to revise the paper. Thanks also to Dr. Anh Vu (Vince) Le, for feedback on an earlier version of this essay, and to Professor Carl Toney (Hope International University) for very helpful and critical perspective on my engagement with Petrine scholarship. All errors of fact or interpretation remain my own.

The three sections that follow will therefore consider first 1 Peter in its original situation, then look at this epistle from a Southeast Asian perspective at the beginning of the twenty-first-century, and conclude with a reading and critical response from the Asian American diasporic context. I will show that different hearings and readings of this letter are not just possible but also viable, but then intend to argue that the *semper reformanda* slogan—the church is reformed and always reforming, or better and technically more accurate: ought always to be reformed[2]—that has come more recently to extend the cry of the Reformation is surely true also vis-à-vis its commitment to the authority of scripture. More precisely, we ought to read scripture both in faith and critically since the deliverances of a prior generation's understandings may not be helpful for the next one. In that case, *semper reformanda* demands a renewed attention to scripture in every generation, to its meaning and message, so that the church—no less the Southeast Asian churches in their various diasporic venues—can be reformed and renewed in order to bear faithful witness in ever new and changing contexts.[3]

DIASPORIC RENEWAL/SURVIVAL IN THE SPIRIT: PETRINE PERSPECTIVES

As part of the Southeast Asian diaspora myself, I am pleasantly surprised to realize that the Asian diasporic existence has a long history that reaches back to, and even goes behind or before, the first-century Jesus movement itself. Peter begins his letter, "To the exiles of the Dispersion in Pontus, Galatia, Cappadocia, Asia, and Bithynia" (1:1b).[4] Such an address clarifies

2. To *be reformed* is more grammatically and theologically accurate, the former because the Latin gerund is passive and the latter suggestive that the church does not do the reforming herself but is reformed by or conformed to the divine word revealed in the scriptures (or for me as a pentecostal, by the Holy Spirit according to the scriptures); for explication, see Nebelsick, "Ecclesia Reformata Semper Reformanda." Thanks to my Fuller Seminary colleague John L. Thompson for alerting me to this matter and directing my attention to this article.

3. This essay brings together my previous efforts along two distinct registers: in Asian American theology, and in theological interpretation of scripture—e.g., in my books *The Future of Evangelical Theology* and *The Hermeneutical Spirit*—so that what is proposed here is a theological reading of scripture (1 Peter, to be exact) from a diasporic Asian location.

4. We do not have to resolve the scholarly debate about whether or not the beginning of the epistle, "Peter, an apostle of Jesus Christ . . ." (1:1a), is true even if, for our purposes, it is just as easy to identify the author of this letter following its self-designation.

this as a circular letter, directed to those of the "Dispersion"—διασπορά (*diaspora*)—which generally had come to be related by that time to the long history of Jews outside of Palestine, since the time of the Babylonian exile five hundred years earlier. Here, the "Dispersion" refers to those who were both temporary and more or less permanent residents in five Roman provinces, of which Asia was the farthest west. We also know that Asia then "was one of the most Hellenized, most thickly populated, and wealthiest of the Roman provinces."[5] Thus we are not surprised to know that another part of the New Testament written to some of its leading churches—the book of Revelation was composed for congregations in the cities of Ephesus, Smyrna, Pergamum, Thyatira, Sardis, Philadelphia, and Laodicea—condemned the reliance on and valorization of affluence in that region.[6]

Yet it was precisely amid such wider regional prosperity that Peter writes to "exiles of the Dispersion": παρεπιδήμοις διασπορᾶς (*parepidemois diasporas*). Later in the letter, Peter addresses them "as aliens and exiles" (2:11a)—παροίκους καὶ παρεπιδήμους (*paroikous kai parepidemous*)—thus indicating that these believers in Jesus were those who were "resident aliens" in these provinces, perhaps particularly in the socioreligious and political senses of that notion.[7] If *parepidemos* usually referred to travelers and ethnic migrants, such a person was also considered to be "a sojourner, and hence without the recognized status even of a πάροικος [*paroikos*]."[8] The latter, on the other hand, also was "not a full citizen and . . . having neither the obligations nor the privileges that fell to citizens, nevertheless did have a recognized status and hence was not totally outside legal protection."[9] As such, then, Peter was writing to messianists who if gentiles lived amid at least an existential sense of being strangers in the present (West Asian) land because of their religious convictions, even if among them were also immigrants from Palestine or other parts of the Mediterranean world, but all of these likely did not enjoy the freedoms and advantages of full citizenship. Probably, these resident aliens, gentile

5. Achtemeier, *1 Peter*, 85.

6. See Royalty, *Streets of Heaven*; I will have to return on another occasion to read the last book of the New Testament from an Asian or Asian American perspective!

7. See Houston, *Leading by Example*, ch. 3; *parepidemoi* appears once more in the NT in the so-called hall of faith: "They confessed that they were strangers and foreigners on the earth . . ." (Heb 11:13b).

8. Achtemeier, *1 Peter*, 173.

9. Achtemeier, *1 Peter*, 173.

and Jewish followers of Jesus both, derived from "mixed economic and social backgrounds."[10]

Although I will treat the recipients of this circular letter as composed of Jews and gentiles, there is some evidence that they were predominantly if not exclusively the latter.[11] From that perspective, it makes sense to understand references to this exilic experience in spiritual terms as much as in political ones. As those "who have been chosen and destined by God the Father" (1:2a), with "an inheritance that is imperishable, undefiled, and unfading, kept in heaven" (1:4), their allegiances were neither with the Roman Empire nor with the systems of this world. But even if this was not an immigrant group of believers in the geographic, ethnic, or social sense, there is also no reason for other readers to eliminate these features entirely either. Although there is little hint from the letter that these were forced exiles, there is much to be said for understanding their diasporic identity as chosen or voluntary, at least with regard to their Christian aspects.[12]

This being the case, it becomes clearer that and why the author urges his readers to commit themselves spiritually and theologically in faith: "If you invoke as Father the one who judges all people impartially according to their deeds, live in reverent fear during the time of your exile" (1:17). Similarly, and by extension, he admonishes: "Beloved, I urge you as aliens and exiles to abstain from the desires of the flesh that wage war against the soul. Conduct yourselves honorably among the Gentiles, so that, though they malign you as evildoers, they may see your honorable deeds and glorify God when he comes to judge" (2:11–12). On the one hand, exilic existence is divinely oriented, focused on the call to holiness that contrasts with the sinfulness of the world (see 1:14–16). On the other hand, exilic spirituality and faithfulness also has historical and political purchase in relationship to their Asian (and other provincial) neighbors. The call to holiness in that respect has a missional character: to live in such a way that unbelievers will be alerted to their evil deeds and character.

That these believers are being maligned by those among whom they lived suggests that they are being persecuted.[13] The author seems aware

10. Achtemeier, *1 Peter*, 57.

11. E.g., Michaels, *1 Peter*, xlix–lv, argues the letter was written primarily to gentiles, proselytes, and God-fearers (cf. Acts 10:34–35).

12. See Mbuvi, *Temple, Exile, and Identity in 1 Peter*, 29.

13. See Williams, *Persecution in 1 Peter*, for a detailed and comprehensive study of the kinds, extent, and context of the persecution endured by these believers in ancient West Asia.

that his readers, "even if now for a little . . . have had to suffer various trials" (1:6). There appears to have been certain groups such as slaves who also experienced unjust distress (2:19–20),[14] but many others must have understood themselves to have "suffer[ed] for doing what is right" (3:17a). Hence, they were warned: "Let none of you suffer as a murderer, a thief, a criminal, or even as a mischief-maker. Yet if any of you suffers as a Christian, do not consider it a disgrace, but glorify God because you bear this name" (4:15–16). Perhaps the situation was intensifying: "Do not be surprised at the fiery ordeal that is taking place among you to test you, as though something strange were happening to you" (4:12). As such, then, the apostolic word was to strengthen resolve: "let those suffering in accordance with God's will entrust themselves to a faithful Creator, while continuing to do good" (4:19).[15] In the end, theirs was a spiritual battle against the devil himself that all believers were subject to even aliens and exiles, so: "Resist him, steadfast in your faith, for you know that your brothers and sisters throughout the world are undergoing the same kinds of suffering" (5:9).

It would appear incontrovertible then that the resident aliens of Asia Minor (and the surrounding Roman provinces) were having to survive amid the antagonism and hostility of the wider culture. Thus, the Petrine challenge was that they embraced their divinely providential status while "bearing the burden of marginal rights, ostracism, and verbal abuse."[16] So even if they were a "pilgrim people" first and foremost because of their ethnic or economic status, their religious, ecclesial, and social commitments were to inspire endurance of the "pain, abuse, and ostracism that Christians as a minority group suffer in a pagan society."[17]

In this context, it is also perhaps unsurprising that these aliens and exiles were enjoined to live in ways that minimized the possibility that they could be accused of being troublemakers. Be law abiding and honorable, was the call:

14. See Smith, *Strangers to Family*, ch. 3, on "Provinces and Households," which details the social locations and relational matrices of various groups—slaves, women, even government-related officials—addressed in the letter.

15. If Dubis, *Messianic Woes in First Peter*, is correct regarding this passage of 4:12–19 as being apocalyptic in nature, then later readers might either dismiss its relevance to their lives if not similarly (apocalyptically) understood or reinterpret their circumstances in this same (apocalyptic) manner; both have happened, but our reading is independent of such extrapolations.

16. Richard, *Reading 1 Peter, Jude, and 2 Peter*, 103.

17. Richard, *Reading 1 Peter, Jude, and 2 Peter*, 23.

> For the Lord's sake accept the authority of every human institution, whether of the emperor as supreme, or of governors, as sent by him to punish those who do wrong and to praise those who do right. For it is God's will that by doing right you should silence the ignorance of the foolish. As servants of God, live as free people, yet do not use your freedom as a pretext for evil. Honor everyone. Love the family of believers. Fear God. Honor the emperor. (2:13–17)

Believers in the Lord Jesus Christ ought not to do anything that would attract negative attention to their lives.

Might such a posture lead to a form of quietism vis-à-vis the surrounding social and political culture? Surely a Marxist kind of political revolution is out of the question. However, there might be at least a subtle, if not overtly subversive, form of Christian response, perhaps a way of life of good deeds that nevertheless manifest a kind of "calculated conformity" or "cautious resistance."[18] After all, if the supremacy of the emperor is accepted, this is actually "for the Lord's sake" (2:13), not to mention that this is acknowledged along with the conviction that "angels, authorities, and powers [are] made subject to him [the Lord]" (3:22b). Further, pagan or heathen social norms are intentionally flaunted and renounced: "You have already spent enough time in doing what the Gentiles like to do, living in licentiousness, passions, drunkenness, revels, carousing, and lawless idolatry. They are surprised that you no longer join them in the same excesses of dissipation, and so they blaspheme" (4:3–4). Thus, did the epistle sketch the possibilities of what might be considered a dual citizenship—of heaven and in the imperial West Asian context—one that enabled both messianic commitment and social survival.[19] Arguably, the letter's opening address to "exiles of the Dispersion" frames, and thereby invites, its recipients to embrace a self-understanding that is *within* but not *of* the imperial regime.[20] There are various indicators, then, that such a peaceable way of life (3:11b) was not devoid of counter-cultural dispositions and conduct.

18. See Williams, *Good Works in 1 Peter*, chs. 8–9.

19. This is the argument of African American NT scholar Shively Smith in her *Strangers to Family*; my strategy, as unfolded in part 3 later, is sympathetic to her reading of this Christian letter but adopts a varying reception stance based in part on the *semper reformanda* principle which retrieval at this time also motivates our re-reading of this portion of the NT.

20. See Horrell, "Between Conformity and Resistance."

In the big scheme of things, however, the goal was endurance of cultural criticism and actual social and political maltreatment, in order to achieve (at least in part) and attain "the salvation of [their] souls" (1:9b; also 2:2b, 25b). Although "rejected by mortals," resident aliens ought to realize that they are "yet chosen and precious in God's sight" (2:4b). As "chosen"—literally, ἐκλεκτός (*eklektos*) or "elect"—of God (1:1; 2:6, 9; 5:13), they were also the scorned of the world: "But you are a chosen race, a royal priesthood, a holy nation, God's own people, in order that you may proclaim the mighty acts of him who called you out of darkness into his marvelous light" (2:11). One ought not go out of one's way to trouble the darkness of the pagans, but yet Christian love, hospitality, and speech (4:8–11) ought to be observable by the world and even remarkable to them.

How might this maltreated group of diasporic Asians find strength to remain faithful? Perhaps because they have been "sanctified by the Spirit to be obedient to Jesus Christ" (1:2b). The Spirit of Christ not only has foretold these torments that are being experienced (1:11–12), but now enables them to give an account to and live before God in the requisite blameless way (4:5–6). More specifically, it is the divine Spirit that empowers their persevering witness in the face of travail and intimidation: "If you are reviled for the name of Christ, you are blessed, because the spirit of glory, which is the Spirit of God, is resting on you" (4:14).[21] These pilgrim people are thereby not alone but accompanied, and indeed formed to be a persevering community, by the Holy Spirit during this stormy season within a hostile *polis*. Such a Petrine pneumatology is consistent with that found in the broader Christian Testament, particularly with regard to the Spirit's enabling faithfulness in this eschatological time between the times: after the ministry of Jesus the man anointed by the Spirit to preach that the reign of God was at hand and in anticipation, amid struggle and suffering, of the full manifestation and expression of the *basileia* to come.

Our brief assessment of the Petrine rhetoric suggests that these aliens and exiles of Asia (and related regions) found renewal by the Spirit of the living God to enable persistence and overcoming in a difficult

21. Dubis, *Messianic Woes in First Peter*, ch. 6, suggests that the Spirit's messianic anointing in Isaiah is not only alluded to here in 4:14 but is also the extended from the individual (Messiah) to the Petrine (exilic) community; the role of the Spirit in enabling navigation between "assimilation [to the world] and defection [from the church" is highlighted by Green, "Living in Exile," esp. 316 and 320–22.

social and political atmosphere. They were not to give unbelievers any occasion to bring accusations even as they were to be law-abiding and honorable before the principalities and powers of their age. If they were without full political, civil, and legal protections, they were nevertheless expected to be responsible resident aliens, contributing to their social world if in no other way than by honoring the powers that be.

RENEWAL IN MANY TONGUES: SOUTHEAST ASIAN CHRISTIANITY IN THE TWENTY-FIRST CENTURY

This Petrine message, I will now suggest, not only remained pertinent to, but arguably also was assumed by, other Asians even if disconnected in space and time. If we fast forwarded to the other side of the Asian continent twenty centuries later, I now seek to portray in broad brushstrokes how Southeast Asian Christian faithfulness can be understood in light of the resident alien posture prescribed in this apostolic letter. To be clear, I will not be producing any documented Southeast Asian readings of 1 Peter even as it would be ridiculous to claim that in the short space of this segment of a theological essay we might do adequate justice to describing Southeast Asian Christianity at the turn of the third millennium.[22] At the same time, I wish to be suggestive about how the conditions under which Southeast Asian Christians have lived, at least in the recent past, might be considered when refracted through a Petrine lens. Some general comments on Malaysia (with a comparative aside regarding Indonesia), Thailand, and Vietnam will be sufficient for our purposes.[23]

Malaysia is of course of personal interest given that is my nation of birth. Of primary import in the context of this discussion, however, are two sets of facts: first, that Malaysia is an Islamic nation (over 60 percent of Malaysians are Muslim), and hence that Christians are a minority population religiously (under 10 percent), and second, that the latter group are also a minority population ethnically, consisting mostly of Chinese and South Asian (Indian) immigrants who live alongside native or indigenous Malays, who are religiously Muslim. Christians thereby live as

22. Those interested in a more extended scholarly account can consult Poon, *Christian Movements in Southeast Asia*.

23. Various chapters in Phan, *Christianities in Asia*, overview Christianity in these and other Southeast Asian nations; my account will be rather general, fitted to our scriptural analysis in many ways, rather than purporting to be an empirical or historical study.

resident aliens in Malaysia in both possible senses of the Petrine notion: as spiritually marginal and as ethnically minoritized. Christian evangelism of Muslims is legally prohibited in this country although cases of conversion of Malays occasionally surface. The point is that explicit efforts to proselytize are not part of the Christian mission or *modus operandi*, at least not with any sustained intentionality vis-à-vis the indigenous Muslim Malays.[24] While apostolic boldness might be proclaimed as a virtue, even that which prophetically denounces unjust governance—e.g., Peter and John's courageous stance: "Whether it is right in God's sight to listen to you rather than to God, you must judge; for we cannot keep from speaking about what we have seen and heard" (Acts 4:19–20)—the majority of the time Christians abide by the general principle we have already seen enunciated in West Asia: "For the Lord's sake accept the authority of every human institution, whether of the emperor as supreme, or of governors" (1 Pet 2:13–14a). By and large, Christian believers "lay low," thus not providing occasion for unbelieving slander. In the various instances in which such persecution is experienced, however, it is hoped that they might be able to testify such has been unprovoked, and in that sense, their resilience is also authoritatively commended by the writer of the letter to that previous generation of (West) Asian resident aliens. The point is that the flourishing of Christians in Malaysia depends in part on how they are perceived: less as agitators of the Muslim center and more as contributors to national prosperity.

Like in Malaysia, Christians are slightly under 10 percent of Indonesians, albeit with various important differences, including that the latter is the fourth largest population in the world. This is important since with almost 80 percent adhering to the Islamic faith (over two hundred million), this island country is the largest Muslim-majority nation on Earth. Yet, and here again contrasting with their northern neighbor, rather than Islam being the official religion, it is one of six recognized by the state ideology of Pancasila that attempts to promote interreligious toleration amid national unity.[25] Protestants are predominant among the Christians in the land and quite vibrant across various sectors. In that respect, while being less dispersed exiles under the threat of political harassment, they are no

24. For more on Protestant Christian strategies for engagement in the Islamic context of Malaysia, see Peter, *Proclaiming the Peacemaker*.

25. "Pancasila" is, literally, *five-principles*, which are the bases for national unity for the Indonesian country and people; see Intan, *"Public Religion" and the Pancasila-Based State of Indonesia*.

less obligated to navigate the challenging path between being a religious minority and bearing an evangelistic witness. As with their West Asian colleagues from the first century, Indonesian Protestants would accept that they also are addressed by these Petrine words: "Like living stones, let yourselves be built into a spiritual house, to be a holy priesthood, to offer spiritual sacrifices acceptable to God through Jesus Christ" (2:5).

If the Southeast Asian Peninsula and further southern Indonesian archipelago are Muslim-dominated, Thailand is officially a Theravada Buddhist country, organized as a constitutional monarchy (the king must be Buddhist) even if currently (since 2014) ruled by the military junta. With around 95 percent Theravadan and almost 5 percent Muslim (primarily in the peninsular strip reaching down to and bordering Malaysia), that leaves very few Christians! But because Buddhist practice on the indigenous ground is popularized, Christian mission efforts have not been hesitant about reaching out to the wider Buddhist population,[26] even if success so far is numerically inconsequential. Precisely because Buddhism is so culturally ingrained, Thais cannot envision Christian conversion in any other sense than as abandonment of their Thai identity. Hence, by and large, this very small groupings of Christians would resonate with the Petrine distinction between their present form of life, consecrated to holiness, and that of their neighbors, at least metaphorically if not literally full of "licentiousness, passions, drunkenness, revels, carousing, and lawless idolatry" (4:3). Christian solidarity would be a precious sensibility since otherwise, faithfulness to the way of Jesus would be overwhelmed by submersion into the prevailing non-Christian—Buddhist—culture and society. Thus, hearkening to the Petrine call would be exigent, if for no other reason than that resources for buttressing Christian identity are scarce in this Buddhist-dominated world: "all of you, have unity of spirit, sympathy, love for one another, a tender heart, and a humble mind. Do not repay evil for evil or abuse for abuse; but, on the contrary, repay with a blessing. It is for this that you were called—that you might inherit a blessing" (3:8–9). So, while not quite exiles in the migrant or diasporic sense, Thai Christians would certainly resonate with the apostolic message as resident aliens devoted to the lordship of Jesus Christ amid the Buddhist imperial system.[27] The question there might be

26. The Southeast Asian Network has long been producing missiological literature for the Thai Buddhist context.

27. See Fleming, *Buddhist-Christian Encounter in Contemporary Thailand*, including his discussion of "Buddhists and nationalism" (141–56).

how to honor their king as their West Asian forebears were requested to do two thousand years before them.

In now finally turning to Vietnam, I confess little expertise and much ignorance. In my understanding, however, there are a number of parallels between the West Asians Peter was addressing and contemporary Vietnamese Christianity, especially of the Protestant sort (we are, after all, celebrating the Reformation). First, imperial Rome could at any point, and did in some instances under specific emperors, persecute the early West Asian believers; the government of the Socialist Republic of Vietnam, meanwhile, as one of five official communist administrations in the world today (with China, Cuba, Laos, and North Korea), can also make life very difficult, if not outright tyrannize Christians in this coastal country. Second, if West Asian messianists were exilic and resident aliens, contemporary Vietnamese Protestants, numbering under 1 percent of the population, are also a severely pressured group.[28] Last but not least, whereas West Asian Christians in the first century were of mixed socio-economic backgrounds, the majority of evangelical and pentecostal Christians in Vietnam are found chiefly among indigenous populations in the rural and mountain regions of the country, and in that sense doubly (or triply, one might argue) marginalized on account of their lower class and geographic locations.[29]

Christians in Vietnam are actually not supposed to be gathering without registering with the government. Yet how to track small groups dispersed in the country- and mountain-sides is not an easy task. Evangelical and pentecostal renewal makes sense in this context since these groups likely engage in minimal direct political involvement, if any, so are less prone to running up against government officials or realities. "Staying low" is part and parcel of their political way of life, even strategy, even as in these spaces they are more inclined to ignore, rather than honor, the socialist regime.[30]

The preceding is obviously both generalized in the extreme and perhaps distorted via the Petrine lens. Still, within this context of celebrating the legacy of the Reformation, the scriptural frame has been helpful, I would argue, in enabling us to appreciate the form of at least Protestant Christianity in Southeast Asia in more or less recent times. Many are

28. Le, "Pentecostal Movement in Vietnam."

29. See Reimer, *Vietnam's Christians*, ch. 8.

30. There are also many nuances in dispositions and approaches; more detail across the spectrum is available in Le, *Vietnamese Evangelicals and Pentecostalism*.

diasporic communities, even if one or more generations have elapsed from when their ancestors moved into these parts of the Asian continent, but all are resident aliens forging lives of discipleship and witness within socio-political and religious domains that are contrasting, if not also inimical, to their Christian faith.[31] This is an important point to confront, particularly as we shift to the American context in the next (and final) part of our essay, since in that sphere, Christians are in the majority in almost every sense, not in the religious, cultural, or political minority as they were in West Asia. So, Southeast Asian resident aliens might find comfort in the closing words of the apostolic missive sent to their West Asian counterparts a long time ago: "Humble yourselves therefore under the mighty hand of God, so that he may exalt you in due time. Cast all your anxiety on him, because he cares for you. Discipline yourselves. . . . And after you have suffered for a little while, the God of all grace, who has called you to his eternal glory in Christ, will himself restore, support, strengthen, and establish you" (5:6–8a, 10). Yet, how might this read in the Asian North American diasporic context? Yes, God's promises will prove themselves true in order to reform and renew our lives and churches, whether across continents or across centuries of time, but can 1 Peter be a force for renewal and revitalization of the faith for Southeast Asians once more transferred across a vast hemispheric divide?

LIMINAL RENEWAL: ASIAN AMERICAN CHRISTIANITY ON THE ECCLESIAL AND POLITICAL MARGINS?

In the last part of this essay, I want to switch contexts one more time, to the Southeast Asian diaspora to the Americas. Of course, we cannot hope to do justice to the historical and ethnic diversity of this reality, much less to its theological dimensions. I write, for instance, as a Malaysian Chinese whose parents migrated to the USA to pastor among the Chinese-speaking diaspora to Northern California, and so I can say little about the Laotian, Hmong, or Vietnamese refugee experiences across the continent for instance.[32] Hence, I will speak more generically from an *Asian American* perspective if for no other reason than expedience, and proceed as if this is in continuity, even if twice removed, with the West

31. See also my short essay "Evangelism and the Political in Southeast Asia."

32. An initial foray toward a Vietnamese American theology is charted by Roman Catholic Vietnamese theologian Phan, *Christianity with an Asian Face*, ch. 11: "The Dragon and the Eagle: Toward a Vietnamese American Theology."

Asian diasporan community to which Peter addressed his apostolic communiqué long ago.

From this contested Asian American site, nevertheless, I wish to explore the fortunes of the Petrine appeal. More precisely, I ask how the apostolic dispatch might be received among those who find themselves, regardless of Asian nation of origin, stereotyped as *perpetual foreigners* or as *model minorities*. These labels, of course, are discriminatory, but I will persist in thinking with and through them, hermeneutically, in order to ask if and how 1 Peter can be a resource for ecclesial renewal across the Asian American diaspora.

Asian Americans are *perpetual foreigners* because for historical reasons and because of their appearance, whites have and always will assume they are from elsewhere than America.[33] Yet they strive to fit in, and do so by playing by the social and cultural conventions—the *rules*—of the host nation. From that perspective, they have acclimated themselves to American culture and, for those who are Christians, to the sub-cultures of American Christianity around the country. For Asian American Protestants, more particularly, they have assimilated with the conservativism of their evangelical hosts, thereby at least attempting to demonstrate their belonging as resident aliens. Yet these historic "absolute aliens" can never do enough to be convincing about their Americanness;[34] they just don't look the part.

First Peter's pleas remain forceful in this Asian American diasporic environment. "Like obedient children," they are urged, "do not be conformed to the [sinful] desires that you formerly had in ignorance" (1:14), even while they are reminded: "You know that you were ransomed from the futile ways inherited from your ancestors" (1:18a). This buttresses the evangelical conversion narrative, surely, that they have left behind their Asian (e.g., Malaysian, Vietnamese, or whatever) practices and cultures, and are to embrace the American—read: evangelical—way of life. The evangelical church has not only sent missionaries across and around the Pacific Rim, but now will oversee the maturation of Asian American believers in their new homeland; hence the rhetoric of the Petrine discourse

33. And also from an existential perspective, when in Asian countries (from which their ancestors originated), at least 1.5 and later generations are also not acknowledged because they sound different (their American accents are unmistakable, or they do not speak the requisite Asian language); for further discussion of the *perpetual foreigner* experience, see Yu, *Yellow*, ch. 3.

34. See Chang, *Citizens of a Christian Nation*, 63.

is directly applicable to Asian American exiles (aliens and strangers) who are mentored and even supervised(!) by their (white) evangelical paternalists: "Rid yourselves, therefore, of all malice, and all guile, insincerity, envy, and all slander. Like newborn infants, long for the pure, spiritual milk, so that by it you may grow into salvation" (2:1–2). When Peter writes: "Now that you have purified your souls by your obedience to the truth so that you have genuine mutual love, love one another deeply from the heart" (1:22), conformity to the truth of the gospel is equivalent with compliance with the norms of the (white) evangelical church. Asian American persistence and flourishing depends in large part on their subservience to and docility vis-à-vis evangelical cultural expectations.[35]

And here is where the *perpetual foreigner* is called upon to live fully into the *model minority* image. The latter, while seriously problematic on so many levels—vis-à-vis not just Asian Americans but also whites and those of other ethnicities—is rooted deep in the nineteenth-century history of Asian American quietism (compared to African American resistance to post–Civil War lynching and Jim Crow)[36] and unfortunately remains profoundly potent. Asian Americans do not want to disappoint—more important: dishonor!—their parents, for example,[37] so they tend to avoid any behaviors that would bring a bad name to their family, clan, ancestors, and by extension, to their people. This means, especially but not only for East Asian Americans who are deeply shaped by Confucian cultural protocols, acting in ways that gain the approval of those outside their family, clan, and people groups, in other words, living deferentially in relationship to whites so as to facilitate their acceptance among the dominant (white) evangelical church and the wider (white) American cultural spaces, whether in their residential communities, employment venues, or other public spaces and spheres.[38] As such, Asian Americans socialize themselves into the model minority orientation, adapting to its assumptions and adopting its values even if they may never have heard about it.

35. Another, more sympathetic but also historically informed, Asian American consideration is Moy, "Resident Aliens of the Diaspora."

36. Chang, *Citizens of a Christian Nation*, is an excellent comparative study that documents the contrasting fortunes of Asian and black American subjects.

37. E.g., Yep et al., *Following Jesus Without Dishonoring Your Parents*; cf. Toyama and Gee, *More Than Serving Tea*.

38. For further discussion of the internalization of the model minority mentality by Asian American Christians, see Busto, "Gospel According to the Model Minority?"

The discursive counsel of 1 Peter reinforces these survival instincts as well as the model minority ideal, however damaging in reality and in the long run. Thus, because of the other-worldly commitments of evangelical spirituality, the Petrine emphasis on heaven (1:4; 3:22) and on spiritual salvation (e.g., 1:9, 22; 2:25), the proper attitude and disposition, regardless of what the circumstances might be, should be on unobtrusive perseverance: "The end of all things is near; therefore be serious and discipline yourselves for the sake of your prayers. Above all, maintain constant love for one another, for love covers a multitude of sins. Be hospitable to one another without complaining" (4:7–9). If perpetual foreigners are to hearken to their superiors and authorities—and these are not just imperial but also ecclesial leaders—then model minorities ought to "suck it up," so to speak, as those exhibiting the spiritual humility and maturity that is properly oriented to the soteriological realities that really matter: "In the same way, you who are younger must accept the authority of the elders. And all of you must clothe yourselves with humility in your dealings with one another, for 'God opposes the proud, but gives grace to the humble'" (5:5). After all, if the Petrine Christians could submit to the reigning authorities amid challenging circumstances (also 2:13, 18; 3:1), then authentic Christian sincerity in the Southeast Asian diaspora will conform any Asian American unruliness and fleshliness to the dictates of the (white) evangelical and political preferences. Peter's call for diasporic self-examination continues to ring loud and clear: "For the time has come for judgment to begin with the household of God; if it begins with us, what will be the end for those who do not obey the gospel of God?" (4:17)—accentuating the need to embody the model minority witness so as to remain irreproachable before (white) Evangelicalism and to be amalgamated to the broader American public square in all possible ways so as to compensate for their phenotype and pigmentation.[39]

Postcolonial biblical scholars like Elisabeth Schüssler Fiorenza have attempted to identify the silenced voices within the cracks of the Petrine letter, whether of those questioning civic withdrawal, or of women, or of slaves or others within the *paterfamilias* and ecclesial circles who were in receipt of the letter.[40] I am less focused on the household codes explicit in this apostolic exhortation than on its capacity to catalyze ecclesial reform and renewal for the Asian American diaspora. If the author of the epistle

39. The preceding is wholly my own, fallible, reading of 1 Peter's reception in the contemporary Asian American climate.

40. See Schüssler Fiorenza, "First Letter of Peter."

to the resident alien believers in West Asia was concerned that this elect people of God would remain a "holy nation" discernible from unholy pagans and be a "royal priesthood" capable of bearing witness and mediating the gospel to an adverse first-century gentile milieu, then I believe we ought to be anxious about how those of us who believe ourselves to be "sanctified by the Spirit" (1:2) can yet remain "a chosen race" (2:9) in a multi-ethnic and multi-racial political space in the twenty-first-century American context. The racialization of America into black and white has definitive implications also for Asian Americans regardless of the hue—darker or lighter—of their skin color.[41] We cannot remain content with being a "chosen race" that enjoys model minority privileges especially when that itself perpetuates injustice across the color spectrum.[42] Yet if we are to renew and revive the Asian American Christian witness in the present, what options are available?

To be sure, nothing comprehensive can be proposed in the time and space remaining. What has emerged over the course of this hermeneutical sojourn, however, is not that the Reformation commitment to *sola scriptura* is unviable, but that any reading and reception of scripture ought to be attentive both to its original contexts and to the contemporary realities. The resident aliens of West Asia written to by Peter were marginal communities in almost every respect: ethnically (possibly), socio-economically and class-wise (probably), culturally (assuredly), and religious (definitively). The Asian American diaspora of the present era may be perpetual foreigners ethnically, but those who are Christians are part of the establishment—more or less—religiously. What I mean is that the evangelical church is both in a post-Christendom phase but yet also one in which it continues to have access to political power, for good or ill. In that respect, Asian American Christians, especially but perhaps not only of the evangelical sort, are both outsiders *and* insiders, albeit in different respects.

41. See my essay "Race and the Political."

42. My point here is the flip side of what raised by Bauman-Martin, "Speaking Jewish": that the Petrine strategy for gentile survival in imperial West Asia was appropriation of a Jewish identity, one that was politically and literally hazardous to Jews in a post-Christendom context; similarly, I suggest an uncritical contemporary Asian American adaptation of the Petrine proposal developed from two millennia ago in another set of circumstances mutes the ecclesial voice of the "model minority" and subordinates the theological integrity of the "perpetual foreigner" to the host church and society.

From this perspective, then, I suggest development of an Asian American perpetual foreigner hermeneutical stance, one that can take advantage of their outsider's (even resident alien) vantage point but yet also enable more apt ecclesial, prophetic, and even political witness than what the model minority mind might feel comfortable with.[43] This might mean that we read 1 Peter again but differently, even as it might mean we read this first Petrine epistle canonically, with other apostolic and scriptural voices, realizing that this letter (along with much if not all of the New Testament) was written by a member of a minority group to others who were on the margins of the dominant first-century political culture. Such a realization helps us to discern when it is important and right to keep quiet and submissive even to our ecclesial and political hosts and when it is imperative and urgent to speak truth to even the imperial powers. Asian American immigrants of whatever generation might seek to settle into our American home, but the truth of 1 Peter is that it calls attention in an undeniable manner to the fact that Christian faithfulness is forged within diasporic spaces of liminality, horizoned by the coming reign of God, and thus never permitting, for any sustained period, anyway, the comfortability that leads to full accommodation to the cultural status quo. Such liminal, hybrid, and dynamic historical life we can and ought to bear witness to from out of our perpetually foreign Asian American situatedness.[44] This scripturally informed perspective, I proffer, would be what the Reformers would have welcomed as part of the church that is reformed-and-always-being-reformed, even as those of us who are attempting to follow the leading of the Holy Spirit will inevitably always need to adjust to be and do what is appropriate for every new time and space.

43. Elsewhere I have sketched such a stance: Yong, "American Political Theology in a Post-al Age."

44. See Lee, *From a Liminal Place*.

CHAPTER 9

"Not Many of You Should Become Teachers . . ."

Whose (Established) Professoriate? Which (Diasporic) Faculty?

"NOT MANY OF YOU should become teachers, my brothers and sisters . . . " (Jas 3:1a). This title from the book of James is at best ironic given that this essay is written by a dean of a theological school and presented to honor its president.[1] Am I saying that our PhD students should (not!) finish their degrees and/or (along with our recent graduates) find other vocations, or even worse, that our PhD programs should not train teachers?! Not at all. But now that I have your attention, let me say that James's warning needs to be heeded even today, although perhaps for many of the reasons deployed in the letter that bears his name to address other matters precisely because its messages continue to be received by addressees who find themselves in dynamically marginalizing contexts that have continued to emerge over time.

I will be arguing that our response to this Jamesean admonition ought to be that "many should become lifelong learners." There will be

1. I am grateful to Mark Labberton for inviting me in the summer of 2019 to become the first dean over (at that time) two of the schools at Fuller Theological Seminary: Theology and Intercultural Studies (which have since been reconstituted as the one School of Mission and Theology); these last few years have been unprecedented for theological educators having had to navigate the global pandemic, and we have been able to support one another through the challenges and celebrate the periodic, if not insignificant, achievements. Godspeed Mark, in this next chapter of your own theological sojourn!

three basic steps to this destination. First (in section 1), I will drill into the fundamental concerns regarding teachers found in this first of the so-called (since the time of Eusebius)[2] Catholic or General Epistles and attempt to sketch a theology of teachers and teaching foregrounded by the letter's apostolic authority. Second (in section 2), I will adopt the perspective of the purported addressees of this letter, "the twelve tribes in the Dispersion" (1:1b), and explore how they might have responded to and perhaps pushed back on such an orthodox pedagogy replete with an orthopraxy coming from the apostolic center, so to speak. Finally, then (in the third and last section), I will identify our present site as a contested one that is "diasporic" in the theological sense consistent with James's usage, but much more dynamically construed in, from, and to multiple directions, and in this glocal diasporic context, the letter's concerns about orthopathy become just as important both for the formation of teachers and students as lifelong learners and for a wider assessment and reception of this Jamesean dictum.

One important caveat needs to be registered. I come to this letter neither as an exegete nor a biblical scholar but as one who has been laboring off and on in the theological interpretation of scripture terrain the last decade.[3] Although I will take into account some of the historical-critical aspects impinging on our thesis, by and large I proceed literarily, canonically, and theologically, specifically to ask about how this Jamesean caution ought to be understood today. Most importantly, I engage this text as a theological educator,[4] one working to live under the authority of this scriptural text, but doing so by attempting to wonder what it means for us to be faithful pedagogues in the present glocal context. Perhaps the author of this letter would think his words about teachers and teaching have been lost in following translation; or maybe he might appreciate how they have prompted fresh consideration of the educational and pedagogical vocation that heeds the spirit, if not the letter, of his missive.

2. In Cruse, *Eusebius' Ecclesiastical History* (2.23.25), 62.

3. Reflected especially (even if not only) in my collection of essays *The Hermeneutical Spirit*.

4. See also my book *Renewing the Church by the Spirit*.

JAMES AND TEACHERS IN THE JEWISH (CHRISTIAN) DIASPORA: WHAT HATH JERUSALEM TO DO WITH ANTIOCH?

Who is James and why is he so concerned about there being too many teachers among those he is addressing? Beyond including himself as one of the teachers within the community—"for you know that *we who teach* will be judged with greater strictness" (3:1b, italics added)—he self-identifies only as "James, a servant of God and of the Lord Jesus Christ" (1:1a). Although there are a number of individuals named James in the early church, only one of them has garnered historical or scholarly support as author of this epistle. Read canonically and in the spirit of the letter's reception history, we can postulate that the authoritativeness of its presentation—one scholar posits fifty-nine imperatives among the 108 verses![5]—is in line with the early church's understanding of the role played by James the brother of Jesus (Matt 13:55; Mark 6:3), who although not included with the twelve apostles nevertheless was singled out as one to whom the risen Christ was manifest (1 Cor 15:7) and then named among the "pillars" of the church in Jerusalem (Gal 2:9a; cf. Acts 12:17; 15:13; 21:18).[6] Thus, the position taken here is that even if James is pseudonymous (which is the hypothesis on the other end of historical-critical discussion of this matter),[7] our canonical and theological approach reads this letter as consistent with and living out of the positionality of the historical James of Jerusalem, also known as James the Just, even if that is not the actual author.

This canonical rationale persists, then, also when we consider the letter's addressees. Even if "the twelve tribes in the Dispersion" were to be interpreted theologically and spiritually as identifying messianic Jews who yearned for the eschatological renewal of Israel, any disjunction between such a figurative consideration and a more literal reference to Jewish believers (in and followers of Jesus, no less) dispersed among the nations beyond Jerusalem and Judea is a false binary.[8] I say this partially because James's inclusion in the Christian canon emerged over the course

5. Witherington, *Letters and Homilies for Jewish Christians*, 388.

6. There is some consensus among scholars about this; e.g., Hartin, *James of Jerusalem*, ch. 3; Bauckham, "James and Jesus."

7. The most recent substantive defense of this pseudonymistic theory is that of Allison, *Critical and Exegetical Commentary on the Epistle of James*, 3–28.

8. Johnson, *Letter of James*, 171, argues that when *diaspora* is framed as either a spiritual condition or a geographic or geophysical experience, "these are false alternatives."

of the post-apostolic period as a result of a consolidation of his letter alongside, and even ahead of, those of the other Jerusalem "pillars," Peter and John, so that together (with James and Jude) they formed a group of (seven) letters representing another set of voices to that of the dominant Pauline Epistles.[9] From this perspective, the Letter of James's canonical location and authority derive from the legacy of James of Jerusalem, and is appropriately read as being addressed to all messianists any and everywhere, perhaps especially those of Jewish descent beyond Judea, in ways consistent with how this historic figure was also seen as playing a key role in the Jerusalem Council's guidance to the churches at Antioch and beyond (Acts 15:13–35). Some such pillar/elder would have understood that it was at least in part his responsibility as teacher to restore to the fold those who had wandered from the truth (Jas 5:19–20), and this would be relevant of course if he was writing to those under his care locally (in Jerusalem even) but also to any and all who were expecting the messianic restoration of Israel wherever they were to be found (including among the Diaspora).[10] By extension, gentile followers of Jesus as Messiah also, even if not explicitly in James's horizon, were invited to receive and embrace his letter especially if they also were anticipating the eschatological renewal of Israel (Acts 1:5).

Having thus urged why we can proceed by taking for granted the authorial self-designation in the letter, we can now begin to situate James's discouragement of pedagogical aspirations. He had already signaled in his introductory remarks that "everyone [should] be quick to listen, slow to speak, slow to anger" (1:19), so his concerns in the text before us about there being too many teachers are a springboard to elaborating on that initial reprimand. Teachers, our tutor forewarns, "will be judged with greater strictness" (3:1b), and this expectation is hazardous since "all of us make many mistakes" (3:2a). What is problematic is the human tongue, which although "a small member, yet it boasts of great exploits," like how a small fire can engulf an entire forest (3:5). Thus, the tongue "stains the whole body, sets on fire the cycle of nature, and is itself set on fire by hell" (3:6). Even worse, the future prospects of containing the tongue are not good: "For every species of beast and bird, of reptile and sea creature, can be tamed and has been tamed by the human species, but no one can tame the tongue—a restless evil, full of deadly poison"

9. See Wall and Lemcio, *New Testament as Canon*, ch. 11.

10. This is the approach of Cargal, *Restoring the Diaspora*, 45–51.

(3:7–8). Yes, the tongue can bless, but as or more often it curses, even if "this ought not to be so" (3:10b).[11] These realities propel the Jamesean pessimism about having more teachers.[12]

The context preceding this passage may provide further perspective for the vigilance against encouraging teachers. James's famous argument for faith as being dead if not including works has propelled a long history of debate about if and how he was responding to St. Paul's argument that, rather than being justified by works, "Abraham believed God, and it was reckoned to him as righteousness" (Rom 4:2–3). James's position, understandably, if read as countering this Pauline stance, is that Abraham's belief was demonstrated in his offering of Isaac on the altar, and that therefore "a person is justified by works and not by faith alone" (Jas 2:24). Although there is no need to resolve the arguments on this score,[13] the following is noteworthy. First, if James represents the thinking of James of Jerusalem, then what we see here is consistent with what we know about how Paul disagreed with Peter and others who presumed to operate under the authority of the apostolic pillars in the decades of the forties or fifties (see Gal 2:11–12).[14] In this case, it is indeed intriguing to consider that James might be seeking to protect those among his audience from the teachings of others, not least against promulgators of the idea that "by grace you have been saved through faith, and this is not your own doing; it is the gift of God—not the result of works, so that no one may boast" (Eph 2:8–9). The ensuing shifting shape of the canon buttresses this hypothesis, even if in a negative manner: whether or not James or Paul were responding to the other, the post-apostolic church certainly felt the discrepancy, and this was itself part of what

11. On this latter point, see Davids, "Controlling the Tongue and the Wallet," esp. 238–39.

12. I have found Keenan, *Wisdom of James*, as more provocative, in a good sense, than other treatments; for instance, Keenan writes: "James is offering a more *radical* critique of speech itself, which calls attention not to what is taught but to teaching itself as an act of language-formed delusion" (216n4). The reference to delusionality in Keenan's rhetoric might be contested, but his Mahāyāna perspective surely prompts reconsideration about the limits of speech clearly identified in James's text.

13. The literature on this issue is huge, and that is an understatement. Even with the many proposals to minimize the tensions, I would insist that such canonical diversity provides needed and valuable theological resources that dissipate if resolved. See also Zetterholm, "'And Abraham Believed.'"

14. This time frame is constrained not only by when Paul's letter to the Galatians is historically dated but also by James of Jerusalem's martyrdom in about 62 CE; on the latter, see Josephus, *Antiquities* 20.9 (in *Complete Works*, 494–95).

marginalized James until the later third and into the fourth century. In other words, paradoxically, James's perceived diatribe against Pauline or any other itinerant teaching prevalent among his addressees may have slowed down his own canonical reception![15]

On the other side of the teacher and tongue passage, James is worried that earthly wisdom sows "disorder and wickedness of every kind" (3:16b) and seeks to instill instead a heavenly wisdom that procures peace. The former generates "conflicts and disputes" (4:1a), thus setting believers on course with the ways of the world that are in "enmity with God" (4:4a). What is needed instead is a humble submission before God (4:6–10) that persists in patient endurance rather than in grumbling and complaining (5:9–11). Yes, all of these threats are demonic in origin (3:15; 4:7), but it is imaginable that James also views loose-tongued teachers as susceptible to these devilish ploys and hence also dangerously capable of misleading the community of faith.

On James's own terms, then, the following are theological implications for the theological professoriate, at least then if not also now. First, the Jamesean authoritativeness presumes a core apostolic tradition, one rooted in the Jerusalem and Judean center, with responsibility for transmitting and guiding further developments, including providing correction when errant teachings are detected. Second, teaching is a perilous undertaking, particularly given the uncontrollable and destructive nature of the tongue, so theological teachers ought to be their own harshest critics and worst censors. Third, those who believe themselves called to theological instruction and education ought to pursue their vocations with humility and gravity, in anticipation of the eschatological renewal that also comes in the form of judgment. Last but not least, theological pedagogues are called to bless God and, by virtue of the parallel that loving God involves loving our neighbors as ourselves (the latter clause being cited in Jas 2:8), are called to bless—and love and care for in the relevant senses—their students also.

15. For how apostolic and other itineration may have intersected with James's concerns, see Hutchinson Edgar, *Has God Not Chosen the Poor?*, 52–54; Draper, "Apostles, Teachers, and Evangelists," 173, is more doubtful about itinerant teachers (there were traveling apostles, he grants) in James's context.

"NOT MANY OF YOU SHOULD BECOME TEACHERS"! WHAT HATH ANTIOCH TO DO WITH ROME, PARIS, AND OXBRIDGE?

Assuming "the twelve tribes in the Dispersion" is to be understood at least, but not only theologically, how might James's message about teachers have been received by those addressed? If there is no disconnection between the theological and the geophysical dimensions of those scattered among the nations—which would also be those who resided among the Greeks or gentiles (see John 7:35)—then one way to explore this matter is to ask how those removed from the Jerusalemite center of apostolic authority would have heard James's words.[16] There is little historic reference discernible in the letter itself, so much of this will be conjectural. Yet I believe the exercise to be a worthy one especially since much scriptural reading can be situated in diaspora perspective.[17]

We can begin by noting that the other two apostolic pillars, Peter and John, are also traditionally believed to have written to diasporic venues, meaning most literally those locations removed from the Judean center. First Peter is addressed explicitly to "the exiles of the Dispersion in Pontus, Galatia, Cappadocia, Asia, and Bithynia" (1 Pet 1:1), while the Apocalypse of John is given to "the seven churches that are in Asia" (Rev 1:4a).[18] We do not need to adjudge the convoluted issues of authorship related to these letters as my point here is that the diaspora even theologically understood surely was a metaphorical extension of the geophysical distinction between Jerusalem and elsewhere, in this case Asia Minor (modern day Turkey), and that, at least historically, two members of this apostolic triumvirate were believed to have been so engaged with these marginal churches—i.e., beyond and removed from Jerusalem—up to and through this region of the Mediterranean.

As already noted, James of Jerusalem is documented also as having been concerned about providing guidance for the churches stretching up through Antioch in Syria and into Cilicia at the southeastern-most tip of

16. Aymer, *James*, provides a framework for such a diasporic reading; our approach adopts the theological professoriate's perspective, now diasporically refracted.

17. I note here my own location and ongoing sojourn as part of the Chinese-Malaysian diaspora to the USA; see my essay "From Every Tribe."

18. See my essay "Diasporic Discipleship from West Asia Through Southeast Asia and Beyond" (also chapter 8 of this volume); I also provide a "perpetual foreigner" or Asian American reading of the Apocalypse to the seven churches in Asia Minor in *Revelation*.

Asia Minor (Acts 15:23).[19] Intriguingly, Luke also tells us that by then, not only was it "in Antioch that the disciples were first called 'Christians'" (11:26b), but also "in the church at Antioch there were prophets and teachers" (13:1). The development of this prophetic community of theological education was no doubt fed by the Jerusalem church that sent elders like Barnabas (11:20) and prophets up north ("down from Jerusalem to Antioch" [11:27] registers a Jerusalem-centric perspective). Yet the Lukan narrative suggests that the movement between Jerusalem and the diaspora was more multi- than mono-directional. On the Day of Pentecost, he tells us, "there were devout Jews from every nation under heaven living in Jerusalem" (2:5), and this nascent messianic community included, if not at that point then shortly after, Antiochenes like Nicholas the proselyte (6:5b).

The ongoing maturation of the Antiochene congregation meant that this community of prophets and teachers developed also an apostolic and missionary dimension (13:3), even as its leadership was not hesitant about challenging the authority of the Jerusalemites when that was deemed necessary (Gal 2:11). Having become a site of sending also rather than only receiving, Antioch also began to manifest its own theological authority. Even beyond Antioch into the further reaches of the Dispersion, the churches of Galatia were also cognizant about collecting offerings for the poor in the mother-church in Jerusalem and Judea (Gal 2:10), and with this sense of financial capacity comes the related sense of maturation and independence.[20] There is therefore much more of an interrelationality between these diasporically marginal communities and the church in Jerusalem. Yes, at an early point, the persecution in Judea prompted a nascent messianic community substantively outward, even to Antioch and beyond (Acts 8:2; 11:19). But the traffic—apostolic and financial—was always multi-directional.

From this perspective it is intriguing to wonder about the concerns regarding the wealthy evident in James's letter. I am not focused here on adjudicating the argument that James was, or was not, writing to an impoverished community, much less one that was exploited by the rich,

19. See also Bockmuehl, "Antioch and James the Just."

20. Schmithals, *Paul and James*, ch. 4, discusses how this collection for the poor in Jerusalem was complicated due to the complex relationship between Jewish Christians and Jews in Palestine, raising the question about whether James extrapolated too much from how Jews in Palestine felt about the law and applied that to how Jews in the diaspora may have felt.

even if there are indicators in the epistle on both counts.[21] Rather, it is clear that James's Jerusalem-centric point of view sets up an oppositional binary between his addressees and those he labels "rich"; between "the believer who is lowly . . . being raised up, and the rich . . . being brought low" (1:9); between "the poor in the world [as] rich in faith and . . . heirs of the kingdom that he has promised to those who love him" and "the rich who oppress you [and] drag you into court" (2:5–6); between his addresses who humbly acknowledge that "if the Lord wishes, we will live and do this or that" (4:15) and those of the merchant class who arrogantly boast, "Today or tomorrow we will go to such and such a town and spend a year there, doing business and making money" (4:13).[22] What this does not take into consideration is that the emerging apostolic community in Jerusalem was already constituted by networks of socio-economic relations such as we see in the book of Acts (e.g., 2:42–47; 4:32–36; 6:1–6),[23] whereas marginalized diasporic communities are struggling with assimilation or integration into their host environments and hence are in need of either establishing or securing networks of relations, patrons in the first-century Mediterranean sense of that notion. Intriguingly, then, those navigating the challenges of such diasporic contexts may embrace the Pauline approach of "becom[ing] all things to all people" (1 Cor 9:23) precisely in order that they can develop relationships in multiple directions, as needed, at least in part designed to undergird the precariousness of migrant communities, but such postures may also have been deemed by nativists like those at the geophysical center as being intolerably accommodationist.[24] Yes, a migrant community may begin with a sectarian form, but its flourishing will require, over time, interaction with the surrounding society. Might James's diatribes against the "double-minded" (1:7; 4:8) be related to his concerns about dual-forked tongues, not only

21. Hutchinson Edgar, *Has God Not Chosen the Poor?*, provides a balanced scholarly discussion across the spectrum of arguments on this matter; Tamez, *Scandalous Message of James*, 45, on the other hand, urges from a majority world perspective that James writes with a "preferential inclination for the poor," precisely because he is addressing those poor and exploited.

22. Maynard-Reid, *Poverty and Wealth in James*, ch. 5, argues that Jas 4:13–17 describes the merchant class operative among the diasporic communities being addressed.

23. See also my *Who Is the Holy Spirit?*, part 2, for the economics of the early messianists as described by Luke.

24. As Wall, *Community of the Wise*, 245, notes, Paul the missionary does not renounce wealth.

capable of blessing or cursing, but also of instructing in the truth or misdirecting poisonously?[25]

Let me hazard to guess that a diasporic reception of James's letter, perhaps such as at Antioch, may have raised an eyebrow when coming upon the injunction, "Not many of you should become teachers, my brothers and sisters," not least since there is a sense in which by the time the letter had arrived, there was already a theological professoriate at this marginal site.[26] This theological faculty at the apostolic sidelines, so to speak, may thus have been led to a more critical self-assessment (which any good theological faculty ought to regularly undertake!), which then also entailed a re-reading of the apostolic missive. The point the pillars of Jerusalem wished to make, so their interpretation might follow, is less to put a moratorium on the forming of teachers as a matter of orthodoxy than to ensure that those theological instructors are living out and embodying the lordship of Jesus (1:1b), the "implanted word that has the power to save your souls" (1:21), and "the perfect law, the law of liberty" (1:25a), all as a matter of orthopraxy. Therefore, the emphasis is on not showing favoritism to the affluent, on faith accompanied by works, on transcendent wisdom manifest in earthly peaceableness, harmony, and on good fruits.

If we think James's point of minimizing the number of teachers was to exert and retain authority at the margins of the apostolic community—relative to the center in Jerusalem, we are hypothesizing—then history has shown this to be a mistaken judgment. And this is not just about the ascendency of other theological faculties, whether those at Antioch or Ephesus where we know the apostle Paul held school for two years (Acts 19:9–10),[27] but about the emergence of multiple centers of apostolic teaching, some clearly geographically centered (like at Ephesus vis-à-vis the legacies of not only Paul but also other apostolic figures, as tradition conveys) but others related to the documentary and canonical evidence (Matthean, Markan, Johannine, Petrine, and other traditioned communities) bequeathed down through the post-apostolic period. While Luke

25. See here Coker, *James in Postcolonial Perspective*, chs. 5–6, esp. his contrast between the nativist James and the hybridized Paul.

26. Painter, "James and Peter," provides overarching analysis of how, as the early Christian mission expanded, these dynamic contexts generated distinct modes of leadership and teaching.

27. E.g., Brown and Meier, *Antioch and Rome*; Trebilco, *Early Christians in Ephesus from Paul to Ignatius*.

records that Paul ended his preaching and teaching days in Rome (Acts 28), the rise of the Roman see is tied in also with other apostolic figures, and beyond that, over the last two millennia, other authoritative teaching sites—at Paris, Oxbridge, and beyond—have continued to appear. The initial negation seems to have dropped off, and instead, the mantra has been, at least as the theological professoriate has expanded, "*many of you* should become teachers"!

MANY OF YOU SHOULD BECOME LIFELONG LEARNERS: WHAT HATH ROME AND OXBRIDGE TO DO WITH PASADENA AND THE ENDS OF THE EARTH?

In this last, shorter, section, I want to transition to our present moment and nexus, more specifically the one occupied by those of us gathered together to honor the fifth president of Fuller Theological Seminary.[28] This site is one that is both central and marginal—diasporic, in that sense—in converse respects. How might we read James's dictum about teachers in particular, and his letter more generally, from this dual-directional locus? Might we adopt an orthopathic approach as appropriately extending the orthodoxy-orthopraxy complementarity? In other words, how might the question of *right affections* be relevant to our consideration of *right beliefs* and *right practices* when thinking about our theological vocation in dialogue with James?

Fuller Theological Seminary has been marginal at least historically, certainly from the standpoint of Rome or Oxbridge. There is certainly the sense that in the history of evangelical theological education, particularly in light of what is captured in the phrase the "scandal of the evangelical mind"—that there is none, so Mark Noll's historical argument in the end of the previous century went![29]—the evangelical theological professoriate in general, and faculty at places like Wheaton College, Baylor University, and Fuller among others, have been exercised to shake off that reputation. Even on the American front, the leading theological lights have been derivative of the seventeenth-century Massachusetts Bay "city on a hill" experiment, by now replete with much longer histories and deeper endowments, and upstarts like those from seventy-plus years

28. [This essay first appeared in the Mark Labberton Festschrift; see acknowledgments above.]

29. Noll, *Scandal of the Evangelical Mind.*

ago in Pasadena have traveled along a "catch-up" road from its diasporic position on the western seaboard. "Not many of you should become teachers!" may well have been the perception regarding the Pacific Rim emanating from the North American centers of theological power back East, and the response on the "left coast" was something along the lines of: "watch us!"[30] Genetically diasporic indeed, and not about to kowtow to the centers of the theological establishment!

Interestingly, to say the least, Fuller Seminary has developed over its approximately two generations into its own theological center, but now in global context. In part but surely not only due to its School of World Mission (from 2005–21: School of Intercultural Studies), we by now have placed graduates in 130 nations around the world. Pasadena has become its own sending site even as it has also emerged as a leading destination especially, but not only, for evangelical students from the majority world seeking theological education. Surely, Fuller has thrived not because it has said to those outside the North American orbit, "Not many of you should become teachers!" but the opposite. We have welcomed students from around the world for study of the terminal PhD degree and then returned many of them to their original sites of marginality. Because of its reputation, however, Fuller has developed a form of theological authority, one manifest through the seminary's convening power, so that while generative of the theological professoriate,[31] the norms of engagement have still been Pasadena-centric, or, put otherwise, oriented around established norms derived from the Euro-, western, and North American academia.

But this is changing. I am not referring only to what some might have observed as the "regionalization" of Fuller Seminary that has gone on for the last forty years and is now concentrated in the emergence of its Houston and Phoenix campuses, but I am gesturing also to the twenty-first-century globalization of theological education[32] that is expressed in the following: (1) digitization transfiguring (flipping!) traditional residential theological education into a multi-sited, multi-cultural, trans-national, and poly-discursive nexus of interactive relationships; (2) mission no longer from

30. Here I am of course playing off the origins of Fuller, driven by its founders' aspirations to have a Pacific coast and "new" version of Princeton Seminary on the East; see Marsden, *Reforming Fundamentalism*, 24.

31. Fuller's PhD programs ranked sixth in placement of ninety-nine faculty across ATS member schools in 2015; see Tanner, "Tenure and Other Faculty Facts at ATS Member Schools."

32. E.g., Yong, "Liberating and Diversifying Theological Education."

the West to the "rest" but from anywhere to everywhere; (3) post-colonial theological thinking displacing Enlightenment rationality with north-south mutuality and east-west reciprocity; (4) post-Christendom forms of the church eclipsing denominationalism with dynamic ecclesial and missional networks; (5) post-modern spirituality transforming Eurocentrism into global and multi-directional experimentation, and so on. The point is that the margins are now the new center,[33] and Pasadena is being resituated in a global ferment. If the capacity of those "beyond Pasadena" to "speak back" is now amplified, the authoritativeness of these resoundings to and from the ends of the earth—remember from where their PhDs were conferred!—also can no longer be sidelined, ignored, or dismissed.[34]

So, how do we hear and respond now to James's prohibition: "Not many of you should become teachers, my brothers and sisters"? Beyond the defiant, "too late!" we might live into the spirit of James's admonition, which recognition of the potency of the teaching platform ought to motivate living into our theological vocations in humility before God (4:6, 10). Our observations through the diasporic lens, however, also urge us to recognize that over time the center and the margins are more fluid than rigid, and thus that theological authority is granted by the gospel under the lordship of Christ than due to any socio-geophysical origination. In that sense, the shifting center relates to the dynamic—and diasporic!—margins in a back-and-forth dialogue. Teachers and students are in some respects mutual learners, and not just in the sense comprehended by the emergent forms of online pedagogy, but in the true Pentecost sense of the divine wind poured out on all flesh located in and from every nation under heaven.[35] Rather than being a mantra evoked by contemporary pedagogical theory, lifelong learning thus becomes part of the spirit-filled life of the mind that engages the theological professoriate situated in many dynamic and continuously interacting sites—and through such interface, grows and develops—with multiple trajectories of audiences. What emerges is not just knowledge (some here might

33. The so-called shift of the Christian center of gravity to outside the Euro-American West; see Jenkins, *Next Christendom*.

34. I am delighted to point out that one of the editors of this book (in which this chapter first appeared; see acknowledgments above), Anne Zaki, is on the one hand a product of Fuller, including her PhD stamped by the honoree of this Festschrift, but also on the other hand with responsibility to shape the contributions of the various essays and corral us as its authors in the volume's preferred directions, from her own perspective and location!

35. See my essay "Incarnation, Pentecost, and Virtual Spiritual Formation."

insert: "dead" orthodoxy) but wisdom: the theologically negotiated and cultivated practice of righteousness and peace (Jas 3:17–18).[36]

But there is one final point: If the addition of orthopraxy might seem to complicate the task of the theological professoriate that has heretofore been focused (especially in the West) primarily on orthodoxy, the Jamesean perspective invokes the further specter also of orthopathy: the sense of a theologically informed and inflected feeling, not merely at the emotional register, but at the deeper and more radical level of the heart, the affections, and the yearnings and hopes that drive even the theological mind, much less theological behavior and practice.[37] James himself determines that it is desire that animates sin, and then death (1:14–15), and that conflicts and disputes derive from "cravings that are at war within" us (4:2). Thus, hearts need to be purified (4:8) and, in the context of considering how the tongue can be disciplined and guided by heavenly wisdom, James insists that enviousness and selfish ambitions, the stuff of "wisdom" from below, need to be rooted out (3:14). Even for theological instructors, if they "do not bridle their tongues [they] deceive their hearts, [and] their religion [theological profession] is worthless," James would say (1:26). The point is that we can pass on right doctrine, and we might even be able to practice "rightly" for a while (in terms of meeting socio-behavioral expectations), but if our hearts are distorted and our passions misdirected, then we might want to reconsider whether we ought to or can be teachers of the faith.[38]

36. The goal of right teaching and instruction is, after all, harmony across the diaspora, so McKnight, *Letter of James*, 276.

37. See my essay "Affective Spirit."

38. This essay has gone through a few iterations. Thanks to my PhD advisees for a stimulating discussion of its first draft; to Jeremy Bone for proofreading; to David Down for earlier comments; and to Joel Green, associate dean of Fuller's Center for Advanced Theological Studies, for inviting its presentation at the annual CATS Breakfast event at the American Academy of Religion and Society of Biblical Literature annual meeting in San Diego, California, November 26, 2019. I am grateful also to the editors of this book for their feedback on the chapter.

PART IV

The Apocalypse

Unveiling Eschatology and Culture

Chapter 10

Unveiling Interpretation After Pentecost

Revelation, Pentecostal Reading, and Christian Hermeneutics of Scripture

Not too long ago, one of the leading voices in the theological interpretation of Scripture conversation, Joel Green, observed that pentecostal biblical scholars have done their part in leading the way to thinking in more tradition-specific ways—*confessionally* may not be the right word given pentecostal wariness, at least historically speaking, about creedalism—about hermeneutics, perhaps partly because of "persons nurtured in the Pentecostal tradition coming to the table of biblical studies rather late, when the rules of the game of critical scholarship had been somewhat loosened, allowing for critical reflection on the Enlightenment project."[1] Green's comments can certainly be profitably analyzed from any number of angles, including discursive trajectories leading from the Enlightenment or those opening up to the postmodern academy, yet he has also clearly put his finger on what seems to be the growing realm of pentecostal hermeneutics, one marked by no less than at least a half dozen major texts in the last decade plus.[2] Within this space one might

1. Green, *Practicing Theological Interpretation*, 11.

2. Leading the way here are Archer, *Pentecostal Hermeneutic for the Twenty-First Century*; Noel, *Pentecostal and Postmodern Hermeneutics*. A number of important edited volumes have also appeared: Spawn and Wright, *Spirit and Scripture*; Martin, *Pentecostal Hermeneutics*; Archer and Oliverio, *Constructive Pneumatological Hermeneutics*. Recently, Keener, *Spirit Hermeneutics*, is new and now making a big splash, and rightly so.

certainly consider whether pentecostal contributions are advancing the hermeneutical discussion even if there might also be worries, at least in some circles of the Society of Biblical Literature, for instance, that to embark on any more qualified forms of interpretative approaches to scriptural reading—e.g., Baptistic, Reformed, or Lutheran, much less pentecostal or Wesleyan—would be nothing more than a sectarian undertaking. Put pointedly in terms of this essay: How, if at all, might specifically *pentecostal* readings of the Bible make a contribution to the broader ecumenical church and theological academy?

An exhaustive response to this question cannot be presented within the scope of this essay, but a preliminary mapping of the scholarly terrain suggests at least three possible types of contributions that we might designate the authorial, the particularist, and the hybridic. The first (the authorial) relates to a reading that is not recognizably pentecostal in character even if accomplished by scholars who are pentecostal by ecclesial affiliation and practice, whereas the second concerns a contrasting strategy that is intentionally and explicitly pentecostal (informed up front by pentecostal perspectives). The third relates to efforts by pentecostal scholars to read as Pentecostals but not only for Pentecostals, what I am calling a hybridic tactic.[3] To be sure, as we shall see, these are more heuristic labels of overlapping sensibilities and interpretive practices than they are ideal types of three wholly distinct or demarcated undertakings. I will sketch the contours of the three approaches in dialogue with three recent books on the Apocalypse written by pentecostal scholars—those by Jon Newton, Melissa Archer, and co-authors John Christopher Thomas and Frank Macchia[4]—before outlining a fourth alternative *theological*, or better, pneumatological, suggestion.

Before proceeding, one final comment is necessary regarding our interlocutors and the fact that each of their works engages substantively the final book of the Bible. Pentecostal biblical scholarship has focused somewhat (although certainly not solely) to date on the book of Acts and its antecedent volume, the Third Gospel, and understandably so

3. I do not capitalize *pentecostal* when used as an adjective but do (*Pentecostal*) when used as a noun (e.g., to refer to persons).

4. Newton, *Revelation Worldview*; Archer, *"I Was in the Spirit on the Lord's Day"*; Thomas and Macchia, *Revelation*. Full disclaimer: this essay began initially as a review of these three recent publications, which we will treat more or less in their order of publication.

given St. Luke's renown as a historian and theologian of the Spirit.[5] Yet it may be precisely for this reason that review of pentecostal readings of the Apocalypse could facilitate assessment of the nature of pentecostal hermeneutics and of its potential contributions to theological interpretation of scripture discussions. Put alternatively, part of the question we will explore in the following is what it means to read the book of Revelation in a pentecostal way. I shall suggest that Newton writes neither denying nor emphasizing his pentecostal perspective but yet his efforts to engage a more general Christian audience and set of concerns nevertheless foregrounds Revelation's apocalyptic horizon that could be understood as related to pentecostal instincts and sensitivities; this is thereby an implicit pentecostal reading, one that is embedded within the author's pentecostal identity—hence what I call *authorial*—and is thereby informed broadly by that pentecostal worldview. Archer's, meanwhile, is explicitly pentecostal in terms of sources, methods, and approach; in that sense it is a *particularistic* perspective on Revelation, although some might wonder about its relevance beyond the pentecostal community. Thomas and Macchia are renowned pentecostal scholars, and we will consider in what ways they attempt to communicate their pentecostal predispositions amid a wider ecumenical audience. By considering these pentecostal "takes" on the book of Revelation, a book that, at least on the surface, may not be seen as overtly constituted by pentecostal-related themes and topics, we shall see if being pentecostal makes an interpretive difference and what such might be.[6] More importantly for the purposes of this essay, the apocalyptic horizons and backdrop to these pentecostal reading endeavors puts in stark relief our question about how pentecostal hermeneutics might further debates in theological interpretation of Scripture.[7] I will argue in the concluding section that something like the proposed

5. E.g., Mittelstadt, *Reading Luke-Acts in the Pentecostal Tradition.*

6. Pentecostal readings of Revelation are growing in number. An almost exhaustive overview is Archer, "Pentecostals and the Apocalypse." If readers of the present review essay are tempted to consider it as supplementing Archer's account, note that my purposes are directed toward the specific interface of pentecostal hermeneutics of Revelation vis-à-vis the also more-or-less recently emerging field of theological interpretation of Scripture.

7. I understand that although in some respects fairly new, the theological interpretation of Scripture conversation is complex. The following reflections do not depend on establishing definitively the contours of this discursive field, but can be considered a preliminary effort by a pentecostal systematician to enter into the discussion. My own mapping of this arena is in the introductory chapter of my *The Hermeneutical Spirit.*

theological—and pneumatological—model is needed to receive the gifts of the other three approaches while redeeming their liabilities.

REVELATION AND THE PENTECOSTAL AUTHOR: AN IMPLICIT PENTECOSTAL HERMENEUTICS

Jon Newton is dean of postgraduate studies and head of research at Harvest Bible College, a ministry training school steeped in Australian pentecostal history but more recently being reconceived within the broader sphere of mainstream Christianity in that region of the world. This may helpfully explain why, although long situated within a pentecostal milieu,[8] Newton writes neither in "pentecostalese" nor only for Pentecostals but, more generally, for the wider Christian community. Yet I will suggest that a closer reading of Newton's vision of "apocalyptic thinking"—part of the subtitle of his book under review—unveils an indubitable pentecostal character.

The Revelation Worldview is neither Newton's first book nor his only book on the Apocalypse. Its predecessor, *Revelation Reclaimed: The Use and Misuse of the Apocalypse*, a much slimmer volume from a mainstream evangelical publisher,[9] derived from the same pool of prior doctoral research (on which more in a moment) and was addressed to a more popular audience. Its goal was to counteract escapist renditions of the book as well as speculative correlations between John's symbols and contemporary events inspired by dispensationalist presuppositions. To the degree that much of modern Pentecostalism, including that of large segments of the Australian movement, is dispensational in its eschatology, to that same degree, *Revelation Reclaimed* attempted to set the record straight about how to read the book responsibly, interpret it biblically in its first-century context, and apply it appropriately today.

Although based on research for which the PhD was awarded at Deakin University (Melbourne, Australia), *The Revelation Worldview* is a "heavily revised version" of the 2006 doctoral thesis.[10] Newton is not wholly or only critical of postmodernism, variously appreciating its critique of modernity and embracing of the intellectual space opened up by postmodern impulses. Nevertheless, if not every story is equal even in

8. For over four decades, Newton admits (*Revelation Worldview*, x).

9. Newton, *Revelation Reclaimed*.

10. Newton, *Revelation Worldview*, ix.

the postmodern climate, then how might the biblical story be understood as viable in the present time? Here is where Newton believes the Apocalypse provides as good a window as any scriptural writing to take up the issues. He hedges his bets that as the culmination of the biblical storyline and height of scripture's symbolic strangeness and density, Revelation both challenges any worldview and provides a bridge for cross-cultural worldview inquiry, analysis, and even adjudication.

In particular, the book of Revelation presents a world-picture (indeed, through a series of visions: cosmology), is suggestive for what and how we know (epistemology), and tells us something about John the Seer's understanding about human beings (theological anthropology). Among other means, then, Newton reads this final book of the Bible to inform, critique, and construct a Christian worldview as inclusive of the following elements: a spirit or spiritual world of angels and other realities, a moral and historical sphere that involves at least in some respects binary choices between good and evil, a prophetically infused realm through which God instructs and transforms human creatures, a corrupt political sphere that requires declared allegiances and decisive action, etc. Although it is clear that for the apocalyptic seer (and those who would adhere to his perspective), "some rival narratives (most notably those of imperial Rome) and polytheistic practices must be refuted and rejected completely, because their claims are ultimately 'blasphemous,'"[11] yet generally there are enough openings in Revelation for a more dialogical interface with other worldviews or narratives.

One of the primary moves Newton makes that undergirds his more relational approach is to interpret Revelation as a love story, a crowning moment or "final chapter" of the biblical narrative about God reconciling the world to himself through Jesus Christ.[12] In this way, Revelation presents a final account, albeit one that redeems rather than only rejects rival stories. Following the Seer's insistence that in the New Jerusalem, "the nations will walk by its light, and the kings of the earth will bring their glory into it. . . . People will bring into it the glory and the honor of the nations" (Rev 21:24, 26), Newton affirms: "the new world order envisaged by John does not imply a uniform culture, but a variety of reformed Christian cultures. . . . Absolute truth coexists with diversity of expression."[13]

11. Newton, *Revelation Worldview*, 308.

12. Newton, *Revelation Worldview*, 261–76 (citation from 274); here Newton builds on the work of McIlraith, *Reciprocal Love Between Christ*.

13. Newton, *Revelation Worldview*, 309.

I digress here to note that Newton does not reference the Day of Pentecost account with regard to the preceding claim. Although I will return to the significance of this disconnect, for the moment, I should add that little is said in Newton's book about Pentecostalism at all. There is one section in chapter 3, "The Reality of the Spirit World," that discusses the movement as constituting a "new" but yet also "old" Christian worldview[14]—new in terms of its recent arrival on the world stage from meager beginnings at the turn of the twentieth century but old with respect to its pluralistic pneumatological imagination believed to be consonant with the NT cosmology. It is arguable even in this regard that there is only one way to understand the spirit-world of the biblical narratives and that such is precisely replicated among the pentecostal masses.[15] Yet this point aside, even with this segment, a pentecostal perspective plays no obvious role and does no unambiguous work in Newton's book.

I suggest then that *The Revelation Worldview* is pentecostal only insofar as its author is self-confessed as a participant in the movement. This is what I mean by *authorial*: Here is a book written by someone with a pentecostal identity, even if that is not hermeneutically foregrounded.[16] Having said this, I would also observe that there are aspects of Newton's pentecostal spirituality that nevertheless appear amid his more generalized argument. These are recognizable primarily in his spirit-infused cosmology and his pneumatological epistemology, among other threads. It is telling in this analysis that Newton goes so far as to indicate, at the end of the previously alluded to Pentecostalism section, that this movement "may then be the form of contemporary Christianity most able

14. See "Pentecostalism: A New/Old Christian Worldview," in Newton, *Revelation Worldview*, 147–50.

15. My own attempts to comprehend, in our late modern context, the biblical witness to the many spirits and the principalities and powers can be found in *In the Days of Caesar*, ch. 4; and *Spirit of Creation*, ch. 6, among other sites. See also Kärkkäinen et al., *Interdisciplinary and Religio-Cultural Discourses*.

16. An even better example of such an *authorial* stance is Fee, *Revelation*. Although a noted pentecostal scholar who has published explicitly on pentecostal-related topics, in this work, Fee is the consummate exegete as defined by modern canons of biblical criticism. Hence he announces as much in the preface: "The purpose of the present book is therefore singular: to offer one New Testament scholar's exegetical reading of the text, with very little concern for anything except to help people hear it for the word of God that it is" (ix). Although arguable from any number of perspectives, my point here is that Fee is a pentecostal by identity but in this volume eschews any notion that such might have anything to contribute to scriptural interpretation. The implication—here I realize I risk reading too much into his prefatory remarks—is that to adopt a pentecostal lens might compromise the exegetical task. We will return to this below.

to express the insights I have discerned in Revelation and speak to the needs of the postmodern world, though its attitude to postmodernism is ambivalent."[17] Here what is implicit otherwise comes into the open, although it does not undermine the overall more general framing of *The Revelation Worldview* as addressing a broader audience about important issues that cut across the Christian spectrum.

REVELATION IN PENTECOSTAL PERSPECTIVE: A PARTICULARISTIC HERMENEUTICS

I deem that Melissa Archer is not more pentecostal than Jon Newton—even if her pentecostal situatedness is in the North American Church of God, Cleveland, Tennessee, context rather than Down Under—but her reading of Revelation is surely more explicitly pentecostal than his. This is in large part because her PhD thesis was supervised by John Christopher Thomas, not only a Johannine scholar but also founder, since the early 1990s, of the *Journal of Pentecostal Theology* and its Supplemental Series, the latter now featuring over forty titles. Thomas has also been supervising doctoral students over the last decade plus from his post at the Pentecostal Theological Seminary in Cleveland, Tennessee, and, via the Centre for Pentecostal Theology associated with the seminary, nurturing along the way in that context a distinctive approach to pentecostal scholarship via a literary hermeneutic. As we shall comment further on Thomas's own commentary on the Apocalypse below, here I focus on the results as manifest in Archer's published dissertation. I suggest that Archer's specific and explicit (*particularist*) pentecostal approach can be seen at least at three levels: thematic/textual, methodological/ecclesial, and spiritual/theological.

Thematically, Archer's reading of Revelation attempts to stay as close as possible to the literary and narrative arc of the text (here consistent with Thomas's literary approach) and in that respect focuses on one of its central motifs: that of worship. Her book begins with an extended review of modern literature devoted to worship in the Apocalypse as well as to the half dozen or more hymns across its chapters.[18] Later in her book, she provides readings—exegesis of, broadly rather than

17. Newton, *Revelation Worldview*, 150.

18. That worship is central to the Apocalypse can be seen also in two other books addressing this connection: Kraybill, *Apocalypse and Allegiance*; Gorman, *Reading Revelation Responsibly*. See also my "Revelation and the Political in the 21st Century."

technically understood (more on this momentarily)—of these passages. Yet what ought not to be overlooked is the distinctive role of worship in pentecostal spirituality as well. Although it is certainly not the case that worship is unique to Pentecostalism, yet there is a sense in which pentecostal theological identity might be found as much if not more in its spirituality, expressed in liturgical practices, than in its written treatises.[19] I suggest that the significance of worship in pentecostal spirituality resonates with a hermeneutical approach to the Apocalypse that foregrounds its primacy. Put another way, Archer is primed to consider worship in the Apocalypse precisely through her formation as a biblical reader in pentecostal worship.

Yet, and here methodologically, Archer's is not merely a personal or individualistic worship hermeneutic. Rather, the pentecostal perspective on display in this book belongs to the movement writ large. As with other Thomas students, Archer deploys a reception-history approach, applied especially to early pentecostal periodical literature, but in this case observing how the first generation of modern pentecostal believers interpreted Revelation, particularly its worship scenes and hymnic materials. What emerges is thus a historically informed pentecostal reading of the Apocalypse, one that perceives how early pentecostal singing, poetry writing, preaching, and worship practices were resourced from the last book of the canon on the one hand, while also leading to and sustaining pentecostal theological understandings and practices on the other hand. Interestingly, and perhaps not unexpectedly, the dispensational emphasis otherwise conspicuous in pentecostal circles finds little corroboration in this early literature, especially as it relates to how the first generation of pentecostal believers received and read the book of Revelation.

What has Archer achieved for theological interpretation of Revelation, then? Three interrelated outcomes commend themselves for consideration. First, the pneumacentric dimension of pentecostal worship sensibilities leads Archer to discern a liturgical outline for the Apocalypse delineated by its four uses of the phrase ἐν πνεύματι ("in the Spirit"): 1:9—3:22 (1:10); 4:1—16:21 (4:2); 17:1—21:8 (17:3); and 21:9—22:5 (21:10).[20] This provides a pneuma-liturgical hermeneutic, one might say,

19. See on this point my "Improvisation, Indigenization, and Inspiration"; cf. Yong, "Worship in Many Tongues"; Yong, "Power of Language."

20. No doubt Thomas, her mentor, was influential in this regard as his own commentary is structured along these lines; whereas he presents the Apocalypse as a "visionary drama" (see Thomas and Macchia, *Revelation*, 7), however, my next set of comments indicate that Archer's might be better considered an audiophonic rendition.

that enables a fresh reconsideration of Revelation's message. Second, Archer's pneumatological approach to Revelation as a set of liturgical narratives also renders more blatant the seer's repeated mantra in the first section of letters to congregations of Asia Minor: "Let anyone who has an ear listen to what the Spirit is saying to the churches" (2:7, etc.).[21] This apocalyptic summons to hear the voice of the Spirit resonates with the oral nature of pentecostal spirituality, which in turn invites development of an aural hermeneutic, indeed a mode of scriptural interpretation that depends on the sonic dimension of verbalizing the text and cultivates at least a bimodal (both visual and oral) perceptivity of its message.[22] Last but not least in this regard, reading and hearing Revelation as the call of the Spirit urges articulation of a theology and practice of worship informed by its apocalyptic witness. Thus Archer's engagement with this book asks "what the Apocalypse reveals about worship" and makes suggestions, first for the pentecostal community, but with implications for Christian worship at large.[23]

Archer's work is best appreciated as extending the conversation opened up by Robby Waddell. Published in Thomas's aforementioned Journal of Pentecostal Theology Supplement Series, *The Spirit in the Book of Revelation* attempted both to provide a constructive pentecostal interpretation of the Apocalypse—indeed it was the first scholarly initiative in this vein—and to sketch the contours of a pentecostal hermeneutic in conversation with John the Seer's work.[24] Waddell's deployment of intertextuality theories and his zeroing in on Rev 10–11 as providing gravitas for his proposals both complicated his task (in some respects, the intertextual and pentecostal hermeneutical visions were mutually informing, but in other respects they could have been equally effective on their own, begging the question about their convergence in this work) and has

21. It is worth mentioning in passing that the most recent extensive analysis of these letters and their pneumatological implications is by pentecostal-charismatic scholar Wilson, *Victor Sayings in the Book of Revelation*. At the same time, his approach is broadly that of Newton's, in what I have called above the *authorial* mode, with pentecostal-charismatic sensibilities operating in the background rather than in any overt manner.

22. Thus ch. 4 of Archer's *"I Was in the Spirit on the Lord's Day,"* which unfolds the substance of her reading of the Apocalypse, is subtitled: "Hearing the Revelation of John." For more on pentecostal orality, see my "Understanding and Living the Apostolic Way: Orality and Scriptural Faithfulness in Conversation with African Pentecostalism," which is ch. 3 in my *Hermeneutical Spirit*.

23. Archer, *"I Was in the Spirit on the Lord's Day,"* 298.

24. Waddell, *Spirit in the Book of Revelation*.

required further elucidation (especially since efforts to identify pivotal texts in any scriptural work, not least those as expansive as Revelation, are inherently contested and contestable). Fast forward to Archer: *"I Was in the Spirit on the Lord's Day"* provides empirical grounding (via recourse to early pentecostal literature) for the pentecostal hermeneutic Waddell labors to construct in the abstract even as it proffers a coherent pneumatological hermeneutic that spans the full scope of the Apocalypse. Arguably, Archer projects the plausibility of a pentecostal reading of the full text of Revelation that is fundamentally informed by pentecostal practice and sources, even if its theological pay-off purports also to have broader ecumenical relevance.

REVELATION IN STEREO: A HYBRIDIC PERSPECTIVE

If Newton is a pentecostal who has written on Revelation and if Archer has produced a kind of pentecostal reading of the Apocalypse, then Thomas and Macchia's *Revelation* is what we might call a hybridic approach, one that both is and yet also is not distinctively pentecostal in appeal. To be sure, Thomas and Macchia are two of the more internationally renowned pentecostal scholars, the former as a NT and Johannine expert and the latter as a systematician, both with extensive publication records. They are hence recognized not just as pentecostal academics who have done scholarly work according to the standards of their respective guilds but as having brought their pentecostal perspectives to bear on their scholarship in substantive ways. Yet, their *Revelation* commentary is nothing like Archer's book, even as the pentecostal accents are identifiable for those who care to notice. I suggest that the hybridity of their achievement can be parsed especially in terms of their commentary's intended audience.

Revelation is the sixth volume in the Two Horizons New Testament Commentary series inaugurated in 2005, although it is only the second one that is coauthored by a biblical scholar and a theologian.[25] Not only is the series carried by a mainline publisher, but there appears to be a general format and structure—each book includes an introductory or orienting section, followed by exegetical commentary, and concluding with theological reflections—intended to bridge disciplinary undertakings that have been historically segregated, at least in the modern era. Thomas's approximately 430-page commentary is actually a condensation

25. The other being Wall with Steele, *1 and 2 Timothy and Titus.*

of much longer manuscript written for the Two Horizons series but then published (in over seven hundred pages), with permission from Eerdmans, under the auspices of an imprint associated with Thomas's Centre for Pentecostal Theology.[26] The shorter version preceding Macchia's theological reflections includes much that is verbatim from the sole-authored commentary, although many paragraphs have been reduced and/or combined (and revised in the process), even as a good deal of material, including some of the most explicitly pentecostal aspects, has been excised altogether.

Intriguingly, although the prefatory comments are clear about the pentecostal provenance of Thomas's scholarship, this is not presented as a *pentecostal* commentary on Revelation. Instead, as the earlier book advertises (in its subtitle), the goal is a *literary* and *theological* interpretation. Thomas's narrative and literary hermeneutical skills are evident in both venues, and he interacts regularly with prior pentecostal readings of Revelation (including Waddell and Fee, among others).[27] However, explicit pentecostal insights are not pronounced even as the feeling one gets throughout this first, longer, section of the book is that contemporary readers ought to pay attention first and foremost to the literary features of the text and that the benefits of such focus can be crafted quite apart from any particularistic insights. To be sure, Thomas is well equipped to have provided a distinctively pentecostal exegesis of Revelation, given his prior efforts in this direction on the Johannine writings.[28] Perhaps the wider audience of the Two Horizons series motivated his predominant literary approach to the text of Revelation.

26. Thomas, *Apocalypse*.

27. Most prominently, Hollis Gause, a pentecostal Church of God scholar whose *Revelation* was written for a more popular audience, especially for pentecostal pastors and lay teachers. Also cited is Skaggs and Benham, *Revelation*, although interestingly, space precludes argument that Thomas's two commentaries, while not being explicitly pentecostal in orientation, are more pentecostal than the Skaggs-Benham book despite its series location. All of this to say that, although it may not be appropriate to label Thomas's exegesis of Revelation as pentecostal, it is more pentecostal than not, comparatively speaking.

28. E.g., Thomas, *Footwashing in John 13 and the Johannine Community*; Thomas, *He Loved Them Until the End*; see also Thomas, *Devil, Disease, and Deliverance*; Thomas, *Spirit of the New Testament*. Interestingly, Thomas's *Pentecostal Commentary on 1 John, 2 John, 3 John* is not as robustly pentecostal, a bit like Thomas's *Revelation* comments, perhaps constricted by the commentarial paradigms reigning in the biblical studies academy today.

Frank Macchia's 220-page consideration of the "Theological Horizons of Revelation" (the title of the second part of this work) reflects his training as a systematic theologian much more so than his work as a pentecostal theologian. What I mean is that whereas Macchia is more than capable of providing a *pentecostal theological* reading of Revelation in light of his previous work,[29] his thoughts are organized according to the conceptualization prevalent in the field of systematics and dogmatics: beginning with the doctrine of God and then proceeding, in order, through Christology, pneumatology, ecclesiology, soteriology, and eschatology. Further, in each of these six sections, the method is consistent: in the first subsection an overview of other NT voices on the dogmatic locus and then in the next subsection, a more systematic consideration of what Revelation says on that specific doctrinal or theological topic. If the earlier summations of NT perspectives are supposed to provide background for the theological interpretation of Revelation's Christology, pneumatology, etc., this is not immediately obvious as the discussion in the latter parts of these six sections engages mostly with the Apocalypse's data. No rationale is discernible for this approach, although what emerges, for interested students, is a kind of biblical theology of at least the six loci within the scope of seventy-five scattered pages (skipping over the Revelation discussions).

When set alongside the other volumes available so far in the Two Horizons series, there does not appear to be a strictly enforced template structuring the "Theological Horizons" portions of these books. There is some indication that authors have been invited to situate the theological aspects of the text they are commenting on within the broader NT and canonical contexts, concluding with some more constructive and contemporary considerations, and this movement is discernible in broad strokes in Macchia's approach.[30] But there appears to have been some latitude provided for this aspect of the assignment, including space for developing the text's central theological motif into a more encompassing framework of analysis,[31] and allowing the possibility of com-

29. Here I am thinking primarily of Macchia's two constructive theologies, *Baptized in the Spirit* and *Justified in the Spirit*, which eschatological horizons, among other elements, could have been pressed into fruitful pentecostal engagement with the text of Revelation (so I would surmise); more on this later.

30. This outline is clear in at least three of the volumes, i.e., Thompson, *Colossians and Philemon*; Green, *1 Peter*; Reese, *2 Peter and Jude*.

31. Friendship is the orienting framework in the theological part 2 of Fowl, *Philippians*.

menting theologically on the assigned scriptural text from a more confessionally defined perspective.[32] Comparatively speaking, then, the question is prompted: What if Macchia had brought the book of Revelation into direct and more extensive interaction with Lukan texts, for instance? If Thomas's literary presuppositions privileged intertextual readings across the Johannine writings (understandably so), then Macchia the pentecostal systematician ought to have been free to deploy for the present task the Lukan motifs and categories so prominent in his other work. Yet the latter appear almost only in Macchia's summaries of the other NT voices, and never in constructive theological engagement with the text of the Apocalypse. Alternatively, perhaps the pneumatological thread running through Revelation may have been more systematically assessed and put to work toward a more elaborate pneumatological theology of the Apocalypse, especially in light of Macchia's prior efforts in this area.[33] But again, pneumatology is here treated only as one of the theological loci, and thereby inhibited from being theologically generative. Given the theological creativity manifest in Macchia's other publications, his contribution to the project appears to have been constrained according to its published form. If so, from my vantage point, this was a missed opportunity for one of the premier pentecostal theologians at work today to explicate a distinctively pentecostal reading of Revelation, one that could have fulfilled the promise latent in the trajectory charted by Archer (and Waddell before her).

REVELATION AFTER PENTECOST: A PNEUMATOLOGICAL INTERPRETATION OF SCRIPTURE?

I have suggested in this review essay that there are a number of ways to understand pentecostal hermeneutics in relationship to the emerging field of theological interpretation of scripture. One might be to emphasize the

32. The commentary on the Thessalonian letters by a Nazarene scholar published also in 2016, for instance, notably features the Wesleyan hermeneutic of holiness, and this in turn frames its interaction with other theological themes in these two early Pauline Epistles: Johnson, *1 and 2 Thessalonians*. The previously alluded to Wall and Steele volume also includes sections considering specifically earlier Wesleyan readings of their scriptural assignments.

33. One expression of such a pneumatological hermeneutic is Lee, *Dynamic Reading of the Holy Spirit in Revelation*; surely this book came around too late for consideration since the bulk of the Thomas-Macchia research and writing were accomplished in the few years after the launching of the Two Horizons series in 2005, as indicated in their preface (*Revelation*, xvii–xviii).

adjective of *pentecostal* hermeneutics and thereby say no more than that someone of pentecostal persuasion, confession, and identity in that sense provides a pentecostal reading even without any explicit pentecostal content, whatever the latter might be; I have suggested that Jon Newton's work on reading Revelation in the postmodern context fits such an *authorial* model. One might also emphasize the noun of pentecostal *hermeneutics* in order to highlight how pentecostal functions adjectivally to shape the interpretive enterprise in a fundamental manner; Melissa Archer's reading of worship in the Apocalypse fits such a *particularist* approach. Last but not least, a more *hybridic* stance might also be identifiable, one that is acknowledgeably pentecostal in derivation even if attempting to address and engage a broader ecumenical readership; *Revelation* by Thomas and Macchia, well-known pentecostal scholars, presents both the promise and the challenge of such a hybridic posture. It is not difficult at this juncture to perceive why more explicit forefronting of pentecostal commitments would commend itself to a pentecostally circumscribed audience, while any attempt to write for the church ecumenical and the wider theological academy will impinge on a more particularistic approach. It would appear that theological operation of Scripture operates within the following parameters: either we are empowered to speak more confessionally to those within our faith communities on the one hand, or we need to translate what some may consider to be our more "sectarian" discourse into accessible language and terminology in order to engage wider audiences on the other hand.[34]

This conundrum—at least perceived, regardless if its reality could be debated—may be in part why theological interpretation of Scripture has so far been markedly general in character, more motivated by adherence to the ancient rule of faith or the trinitarian articles than carried by confessional currents.[35] The dilemma is apparent in the pentecostal read-

34. Of course, the reality is much more complicated than the either/of this sentence suggests, especially in our late or postmodern context, in which there is widespread acknowledgment that there is no view from everywhere and only specific views from somewhere; yet, we also cannot rest on our laurels that just because we have our views from our sites does not mean they have equal warrants with those from other sites. In my own work I have surely not been shy about advocating for a pentecostal hermeneutic and a pentecostal theological method, but there are more and less sectarian ways to hold forth one's particularity, and any catholic argument will have to more on the former track. See my *Dialogical Spirit*, for further discussion of the one (particularity) and the many (universality).

35. With the exception of the Wesleyan tradition; see, e.g., Green and Watson, *Wesley, Wesleyans, and Reading Bible as Scripture*.

ings of Revelation surveyed in this essay. Is a pentecostal hermeneutic only valid for the pentecostal community, à la Archer's published thesis, but a more general hermeneutical approach required for an argument with wider cache, as in Newton's project? Or is a hybridic orientation ultimately unsustainable, capitulating to other hermeneutical options (such as Thomas's literary approach) or theological frameworks (as in the genre of systematic theology that structures Macchia's discussion)?

I would like to suggest in light of the preceding that a fourth, theological, alternative is at hand, one that gains potentially from pentecostal scholars but not only from them. More precisely, I recommend that such gravitates toward the pneumatological trajectory—Third Article theology, more particularly—that has emerged in the contemporary theological landscape but yet, from a pentecostal standpoint, is grounded centrally in the Day of Pentecost narrative of the Spirit's outpouring on all flesh.[36] There is no space here for a full discussion,[37] so I limit myself to a few general remarks and then to a basic application to the book of Revelation.

The most important aspect of any pentecostal approach to Scripture that aspires to be ecumenically relevant, I suggest, is less that it derives from the particularity of the pentecostal ecclesiality (although this is certainly not unimportant) but that it builds on the pentecostal story itself, the work of the Spirit unleashed in and through the Day of Pentecost outpouring. The credentials of such a pentecostal hermeneutic, then, are founded not in the idiosyncrasies of pentecostal spirituality but in the scriptural narrative's attestations regarding the foundational and universal work of the Spirit poured out "upon all flesh" (Acts 2:17). This theological, indeed pneumatological, starting point both invites explicit pentecostal reflection on how the work of the Spirit initiated in the pentecostal economy of grace not only extends but also fulfills that promised in the incarnational ministry of the Son, and also buttresses the trinitarian appeals prevalent across current theological interpretation of Scripture discussion via a more robust pneumatological formulation.[38] In this respect, the proposal for a pneumatological reading of scripture

36. My own contribution is *Spirit Poured Out on All Flesh*; for the wider conversation, see, more initially, Kärkkäinen, *Toward a Pneumatological Theology*; more recently, Habets, *Third Article Theology*.

37. The contours of such a pentecostal and pneumatological interpretation of Scripture are on display in my *Who Is the Holy Spirit?*

38. These are claims I hope to make good on in my book *The Hermeneutical Spirit*; see also my *Spirit of Love*, for a dialogical explication of pneumatological hermeneutics and pentecostal theological method.

after Pentecost not only strives to understand how the NT authors read their sacred texts after the Spirit's gifting but also seeks to receive all of these early Christian writings as pentecostal treatises written *in* and carried *by* the Spirit. I suggest that such provides a more radical pentecostal grounding, based not only on contemporary pentecostal experience but on *the* pentecostal character of Christian life and faith after Easter. At the same time, the normativity of this primordial Pentecost begs for elucidation, and this can arise out of any community that is formed by the ongoing work of the pentecostal Spirit. Put in other terms, such a pneumatological hermeneutic welcomes the specificity of pentecostal situatedness but only as one among many expressions of the "fellowship of the Holy Spirit" (2 Cor 13:13) in this dispensation, each strand adding something important and significant to the overall "choir" of the Spirit. As such, then, it is poised to promote a pneumatological and pentecostal reading of Scripture that has wider purchase, for the church catholic and also for the theological academy.

Arguably, any Christian theological interpretation of Scripture will be pneumatological and pentecostal in some sense according to what I have here outlined.[39] In that respect, such a hermeneutical lens might also prove fertile for reading Revelation. Reconsidering the three texts under review from this perspective, Newton's postmodern Apocalypse can be understood also as post-Pentecostal, after the Pentecost outpouring of the Spirit and the harnessing of the many late modern tongues for witnessing to the redemption of the triune God. Archer's apocalyptic worship invites all messianic followers to become pentecostal worshipers, not in the literal sense of attending local pentecostal congregations but in the Lukan sense of giving allegiance to Christ's lordship amid the imperial claims of all times betwixt-and-between Pentecost and parousia. Thomas and Macchia's efforts between two horizons—that of the NT and the present time—can be understood in terms of contemporary Spirit-inspired faithfulness informed by Revelation's Spirit of prophecy that empowers Christian witness "from every nation, from all tribes and peoples and languages" (Rev 7:9). Pentecostal readings would here be welcomed, including applications to pentecostal environments and contexts,[40] but

39. See, for instance, explication of such a pneumatological reading of various NT texts in the third part of each of chs. 2–12 in my *Renewing Christian Theology*.

40. For instance, Keener, *Revelation*, 249–51, appropriately considers the diversity and pluralism of Rev 7:9 in light of the modern pentecostal movement. Note that Keener is a pentecostal NT scholar and that this commentary series is organized

beyond that, extending to pneumatological considerations of the text and the world as in some respects intertwined since with the work of the Spirit of Pentecost.

I aver that such a pentecostal-and-pneumatological horizon not only makes overarching sense of distinctive pentecostal approaches to Scripture—to the Apocalypse in particular, as considered in this essay—but is also consistent with theological interpretation of Scripture initiatives to reconnect biblical studies and theological understanding and practice. Whether the latter claims holds in the longer run can only be adjudicated by explicit enactment of such a pneumatological paradigm, foregrounding in each case the question of how to understand the biblical text afresh in light not just of incarnation and Easter (and ascension) but also of the pentecostal visitation of the Spirit of God.[41] For those who then conclude that since all Christian reading is in this sense pentecostal and pneumatological, and therefore that none is such, my response is to insist that this pentecostal and pneumatological turn is not for its own sake but for the sake of the gospel and the coming divine reign. Even if the pentecostal character of this proposal is subsumed within the trinitarian models gaining currency in the current theological climate, the end result can only be deeper and more, rather than shallower and less, theological—i.e., trinitarian, evangelical, and eschatological—interpretation of Scripture. This unveils the truth of the pentecostal claim: that reading Revelation in particular and Scripture in general after Pentecost involves life in the Spirit so that all theological interpretation of Scripture is at least pneumatological as well.[42]

---

sequentially, with exegetical treatments of the scriptural texts (in this case Revelation) in their original contexts (in sections titled "Original Meaning") preceding theological applications to post-biblical contexts (in sections titled "Contemporary Significance"); the pentecostal references here occur in the latter segment. My proposal does not invalidate the structured division of labor but recognizes both that the meaning-significance distinction is problematic and that theological interpretation is only with difficulty considerable as a later addendum to exegetical "foundations." For my own constructive approach to these complicated matters, see Yong, *Spirit-Word-Community*.

41. My own efforts are in gestation (published later) in my *Revelation*. Perceptive readers will no doubt observe that my delving into the book of Revelation relates to my recently having accepted this assignment.

42. Thanks to Joel Green for the opportunity to review for the *Journal of Theological Interpretation* and to test out my ideas generated in other contexts within this new and emerging domain. Craig Keener and, especially, Robby Waddell, also gave me helpful comments on an earlier draft of the paper, for which I am very grateful. Any errors of fact or interpretation remain my own.

Chapter 11

"To Him Who Loves Us and Freed Us from Our Sins by His Blood. . ."

A Pentecostal Unveiling of Apocalyptic Love

The last book of the biblical canon does not often get consulted when thinking about theology of love.[1] While we will consider various reasons why across the scope of this essay, one place to begin is to note the relative absence of this notion in Revelation and then ask if and how one verse where it is explicitly thematized (in Rev 1:5) could provide a sturdy enough platform for theological reflection on this topic. The following analyzes this and a half dozen other texts on divine and human love in the Apocalypse, considering first the conjunction of *why love* and *why Revelation*, and then proceeding both intertextually-canonically (especially in light of the various cues to John the Seer's reliance on the Old Testament and vis-à-vis the broader Johannine witness) and pentecostally (after the Day of Pentecost outpouring of the Spirit and according to the reception and reappropriation of this theme in Revelation) in order to explore both the ambiguity and complexity of love in a fallen world on

1. John Christopher Thomas [the honoree of the book this essay originally appeared in] was the lead editor of the Journal of Pentecostal Theology Supplement Series that welcomed my doctoral dissertation soon after its defense. I recall feeling buoyed upon receiving his feedback to and acceptance of my submission in the summer of 1999. It is an understatement to say that he has paved the way for pentecostal scholars and theologians like myself. This chapter is written with gratitude for his efforts, which legacy will continue to expand as he is surely far from exhausting his contributions.

the way to the New Jerusalem.[2] I will urge that divine love at the end of the Christian canon cannot but be conceived relationally and trinitarianly, and that this is also intertwined with human response that is enabled by the Spirit of God—or the seven spirits, so named by the Seer (Rev 1:4; 3:1; 4:5; 5:6)—particularly if we read John's perspective as emerging from the underside of history.

LOVE BEFORE AND IN REVELATION: AN INITIAL ANALYSIS

"Of making many books there is no end," a certain preacher said long ago (Eccl 12:12), and this certainly applies to writing about the theology of love.[3] Why then attempt to develop this topic via engagement with the book of Revelation, especially when it has been unmistakably stated that love "is not . . . a dominant theme in this apocalypse"?[4] This first section begins by providing preliminary justification for our focus and then identifying the basic resources at our disposal from the Apocalypse. We shall see that Revelation's ethos and contents accentuate both the promise and the problem for any effort to develop a theology of love.

Love and Revelation: Warranting the Inquiry

Modern Western notions of love have foregrounded, albeit rarely doing so consciously, their affective or emotional (first) and behavioral (second) character. Hence from a theological perspective, *love* has been generally understood orthopathically (related to the right affections or feelings) or orthopraxically (related to the right actions), but less so orthodoxically (related to right teaching or doctrine). Perhaps the promise and challenge

2. This essay extends to the book of Revelation the emerging project of pentecostal interpretation of scripture; see Yong, *Hermeneutical Spirit*.

3. My initial foray into theologies of love was like diving into an ocean of prior considerations, but somehow I surfaced long enough for air (to maintain the metaphor) to add to the debris: *Spirit of Love*. As the book of Revelation was largely absent from the exegetical chapters of that earlier work, the following advances the arguments developed therein, albeit along the apocalyptic register of the final biblical text.

4. Ford, *Revelation*, 378. Other books on Revelation with love in the title are misleading in that they are not expositions of the notion: Francis, *Apocalypse of Love*, is a psychological reading in dialogue with the mystical tradition, and two others—Fallon, *Apocalypse*; Farley, *Apocalypse of St. John*—are more or less in the genre of traditional commentaries.

for theologies of love are precisely that they are attempting to analyze, comprehend, and conceptualize what is felt and done (expressed in actions).

Yet with respect to the orthopathic and orthopraxic dimensions of love, perhaps dialogue with the book of Revelation is appropriate seeing that the latter's symbolic message functions less cerebrally than affectively, being designed to orient, capture, and motivate human hearts first and foremost instead of dialectically convincing human ratiocinations.[5] Still the question persists about what theological analysis can accomplish in this case, especially if the text that we are attempting to understand is now also said to operate more so at the level of feeling and doing than conceptually. While relying on the efforts of biblical theologians to enable appreciation of the "narrative coherence" of the scriptural witness, systematic theologians suggest such needs to be followed with assessments of the "logical coherence" between the world of the Bible and that outside its pages. Our reading of Revelation to come therefore will attend to what is said about love not just at the textual—both internally within and externally without (canonically)—level but also with regard to how its message comports with the realities with which the book engages and to which it points, and herein the rhetorical and the ontological are intertwined.

One important set of considerations this prioritizes relates therefore to the eschatological scope of Revelation. If God is love, as the Bible so noticeably insists (1 John 4:8, 16) and as we shall return to comment on further below (in the next section), then it would seem that the end of the creation story cannot but climax toward, in, or with love. Should not the final scriptural book, no less eschatologically oriented than is Revelation, therefore also bear witness to this loving finale? Yet the ambiguity of the Apocalypse precisely in this regard, particularly the violence within and through which the narrative unfolds, should prompt further consideration of what it means to talk especially about divine love. More pointedly, if God so loves the world and even "desires everyone to be saved and to come to the knowledge of the truth" (1 Tim 2:4), which is emphasized not only among pietistic Christians but also among those with modern liberal sensibilities, then that Revelation's ultimate eschatological images include a multiplicity of woes (8:13)—death of a fourth of the earth (6:8), and then another third (9:15), even of aquatic life (16:3), life-taking

5. Johns, *Lamb Christology of the Apocalypse of John*, 157, notes that there is little logical argumentation in Revelation; instead, "the Apocalypse is primarily a book of pathetical persuasion. . . . Pathical persuasion persuades by exciting the emotions and imagination of the audience." See also Kraybill, *Apocalypse and Allegiance*.

earthquakes (11:13), massive carnage by the sword (19:19–21), and destruction through the cosmic elements (20:7–9), etc.—does not compute. How might we understand this apocalyptic witness to God who loves with the life of his Son but then also seems not just to sanction violence but also to celebrate its gruesome deployment?

Fundamentally then, our scriptural—in this case: Apocalyptic—exploration of love is also a theological one. Numerous books have been written to argue the case that the Johannine witness to God being love is not just one among other central attributes regarding the nature of God but the overarching horizon within which to understand God in relationship to all else, including the pain, tragedy, horror, and even violence of history.[6] The exclamation point that is the final book of the Christian canon does not deny this assertion, but its narrative insists that simplistic and pious understandings of such love that ignore the underside of creaturely existence are not comprehensively biblical. Any serious biblical discussion of love then ought to pause long enough to weigh Revelation's contributions to the topic while being open to reconsidering conventionally defined aspects of love in light of the Apocalypse's witness.[7]

Love in Revelation: Sketching the Theme

But clearly theologians of love who come to Revelation have little to work with beyond a few cursory references.[8] There are four appearances of the term early in the book, in the letters to the seven churches more precisely, two each of which are about divine and human love. Jesus declares his love for those in Philadelphia and Laodicea, in the former case in relationship to unveiling divine love for that congregation to their enemies (3:9) and in the latter case to reprimand congregants to repent and persevere through disciplinary reproof inflicted by God (3:19). Before that, the love of the members of the churches at Ephesus (2:4) and Thyatira (2:19) are recognized and extolled, albeit not without cautionary admonishments. Other than this, with the exception of the opening greeting to which we

6. Most recently, compellingly, and provocatively being Oord, *Uncontrolling Love of God*.

7. Most biblical theologies of love either proof-text from the Apocalypse or ignore it altogether; e.g., Morris, *Testaments of Love*; Palmer, *Love Has Its Reasons*, are respective examples.

8. The following texts are at the heart of the two-page discussion of love in Revelation in Furnish, *Love Command in the New Testament*, 169–70.

will come momentarily and a passing allusion to the saints who loved God more than their own lives (12:11), the Seer says nothing about love throughout the main visions of the book. At the very end, there are two apparently final intimations, one regarding the deity's protection over his "beloved city" (τὴν πόλιν τὴν ἠγαπημένην) witnessed to via consuming judgment upon the enemies of the saints (20:9), and the other about the exclusion from the New Jerusalem of "everyone who loves [φιλῶν] and practises falsehood" (22:15). No doubt any systematic articulation of Apocalyptic love is hampered by the scarcity of references.

Significantly, however, John opens his book with a greeting to the churches that are encouraging for our purposes:

> [4] Grace to you and peace from him who is and who was and who is to come, and from the seven spirits who are before his throne, [5] and from Jesus Christ, the faithful witness, the firstborn of the dead, and the ruler of the kings of the earth. To him who *loves us* and *freed us* from our sins by his blood, [6] and *made us* to be a kingdom, priests serving his God and Father, to him be glory and dominion for ever and ever. Amen. (Rev 1:4–6, emphasis added)

Crucially here, divine love is christologically defined so that any quest for an apocalyptic theology of love cannot but spring off the revelation of Jesus Christ. This is as it should be since the visions of this book are ultimately not only from Jesus but also about his (and God's) triumph, even if through the shedding of his blood (as the slaughtered Lamb).[9] Yet even more important for us is the doxological exaltation of Jesus' ongoing love for the churches, denoted in the present participle—and here compare the verb forms italicized in the quotation above—contrasted with the aorist character of his bloody death and his founding of the new people of God as "a kingdom" of priests.[10] Read in this way, Christ's love for the saints, prominently defined in turns of his painful and innocent death (the latter sensibility following from the Lamb imagery that is pervasive in the rest of the visions), undergirds his entire revelation and in that sense at least invites and perhaps even justifies reading the book from this horrendous but yet agapeic point of view. Divine love thus refracted christologically is intense (the Son shedding his own blood and

9. As in Johns, *Lamb Christology of the Apocalypse of John*; cf. Tonstad, *Saving God's Reputation*.

10. De Villiers, "Love in the Revelation of John," 159, begins with Rev 1:5 and then proceeds with detailed exegesis of the six other epithets in this greetings and shows how they are thematically developed throughout the book.

embracing death in order to liberate human creatures from their sins; cf. 5:9; 7:14; 12:11; 19:13) and yet also transformative (resulting in the inauguration of the divine rule; cf. 1:9; 5:10; 11:15; 12:10), even as it disciplines (surely no comforting notion here!) those who are loved in order to nurture love in and through their lives (cf. Rev 2–3).[11] From this perspective, this doxological greeting in the prologue to the book arguably provides a hermeneutic of love with which to reconceive the meaning of the Apocalypse with all of its ghastliness and dreadfulness.

Beyond such a hermeneutical approach, however, Roman Catholic biblical scholar Donal McIlraith has also argued that an "imagery of love" can be discerned as dominating the entirety of John's vision after the letters to the seven churches.[12] McIlraith proposes what he calls a *bridal reading* of the book, one based on the nuptial imagery evidenced in the crowning vision of the marriage of the Lamb and his bride, the saints of God (19:7–8), the great banquet or marriage supper (19:9), the beloved city into which the Lamb and his bride withdraw (20:9), the bride's being adorned (21:2–3, 9), and the Spirit and the bride's liturgical "calling" toward consummation (22:17). Even if this bridal metaphor does not appear until the nineteenth chapter—which would be the primary criticism of McIlraith's theory—yet given the way in which the book ends, it might be granted that the bride is from the beginning called toward the wedding, growing throughout the narrative in her responsive love of "faith, service, and endurance" toward the one who first loved her with his blood,[13] and demonstrating that love with her ongoing perseverance against and resistance to the seductions of Babylon and its harlotry. The latter are finally banished, so that the grand final party is not necessarily one of unequivocal bliss but rather an emergent venue wherein the celebrants consume nothing less than the flesh of the adversaries of God (19:17–21). Hence on this reading, the Lamb and bride's "relationship of love as nuptial bond" is not for those who cannot stomach dreadfulness; instead, as already denoted, it is ultimately about christology, and only secondarily about ecclesiology and eschatology.[14]

If the doxological greeting at the vanguard of the Apocalypse suggests that the love of Jesus Christ undergirds the entire divine revelation, the matrimonial imagery dominant in the capping vision confirms the

11. De Villiers, "Love in the Revelation of John," 163–65.

12. McIlraith, *Reciprocal Love Between Christ and the Church.*

13. McIlraith, *Reciprocal Love Between Christ and the Church*, 72.

14. McIlraith, *Reciprocal Love Between Christ and the Church*, 202–4.

possibility of receiving the full prophecy as the uncovering of divine love. In this reading, then, divine love preserves the people of God, vindicates those who persevere in the face of opposition, and admonishes them toward faithfulness. Such an orientation begins to grasp how a book that precipitates as full a range of affective responses beyond that of sentimentality can yet contribute to a theology of love. Yet we must press further into this apocalyptic missive precisely because of its capacity to nurture affectivity that is counter-intuitive to conventional feelings of orthopathic love.

REVELATORY LOVE AS INTRATEXTUAL-INTERTEXTUAL PROBLEMATIC: A SELECTIVE ASSESSMENT

Although the preceding has begun to identify why few have attempted to develop a theology of love from Revelation, our analysis can gain from further specificity. If love has a pathic dimension, then not only does the violence of the book nurture contrary feelings of affectivity, but its overall narrative arc is sustained by the sense that its intended audience lives amid unfriendly and adverse others. Hence the apocalyptic community (if we can use this descriptor) is repeatedly warned against those within and without who are foes rather than friends, and who even seem to be the source of persecution. In effect, readers are both galvanized against these oppressors, calling on their deity for their exoneration, and eager to realize visitation of divine vindication on those who oppose the people of God (cf. Rev 6:10; 18:20; 19:2). Hence the enemies of God are finally destroyed, whether in battle or via the final condemnation in the everlasting lake of fire (20:10–15).[15] The point is that the book foregrounds divine judgment of and over, rather than love toward, the enemies of God and his people.[16] While this ensures that any theology of love from Revelation is intertwined with rather than exclusive of judgment, it also suggests why the theme of love is not readily associated with the main lines of its message. Love is not the primal feeling aroused when reading this book.

15. Intriguingly, however, if we adopted a hermeneutic of love (from the 1:4–6 framing) for the entirety of the visions, then even at the height of what appears to be divine judgment on sinners, the outpouring of the bowls of wrath in Rev 16, there are hints that such actions are intended to bring the enemies of God to penitence precisely in the twice repeated assertion following bowls four and five that the peoples of the earth persisted in their cursing of God and resisted repentance (6:9, 11); I am grateful to Jordan Wessling for this insight.

16. Thus for instance the efforts to address the question of divinity in relationship to violence; e.g., Bredin, *Jesus, Revolutionary of Peace*.

An additional complicating factor to grasping the meaning of Revelation is that the Seer speaks throughout in semiotic and symbolic imagery. If John begins his prophecy (1:3; 22:7, 10, 18–19) with these words, "The revelation of Jesus Christ, which God gave him to show his servants what must soon take place; he made it known [ἐσήμανεν; *esémanen*] by sending his angel to his servant John" (1:1), then he also indicates that this *making known* involves to "show by a sign," to "give [or make] signs [or signals]," or to "signify."[17] In other words, Revelation is a thoroughly symbolic book. On the one hand, this makes it understandable that its symbolism fires up the imagination and grips human hearts as much as it informs critical cognition. On the other hand, it also exacerbates efforts to think theologically about the Apocalypse. How might we sort through the barrage of feelings and range of emotions generated by the book while working toward a theological formulation? How in other words can we understand what love means when its inarguable semiotic character is also affectively tinged in multiple directions through the text of Revelation?

A related challenge, but one that points a way forward for our assessment, is that the symbolic world of the Apocalypse is thoroughly imbued with material drawn from the scriptures of ancient Israel. One scholar suggests that there are almost six hundred allusions to the Old Testament in Revelation.[18] Surely there is neither time nor space here for a complete analysis of the ways in which the First Testament's understanding of Yahweh's love may, or not, have informed that of the Seer's. At the same time, it may be helpful to highlight some connections to illuminate how the Apocalypse's semiotics of love can be illuminated from ancient Israelite perspectives. Such considerations then can be compared and contrasted with a brief appraisal of revelatory love in the New Testament context, especially the Johannine writings. We will show that a canonical frame does not eliminate the challenges confronting formalization of an apocalyptic theology of love but does clarify its affective contours.

17. Beale, *John's Use of the Old Testament in Revelation*, 296; brackets are Beale's.

18. Moyise, *Old Testament in the Book of Revelation*, 14–16; from among all these allusions, there are almost no—maybe only one? (Rev 2:27 from Ps 2:9)—direct quotations from the First Testament!

Old Testament Anticipations

If the scriptures of Israel are known at all for a revelation of love, what comes through is Yahweh's love for the people. This is consistently portrayed throughout the First Testament in terms of Yahweh's marriage to Israel, most poignantly manifest in the Song of Songs, but also centrally orienting the ministries of both major and minor prophets.[19] The temple and Torah were also representative of divine love for Israel, so that the destruction of the latter in 70 CE shifted locus of such love exclusively to the former. From this perspective, McIlrath's bridal reading of Revelation as well as his lifting up the conjugal imagery in the book makes eminent sense. A number of tangents connecting the Old Testament and the Apocalypse can then also be delineated.

First, as is indisputable throughout the Old Testament, Yahweh loves Israel with a unwavering and undying love. This is obvious when we look at two books that play prominent roles in the Seer's construction: Exodus and Isaiah. Whereas the former narrative of escape from Egypt plainly provides foundational imagery for Revelation's seals, trumpets, and bowls, and even presents a song of deliverance (Exod 15:1–21) that is alluded to—albeit quite distinctively, mentioning Moses' name—by John (Rev 15:3),[20] the latter appears to have been a book so thoroughly absorbed by the apocalyptic author that allusions can be traced almost unequivocally to almost every segment of its sixty-six chapters.[21] As the Hebrew scriptures show God loves Israel so much that God saves her despite her faithlessness, so also Revelation reveals God's preservation of God's people through their precariousness. The Exodus narrative is consistent in this regard in depicting Yahweh as having "steadfast love" for the people (15:13), even to the thousandth generation (15:13; 20:6; 34:6–7). Similarly, Isaiah reiterates regularly that Yahweh loves his people with steadfastness, whether when assailed by the Assyrians (16:5; 22:4), in exile (43:4; 54:8, 10), and even confronted by their vulnerability in

19. See Lyke, *I Will Espouse You Forever.*

20. See, respectively, Schüssler Fiorenza, *Revelation*, 57–73, on how the plagues accomplished Israel's deliverance from Pharaoh are developed in Revelation; and Smalley, *Revelation to John*, 380–94, on Rev 15:1–8 as a "new exodus" for the people of God anticipating departure from Babylon.

21. Fekkes, *Isaiah and Prophetic Traditions in the Book of Revelation*, 280–81, provides a summary that shows John's allusions to come from all portions of Isaiah except chapters 14–20, 27–33, and 35–39; further, although Isa 1–10 is mostly untouched, there are two allusions to 6:1–4 (in Rev 4:8 and 15:8).

the post-exilic context (63:7, 9).[22] The message in these Old Testament texts is clear: Yahweh will not give up on his people. Translated into the apocalyptic milieu, there is a similar idea: the deity of Israel who loves the church will not only free them from the sins of bondage (as Israel was delivered) but will also preserve and transform them into inhabitants of the divine reign (cf. Rev 1:5–6).

Further, for as small a book as is Daniel, there are a disproportionate number of allusions identifiable in Revelation.[23] Yet our remarks are reinforced on the Danielic register since this ancient prophet also recognizes the unfaltering love of Yahweh for God's people, regardless of their fickleness (Dan 9:4–5). Further this small prophecy also identifies its main protagonist as one "greatly beloved" of Yahweh (10:11, 19). Here Yahweh's love for the prophet is comforting amid visions of cosmic providence involving "global" (imperial) and cosmological (spiritual and angelic) powers. Perhaps Daniel's visionary exhortation undergirds the Seer's confidence that despite upheavals of cosmic proportions, the God who upholds and judges the world and its creatures yet loves and cares for individuals, John and his compatriots (and readers) included.

There is one more point worth mentioning in what will still be a very cursory treatment of the intertextual dimensions of Revelation's theology of love: that related to the marital imagery found especially in the book of Ezekiel. John's vision of judgment on Babylon, the "great whore" (17:1), and of the salvation of God's people from out of the whore's clutches, has been shown to be indebted at least in part to Ezekiel's prophecies, particularly those exposing the sexual misconduct, fornication, and adultery of Israel (Ezek chs. 16, 23) and the elegies lamenting and pronouncing judgment on Tyre (chs. 26–28), understood as the object of Israel's unfaithfulness.[24] Yet it is also precisely in these Ezekielian prophecies that there are innumerable references not to divine love but to Israel's lovers (e.g., 16:33–37; 23:5, 9, 22). So while nothing is said about Yahweh's love for Israel, replete throughout the Hebrew canon are many indications that the love of the latter had been redirected from her husband, to remain

22. I am referring to the scholarly division of first, second, and third Isaiah corresponding to three different periods, even if my claim here is not dependent on such a historical reconstruction; see further my treatment of Isaiah in Yong, *Mission After Pentecost*, §§4.1–4.3.

23. See Beale, *Use of Daniel in Jewish Apocalyptic Literature*.

24. If Tyre is "the Great Prostitute," then Rome or Babylon is the "great whore" (Rev 17:1; 19:2); see Ruiz, *Ezekiel in the Apocalypse*, 527, 537.

with the nuptial metaphor, but now negatively construed. Similarly in Revelation, while affirmations of God's love for the churches are present, even if few in number, there are also constant refrains that the people of God ought to be wary of seducing Jezebels that might mislead them into the comforts of Babylon. If divine love in Ezekiel is spurned and Israel's love misdirected, in Revelation God's love manifest in Jesus Christ is or ought to be requited by human creatures. (And some do, including the 144,000 virgins [Rev 14:3–4], which language and imagery of chastity not only contrasts with that of whoredom but is also used repeatedly to describe a faithful Israel in the prophetic literature.) There is therefore something of an open question, something at stake, in the bridal imagery of the Apocalypse: will the love of God be embraced or rebuffed by those to whom such is bestowed?

Johannine Contexts

I now want to take a brief look at the broader New Testament context for re-situating Revelation's theology of love. Here of course, we might wish to simply sketch the theology of love prevalent across the Johannine literature. The immediate problem that greets us is that there is no consensus among scholars that the author of the Apocalypse is the same John as that historically attributed as author of the Fourth Gospel or the elder of the epistles. One proposal regarding common authorship prioritizes Revelation to suggest that the heresies warned against in this initial book do unfortunately come to fruition as reflected in the later epistles.[25] From this perspective, apocalyptic love is necessarily inclusive of sanctifying judgment: "John's theology of salvation through judgment thus includes a very positive understanding of judgment itself. It is real; but it is ultimately an expression of God's love, and it is designed to lead to the wholeness of humanity."[26]

Yet even without resolving the question of authorship, there is certainly the perception of a Johannine circle, one in which the named prophet behind Revelation could have been associated with. What seems common to this so-called Johannine community is its sectarian defensiveness, perhaps in response to either persecution or marginalization

25. Smalley, *Thunder and Love*, 125–37.

26. Smalley, *Thunder and Love*, 148–49.

(self-imposed or otherwise) from the dominant sector.[27] In this context, rather than reproducing the call to love the enemy found in other parts of the New Testament,[28] the churches are commended or chastised for loving or not their God and are warned about tolerating the opposition (parallel to the admonitions in the other Johannine writings against false teachers, etc.). Pheme Perkins notes additionally that Rev 13:16–17 "advocates socioeconomic isolation from the life of the cities in Asia Minor. . . . Clearly, survival in a world where significant participation in the larger culture is impossible will require communal solidarity. . . . Separation from the socioeconomic life of the ancient city is the only way that the believer can remain untainted (Rev. 18:4–5) and not share the fate that awaits the rest of humankind."[29] Hence she concludes:

> Since its price [of "patient endurance and suffering"] may include socioeconomic withdrawal from the life of the cities, love among the elect expressed as solidarity and mutual support must have played a more prominent role than the meager references in Revelation itself might suggest. . . . If "love of enemy" means compromising the gospel witness, then it cannot be Christ's word to the church. If "love of neighbor," that is, associations with the non-Christian neighbor, also exposes individuals to the danger of being denounced and persecuted, then some form of social withdrawal may be the only policy. Revelation does not advocate rushing into martyrdom or punitive exile. Some, like the seer, may have that testimony thrust upon them. For the rest, love as communal solidarity, patient endurance, and refusal to compromise with the powers of evil are the key to survival.[30]

In short: Revelation's depiction of the Christian life as combating the powers of darkness calls for vigilance, resistance, separation, not loving one's enemies, especially if such interactions risk contamination by these others.

Whatever the historical connections, if any, the contrast between what these other Johannine writings say about love and that found in the Seer's visions are quite stark. Both the Gospel and the epistles mention love dozens of times while the former says that God loves the world (John 3:16) and advocates the love commandment (13:34–35), and the

27. I discuss Johannine sectarianism elsewhere: "'Light Shines in the Darkness.'"

28. Perkins, "Apocalyptic Sectarianism and Love Commands," 288–89.

29. Perkins, "Apocalyptic Sectarianism and Love Commands," 292–93.

30. Perkins, "Apocalyptic Sectarianism and Love Commands," 294–95.

latter explicitly repeats that "God is love" (1 John 4:8, 16).[31] Revelation, as is well known, not only clearly communicates divine love for the entire people of God, as represented by the seven churches,[32] but also just as unambiguously declares those not included among the audience and the "us" who are loved by God (1:5) are enemies of the divine outworking in history and will be judged and devastated, even ultimately so with death and destruction in the lake of fire. Further, the Gospel also presents a love narrative, one that involves family members, beloved disciples, and Jesus' own exemplary and ideal (paidagogic, even) love.[33] Revelation, as we have seen, does not feature love as a prominent theme, much less open up a love story in any clear sense. The final wedding feast between the bride and bridegroom and succeeding images suggests a consummation of the love that motivated divine liberation of human creatures from sins and commitment to ensure the bride's arrival at the wedding. But in between, there is little reminder that it is divine love that is prevailing. So however strong the glimpses of God's universal love are in the wider Johannine corpus, the social and religious pressures exerted on this apocalyptic community patently have constrained such expressions in a sectarian direction.

APOCALYPTIC LOVE: A PNEUMATOLOGICAL AND PENTECOSTAL PRAXIS

Whither then the quest for an apocalyptic theology of love? The preceding suggests that any way forward has to navigate the affective and rhetorical dimensions of the text while keeping in mind broader canonical connections—no easy task indeed. Yet that the divine love is both manifest in the vulnerable love of Jesus Christ (1:5) and that the identity of the latter is bound up with "him who is and who was and who is to come, and [with] the seven spirits who are before his throne" (1:4) invites a trinitarian reconceptualization of our problematic. Further, that McIlraith's nuptial reading culminates with the call of the Spirit (see 22:17) further accentuates the plausibility of a more specifically pneumatological consideration

31. Jackman, *Message of John's Letters*, 18; cf. Lussier, *God Is Love According to Saint John*.

32. The seven churches can be understood as representative of John's cosmic or catholic—"universal," for du Rand, "'Let Him Hear What the Spirit Says,'" 44, 48–49—ecclesiology.

33. See van Tilborg, *Imaginative Love in John*.

of the Seer's theology of love. What if we were to follow such clues in re-reading apocalyptic love? In this final part of our essay, I suggest that such an approach foregrounds the interrelated character of divine and human love while also emphasizing the role of human response to, and participation in, the love of God by his Spirit.[34]

The Spirit of Love in Revelation

Prioritizing a pneumatological perspective on love inevitably prompts wider questions about the role of God's Spirit in the Apocalypse. While there is certainly no space for any kind of comprehensive discussion,[35] suffice for our purposes to say that not only is the book of Revelation pneumatically structured—thus the four instances of the Seer's being "in" or "carried" by the Spirit (Rev 1:10; 4:2; 7:3; 21:10) might be indicative of new sections of the book[36]—but it is also presented as a prophecy (1:3; 22:7, 10, 18), and more precisely in pneumatological terms: "the testimony of Jesus is the spirit of prophecy" (19:10).[37] Perhaps not surprisingly, however, the unveiling of Jesus Christ that is at the heart of the book's message is intimately intertwined with the "seven spirits of God" (4:5; 5:6; also 1:4). Readers across the Christian tradition see these seven spirits as hearkening to Isaiah's (11:2) sevenfold messianic spirit or, more probably, to Zechariah's (4:1–6) spirit related to the seven lampstands.[38] The Seer both suggests that the seven churches to which he is writing are graced by these seven spirits (1:3–4) and that the words to the seven churches are from "him who has the seven spirits of God and the seven stars" (3:1). In that respect, the revelation of Jesus Christ is also a revelation of the seven spirits, and the revelatory apocalypse is also the

34. Our discussion here anticipates and is consistent with the argument that says: "The pneumatological perspective on Revelation lends meaning to the all-containing vision. Although quantitatively the Spirit is seldom mentioned, his deeds in Revelation are qualitatively active: so much so that Revelation was realized *in coram Spiritu*"; see de Smidt, "Hermeneutical Perspectives on the Spirit in the Book of Revelation," 44.

35. An excellent point of entry is Waddell, *Spirit in the Book of Revelation*.

36. E.g., Thomas, *Apocalypse*, 2–6.

37. Even if 19:10 might not be a direct reference to the divine Spirit, there are pneumatological aspects to this text; Bauckham, *Theology of the Book of Revelation*, ch. 5, discusses the spirit of prophecy in more detail.

38. E.g., Tanner, "Climbing the Lampstand-Witness-Trees."

unconcealing of the Spirit of God, and that precisely in and through the Spirit's prophecy (this book).[39]

Such a pneumatological framing is particularly relevant when thinking about love. As already mentioned, the word's predominant matrix is in the opening chapters, especially with regard to the seven churches. Within this milieu, it is important to be reminded that the visions of the book are directed precisely to these churches (1:4, 11, 20) and that the Spirit is not only the one that inspires the apocalyptic prophecy but is also desiring that these prophetic locutions (words) achieved certain perlocutionary effects. Thus at the end of each of the seven messages to these churches, either before (in the first three cases) or after (in the last four cases),[40] the call is repeated: "Let anyone who has an ear listen to what the Spirit is saying to the churches" (2:7; also 2:11, 17, 29; 3:6, 13, 22).[41] These letters capture in nuce both the encouragement of the Seer and his warnings. They indicate for our purposes the prophetic and pneumatic character of the revelatory message: attend, and be oriented toward or turn in the Lord's direction. With respect then to the role of these letters and the pneumatic mantra that concludes each one, the apocalyptic communiqué is fundamentally pneumatological in its dynamic. In that sense, the Apocalypse is also at least proto-trinitarian,[42] revealing the Word of the one on the throne, through Jesus Christ, by the (seven) Spirit(s).

If pneumatologically charged, how does this shape our understanding of love in these letters, or how can we understand love within their scope? To the Ephesians it is said, after extolling their "patient endurance" (2:2): "But I have this against you, that you have abandoned the love [*agapon*] you had at first" (2:4). The Thyatirans (the fourth church addressed), on the other hand, are recognized for persevering even further

39. For more on Revelation's pneumatology, Bauckham, *Climax of Prophecy*, ch. 5.

40. Wilson, *Victor Sayings in the Book of Revelation*, 74–75, summarizes the various theories about why this is the case; I have not found any satisfactory explication.

41. Richards, *What the Spirit Says to the Churches*, is a Roman Catholic interpretation that uses the Spirit-saying as a trope to emphasize the contemporary relevance of Revelation (as opposed to its significance being relegated to the original audience)—which is the "key" highlighted in the volume subtitle—and hence does not at all develop any constructive pneumatological hermeneutic or reading as those picking up the text might expect.

42. Here recognizing that any "trinitarian" readings of the New Testament are influenced by post-Nicene developments, and that there are dangers of anachronism when urging Revelation, for instance, as commending a trinitarian theology; for further discussion of the Apocalypse in these regards, see Bucur, "Hierarchy, Prophecy, and the Angelomorphic Spirit."

so that their "last works are greater than the first" (2:19). The former are admonished to return to their first love while the latter are applauded for never having forsaken it. Then the divine love doxologically celebrated at the beginning (1:5) reappears to bolster the Philadelphians: "I will make those of the synagogue of Satan who say that they are Jews and are not, but are lying—I will make them come and bow down before your feet, and they will learn that I have loved [*agapesa*] you" (3:9); here not only is the love of God reassured but the divine judgment is simultaneously threatened against those who love neither the deity nor seven churches. Last but not least, the Laodiceans, whose (legendary) lukewarmness is associated metaphorically with affluent but shameful nakedness—with all its connotations against the backdrop of Yahweh's faithfulness contrasting with the infidelity of the people of God in the Old Testament and then also in Revelation—and leaves them perilously close to being spit and emitted out of the divine presence, are told: "I reprove and discipline those whom I love [*phileo*]. Be earnest, therefore, and repent" (3:19).[43] So divine love both protects and exonerates the people of God on the one hand, but also reprimands and chastises them on the other hand.

Yet note that the primary message of the seven letters urges focus on the Spirit's words, pressing the churches on toward the New Jerusalem in the midst of challenging circumstances and beguiling allurements. God's love promotes and empowers, even as the churches are acclaimed (or rebuked) for response in kind (or not). If within the larger scheme of this apocalyptic prophecy, the work of the Spirit is to enable devotion to the person and witness of Jesus Christ who loved the people of God even to his death, then the theme of the seven letters invites participation by the Spirit in that love, even under pressured and seductive conditions.

Apocalyptic Affections and the Praxis of Love

We must now venture some summary remarks about apocalyptic love. First, it has been suggested that even if explicit references to love are

43. Smalley notes the use of divine *phileo* rather than *agapeo* in this text and speculates about its appropriateness vis-à-vis the Laodiceans, traditionally believed to be "those who deserve it [God's love] least" (*Revelation to John*, 100). I have not found any better elucidation, but the one proposed seems undeserving of recognition as an explanation, certainly not one that is better than simply seeing *agapeo* and *phileo* as semantically synonymous in Johannine literature, the Apocalypse included. On this point, see the section "Lexical Issues," in Wilson, "New Love of the Ephesians."

sparse in this book, the doxological acclamation that discloses Jesus Christ and his love and the marital cord that fully emerges at the end justify reading even the gory details of the book as unfolding through the narrative of divine love. But second, even if God's love manifest in Jesus Christ provides a leading thread for explicating the movement of the book, human reception of and participation in the divine love is crucial for its fulfillment. In other words, Revelation's theology of love is a fully interrelational one, presuming surely divine initiative but fully involving creaturely response.

The relationality of apocalyptic love is further buttressed from our proposed pneumatological angle. The pneumatic injunctions punctuating the seven letters not only mandate attention to the Spirit's prophetic sayings but also are a means of "emphasizing the need for response."[44] Yet the capacity for response is pentecostal, dependent in that sense on the outpouring of the Spirit on all flesh on the Day of Pentecost. From this pentecostal site, Revelation's readers and hearers are enabled to "stand in solidarity with John, Jesus, and the Spirit."[45] More precisely, it is in such solidarity of witness that the church not only embraces divine love but witnesses to such love to an otherwise (and sometime) oppositional world. In effect, it may well be through such witness that an unfriendly world comes to experience the love that the people of God now enjoy, and this itself is consistent with the wider Johannine assertion that the community's love is the means through which those outside will recognize discipleship on the messianic way (John 13:34–35). In this sense, then, John's Apocalypse can be read as a "pentecostal" text, in that his message was one of empowering his readers to persist in their witness of the one who has loved them and inaugurated their priestly reign.[46]

Yet our pneumatological approach to Revelation's theology of love functions not just at the levels of cognition (providing us information about divine love) or behavior (enabling transformation of our deeds) but also at the level of affect. Love, after all, is neither merely an idea nor even a set of activities but is an affective disposition. Revelation's symbolic imagery, as already noted, functions at this affective dimension, nurturing anxieties about the evil of the world and of the wrath to come on the one hand but also cultivating desire for and reorientation toward God—and the wedding celebration to come—on the other hand. For this

44. Koester, *Revelation*, 264.

45. Thomas, *Apocalypse*, 122.

46. See Menzies, "Was John the Revelator Pentecostal?"

work on the human heart, so to speak, the Spirit of prophecy is also the one who addresses the creaturely gut and who is at work amid the hostilities and trials of life. Persistence through the cruel and grueling oppositions of life require nothing less than fully devoted hearts, and this also is the work of the divine Spirit.[47] In short, the Spirit of prophecy not only communicates God's love and will to the churches but also empowers creaturely pathos, love, and action in response.

For the moment, then, our analysis concludes, however tentatively, that Revelation's theology of love is indeed apocalyptic. Divine love is perceived in life's ebbs-and-flows and ups-and-downs, and is experienced amid suffering and hardship.[48] That is why such is felt to be obscure, not least also because it summons if not demands our persevering consecration to Christ's love. This is additionally burdensome for those either already marginal from the socio-economic or political powers-that-be or who find themselves tempted by these forces—that John calls the "great whore"—and then are further persecuted for settling into that embrace. For the love story to end happily ever after, then, we need nothing less than the seven spirits of Pentecost to fall upon us afresh, to both prophesy and assist those who are frail to not just cling to, but grow in, our first love. And this further and ongoing outpouring of the (seven) Spirit(s) may be particularly critical if the reality of God's love for the world (John 3:16) depends on its full actualization and realization on the persevering love of those who have been freed from their sins by his blood.[49]

47. For more on my pentecostal hermeneutic of Revelation, see Yong, "Unveiling Interpretation After Pentecost" (also chapter 10 of this volume); cf. Yong, "Kings, Nations, and Cultures on the Way to the New Jerusalem" (also chapter 12 of this volume).

48. Moffatt, *Love in the New Testament*, 218–21.

49. An earlier version of this chapter was presented to a seminar meeting of the Analytic Theology initiative at Fuller Theological Seminary, Pasadena, California, on February 8, 2017, which theme that year was devoted to divine and human love. Thanks to Oliver Crisp for the invitation to join the seminar's multi-year project, and to seminar members for the insightful questions and comments that have made this a better essay. Mark Wilson, a fellow student of the Apocalypse, also provided valuable feedback. I am grateful to Blaine Charette and Robby Waddell for inviting my contribution to this important honoree volume and for their feedback on an earlier draft of this essay. All errors of fact and interpretation, however, remain my own responsibility.

Chapter 12

Kings, Nations, and Cultures on the Way to the New Jerusalem

A Pentecostal Witness to an Apocalyptic Vision

Although few would reject the multinational and multicultural character of the church in an era of world Christianity, and particularly now that its center of gravity has definitively shifted to the majority world, what that means has been and remains heavily contested (not least in the age of Brexit and Trump).[1] This essay presents some very preliminary reflections on theology of culture by looking at the book of Revelation from a pentecostal perspective.[2] As the justification for our focused analysis will be generated over the course of the argument, it needs to be said up front only that our goals are modest: to tease out some implications for contemporary multicultural belief and practice from the book's eschatological images. We will begin by looking at the promise and challenges of the Apocalypse when approached with questions for

1. Thanks to S. David Moore for inviting my contribution to this work. Jack Hayford's legacy as pentecostal leader and statesman is secure. This essay is intended to be my own humble contribution to a book that seeks to recognize and honor that renown, and even then, his achievements precede me given his own treatment of the Apocalypse: Hayford, *E-Quake*. Jack's emphasis almost two decades ago that this last book of the biblical canon is fundamentally about the sustaining power of worship during difficult times remains in need of rearticulation, and the following can be read, particularly in the final section at the end, as doing little more than echoing aspects of this important message for the purpose of empowering a multicultural church in a hostile world.

2. Rhoads, *From Every People and Nation*, leads the way at this point.

theology of culture, continue by proposing a pentecostal hermeneutic for this final canonical book, and conclude by reconsidering the message of Revelation from this interpretive site. In brief, we will argue that the apocalyptic rendition of the nations, kings, and peoples of the world will not encourage any cheaply obtained multiculturalism but instead demands performative commitments with potentially prohibitive costs, apart from a fresh Pentecost.

Two caveats before we proceed. First, I am neither a biblical scholar nor an expert on Revelation. However, I have gradually waded into the newly emerging field of theological interpretation of scripture and have recently proposed a pentecostal intervention in this area.[3] The following extends my efforts in this direction, albeit focused on the book of Revelation. Even with my prior work on theology of culture and political theology,[4] there is still a great need to root such reflections deeper in the biblical traditions. Second, then, it is important to realize that any attempt to lift a coherent view of *culture* off the biblical pages is anachronistic since this notion is itself of later development rather than embedded within the Bible's concepts and notions.[5] Our approach will be to work primarily with Revelation's references to the nations and kings of the world and to extrapolate from these implications for thinking about the cultural realm.[6] I hope to show there is much to be gained from hovering over the Apocalypse with regard to these matters.[7]

NATIONS AND KINGS IN APOCALYPTIC PERSPECTIVE: REVELATION AND THEOLOGY OF CULTURE?

Let us begin with an image from the New Jerusalem, unfolded (Rev 21:9—22:5) within a broader vision of the new heavens and new earth (21–22). We start at the end, not only of Revelation but also of the Christian canon

3. See Yong, *Hermeneutical Spirit*.

4. See my book *In the Days of Caesar*, ch. 5 of which is a theology of culture.

5. Edgar, *Created and Creating*, 53–54, 226–31, are especially relevant in this regard, with the former pages denoting that the word *culture* does not appear in scripture (so that Edgar's dominant approach is to develop a Reformed version of the so-called cultural mandate via the salvation history narrative), and the latter considering images in the Apocalypse to suggest that the activity of human cultural creation and creaturely creativity will persist in the New Jerusalem.

6. For a missiological perspective on *culture*, see Yong, "Culture."

7. I also outline a political reading of the Apocalypse in Yong, "Revelation and the Political in the 21st Century," so here we attempt a theology of culture.

because of our conviction that our eschatological hopes—for good or ill, both being live options, as we shall see—inevitably shape our aspirations and commitments in the present life.[8] While we will develop this notion further later, for now let us see how John depicts the kings and nations of the world vis-à-vis the New Jerusalem:

> 22 I saw no temple in the city, for its temple is the Lord God the Almighty and the Lamb. 23 And the city has no need of sun or moon to shine on it, for the glory of God is its light, and its lamp is the Lamb. 24 The nations will walk by its light, and the kings of the earth will bring their glory into it. 25 Its gates will never be shut by day—and there will be no night there. 26 People will bring into it the glory and the honor of the nations. 27 But nothing unclean will enter it, nor anyone who practises abomination or falsehood, but only those who are written in the Lamb's book of life. (Rev 21:22–27)

A few remarks are in order by way of launching the discussion. First, God is at the center in every respect. The temple that is central to the biblical traditions now is displaced by the Lord God the Almighty and the Lamb, and the sun and the moon that have "governed" the world (e.g., its rhythms) since the primordial creation also defer to and give way to the deity. Hence whatever we might want to say about nations and kings in this text ought to recognize that their role also is a subordinate one. John mentions them here only since their role is to lift up divinity: The nations enter into the temple which is the divine presence, and whatever glory kings possess in any conventional reckoning here contributes to God's gloriousness.[9] Hence our takeaways from this passage for any political theology or theology of culture should be decidedly *theological*, recognizing that the Apocalypse is concerned not first and foremost with nations or kings but with the God who is creating all things new.

Second, however, we also ought not underestimate the way in which these images herald the universal rule and reign of the Lord God Almighty. The *nations*—consistently rendered as such from *ethne* in the original Greek—refer indiscriminately to all the peoples of the earth who were not-Jews: gentiles, in first-century and even present-day idiom.[10] The

8. Thus I begin my one volume systematic theology with eschatology; see Yong, *Renewing Christian Theology*, ch. 2.

9. Blount, *Revelation*, 393, suggests that here, the contrast is with "the gifts and treasures [brought] to demonstrate homage and fidelity to Rome."

10. See Eller, "How the Kings of the Earth Land in the New Jerusalem," 25.

image announces the fulfillment of the post-exilic prophecy of Isaiah: "the Lord will arise upon you, / and his glory will appear over you. / Nations shall come to your light, / and kings to the brightness of your dawn" (Isa 60:2b–3).[11] The Abrahamic promise "in you all the families of the earth shall be blessed" (Gen 12:3b), episodically revived in Israel's history but mostly languishing across the millennia, here finds its fulfillment. Yet this is not any simplistic universalism either, as those who remain excluded outside the New Jerusalem are also clearly identified.[12]

The point to be made is that God's glory receives from that of the nations and kings of the earth. The final consummation thus sanctifies and purifies the contributions of all those who were not-Israel so that the new and final people of God includes the distinctive attainments of the world's nations and kings. Theologies of culture, understood broadly in terms of the polis to include peoples and nations and their leadership, hence can do no better than to build on this eschatological vision. The New Jerusalem includes, rather than negates, the donation of the nations and their cultural achievements to the glory and honor of God's reign.

Yet the well-known obscurity of this final book of the Bible will not allow us to leave things as simply as the above discussion suggests. The question that immediately emerges is how to understand the presence of nations and kings in the New Jerusalem when the final battles in the preceding chapters clearly depict their apocalyptic destruction. The rider on a white horse is unveiled with "a sharp sword with which to strike down the nations" (Rev 19:15), and proceeds to prepare the "great supper of God" (19:17) from "the flesh of kings, the flesh of captains, the flesh of the mighty, the flesh of horses and their riders—flesh of all, both free and slave, both small and great" (19:18). Indeed the final celebration, the great banquet of divine triumph, arises from out of the annihilation (19:21a) of "the kings of the earth with their armies" (19:19a). And just so that there is no mistake, after the millennial reign,

> [7] Satan will be released from his prison [8] and will come out to deceive the nations at the four corners of the earth, Gog and Magog, in order to gather them for battle; they are as numerous

11. Mouw, *When the Kings Come Marching In*, is a beautiful meditation of the intertextual connections between Isa 60 and Rev 21–22.

12. Any universalistic implications—argued strenuously, for instance, by Jersak, *Her Gates Will Never Be Shut*—are better understood vis-à-vis Israel's salvation history than with reference to the totality of individual persons much less to the entirety of ethnicities, nation-states, or people groups; see du Preez, "Exegetical Notes."

> as the sands of the sea. [9] They marched up over the breadth of the earth and surrounded the camp of the saints and the beloved city. And *fire came down from heaven and consumed them.* (20:7b–9, italics added)

There are no survivors from among the nations, neither from the pre-millennial conflagration nor assuredly from the post-millennial apocalypse. If the kings of the earth and their nations will be abolished in this way, from whence do they arrive into the New Jerusalem?[13]

But there are deeper issues. It is not just that the kings and nations mysteriously resurface in the New Jerusalem, but that by and large, they appear repeatedly in the apocalyptic revelation as opposed to the divine rule and thereby as deserving of obliteration. Most pervasively, the kings and nations of the earth have eagerly embraced the impurities and immoralities of "Babylon the great, mother of whores and of earth's abominations" (17:5b).[14] It is with the worldly (Babylonian) system that "the kings of the earth have committed fornication, and with the wine of whose fornication the inhabitants of the earth have become drunk" (17:2; cf. 18:3, 9). But not only is Babylon "the great city that rules over the kings of the earth" (17:18b), she also "has made all nations drink of the wine of the wrath of her fornication" (14:8) and her demonic trinity—the dragon, beast, and false prophet—has gone "to the kings of the whole world, to assemble them for battle on the great day of God the Almighty" (16:14). John writes that, deceived by Babylon's sorcery (18:23), "the nations raged" (11:18a, here alluding to Ps 2:1), not only acting in utter disregard for Jerusalem—they "trample[d] over the holy city for forty-two months" (11:2b)—but also devastating the creation: the nations are those "who destroy the earth," and thus John sees in turn that they will be destroyed by the divine wrath (11:18b). No wonder, then, the kings and nations of the earth are so easily deceived and mobilized against God and the Lamb in the two final great battles that sandwich the millennium.

The challenges for theology of culture are now more clearly decipherable. If nations and kings are to be present in the New Jerusalem, they not only will need a miraculous preservation through the final carnage

13. Thus the "salvation" of the nations and the "damnation" of all that is impure "stand in some tension with one another and are never fully reconciled in the Apocalypse"; see Thomas, "New Jerusalem and the Conversion of the Nations," 244.

14. Hence, as Baines, "Identity and Fate of the Kings of the Earth," argues, the kings of the earth symbolize those caught in the grips of socially and culturally sinful accommodation.

but will require remarkable redemption and transformation. Revelation suggests that their historical arc is aligned not with but against truth, beauty, and goodness. More comprehensively, the whole world lies under the deceptive power of the Satan (12:9; cf. 20:3, 10a), even as "the whole earth followed the beast" (13:3b), and "all the inhabitants of the earth will worship it" (13:8). It is unlikely, impossible even, for the world and its cultures, historically opposed to God and his people, to be eschatologically reoriented in the New Jerusalem.

Whither then theology of culture in this apocalyptic scenario? Or perhaps more accurately: Whither theology in a culture of apocalypse?[15] Even as the final redemption suggests that nations and kings will honor and glorify God, the predominant narrative in the book of Revelation announces otherwise: of their dishonoring the divine and exalting themselves. The world left on its own, it seems, will be galvanized for any purposes except those intended by its creator. The kings and nations of the earth, representative of its peoples and cultures, appear in these eschatological times to be resolute in their rejection of the truth, tenacious in their resistance to his ways, and steadfast in opposition to his people. The cultures of this world, from this apocalyptic perspective, would appear to be irretrievably corrupted by all that is divergent from the divine reign and rule.

THE SPIRIT SAYS "COME!": DE-APOCALYPTISIZING THE NATIONS AFTER PENTECOST

Commentators have responded variously in their efforts to render a more coherent account of the presence of the nations and kings in the New Jerusalem, ranging from suggestions that although the nations and kings "likely include some who have persecuted God's people," here "they have repented and will be allowed entrance to the city,"[16] to arguments that rather than any conversion of pagan or idolaters at the end, the final vision concerns only those with prior allegiance to the Lamb's will.[17] Without presuming the invalidity of these suggestions,[18] the approach taken in the rest of the essay will be a more decidedly pentecostal one. We will suggest

15. See Warner, "Angels and Engines."

16. Beale, *Book of Revelation*, 1097.

17. See Schnabel, "John and the Future of the Nations."

18. McNicol, *Conversion of the Nations in Revelation*, has a complete discussion.

a reading of the nations and kings in the book of Revelation—and by extension of their peoples, tribes, and languages—from a post-Pentecost perspective. This is less a reference to the pentecostal sensibilities of the modern revival and renewal movement (although there is no intention here to exclude such stances) than it is to the vantage point provided by the Day of Pentecost narrative.[19] In other words, while my own pentecostal hermeneutic cannot be easily dissociated from the modern pentecostal-charismatic movement within which I have been raised and have been in lifelong dialogue, I seek to ground the interpretive moves made here first and foremost in the Acts narrative.[20]

What, however, does it mean to adopt such a pentecostal posture? I suggest that Luke's Pentecost account invites a universal (not universalist) horizon appropriate to our tasks. Three interrelated considerations are germane in this regard. First, the promise of the Spirit empowers messianic witness "in Jerusalem, in all Judea and Samaria, and to the ends of the earth" (Acts 1:8b). And while Acts shows that the gospel does arrive in Rome—considered to be the "ends of the earth" from the apostolic Jerusalem-centric perspective—in the book's final chapter, the initial response to the promise was on the Day of Pentecost when there were both Jews and proselytes (2:10b) "from every nation under heaven living in Jerusalem" (2:5b). The listing of those from the gathered crowd who heard the apostles speaking to them in their own languages from around the Mediterranean world is a selective and partial one drawing from the universal enumeration of the seventy (or seventy-two) nations in the Old Testament.[21] Second, then, Luke records Peter confirming initial fulfillment of the pentecostal promise to and from the "ends of the earth" by resorting to the prophet Joel: "In the last days it will be, God declares, that I will pour out my Spirit *upon all flesh*" (2:17a, italics added; see Joel 2:28a). If there was any doubt that the divine witness would extend to the furthest horizons of the apostolic imagination, this Lukan-Petrine clarification was that yes: the promise of the Spirit belonged just as well to those who derived from the regions of despised Romans, dishonest Cretans, and estranged Arabs—these three mentioned in Acts 2:10–11

19. Here I develop the preliminary steps previously charted in this direction: "Unveiling Interpretation After Pentecost" (also chapter 10 of this volume).

20. My previous efforts in biblical scholarship have focused on Luke and especially Acts—see, e.g., Yong, *Who Is the Holy Spirit?*—but here I apply the hermeneutical approach developed in that venue to Revelation.

21. See Yong, *Spirit Poured Out on All Flesh*, ch. 4.

(among those from other regions)—regardless of how local Palestinian populations might have felt about these peoples.[22] Last but not least, shortly thereafter, Peter again, this time in this sermon in Solomon's Porch after the healing of the lame man at the Beautiful Gate, emphatically pronounced that the universal salvation of God was being fulfilled as anticipated by the prophets of old:

> [19] Repent therefore, and turn to God so that your sins may be wiped out, [20] so that times of refreshing may come from the presence of the Lord, and that he may send the Messiah appointed for you, that is, Jesus, [21] who must remain in heaven until the time of universal restoration that God announced long ago through his holy prophets. (Acts 3:19–21)

Jesus is the promised Messiah, and his gift of the Spirit (2:35) brings about the restoration of Israel, which benefits are not just for Jews but for the whole world.[23]

Yet the universality of the Spirit's outpouring does not translate into any blanket universalism, at least not yet. Clearly there are contingencies involved, for instance, that hearers (those listening to the Spirit-filled Peter in Solomon's Porch for example) would repent; "everyone who calls on the name of the Lord shall be saved" (2:21) is how the text of Joel's appropriated prophecy concludes. Hence also at the end of his Day of Pentecost message, Peter reiterates: "Repent, and be baptized every one of you in the name of Jesus Christ so that your sins may be forgiven; and you will receive the gift of the Holy Spirit. For the promise is for you, for your children, and for all who are far away, everyone whom the Lord our God calls to him" (2:38–39). Yet the response of listeners presumes also a prior occurrence: that recipients of the Spirit bear witness as empowered to do so (1:8). Thus are the eschatological promises of God to be fulfilled in the "last days" (2:17a): the outpouring of the Spirit enables witness to the Messiah to the ends of the earth and draws forth repentance for the messianic time of deliverance. The Lukan eschatological vision of God's salvation is thus comprehensive, even as it involves human participants in proclaiming and heralding in the present time the arrival of the divine reign.

22. Recall that it was well known regarding the Cretans: "It was one of them, their very own prophet, who said, 'Cretans are always liars, vicious brutes, lazy gluttons.' That testimony is true" (Titus 1:12–13).

23. See Turner, *Power from on High*; cf. also Lennartsson, *Refreshing and Restoration*.

Such a pentecostal eschatology is therefore far removed from any dispensational emphasis on futuristic or otherworldly developments.[24] Rather, the Day of Pentecost inaugurates the eschatological time, the "last days," of the Spirit. God's eschatological salvation thus accomplishes divine redemption in the present era, not just in the life to come. In that respect, apostolic eschatology is as much about our contemporary response to and participation in the last days work of the Holy Spirit.[25] Acts not only describes what happened two thousand years ago but invites readers to experience the pentecostal gift that remains available to all, and then to live into that apostolic way of life charted by the Spirit's enablement. So if the Spirit's outpouring "on all flesh" is not intended literally on the Day of Pentecost, then the continued reception of the Spirit among all generations and the responses of such Spirit-filled believers to the ends of the earth since may yet anticipate the universal restoration of the imminent divine reign.

What does it mean then to read Revelation not just after Good Friday, Easter, and the ascension, but after Pentecost? Clearly, Revelation summons a christological and incarnational hermeneutic, grounded in the "revelation of Jesus Christ" (Rev 1:1). Yet John the Seer also calls his book a "prophecy" (1:3) and explicitly says that "the testimony of Jesus is the spirit of prophecy" (19:10), thus bidding readers to approach this as a Spirit-inspired text. There are innumerable other references to the divine breath (*pneuma*) that serve as cues to reading Revelation pneumatologically. The letters to the seven churches each conclude with a pneumatic invitation: "Let anyone who has an ear listen to what the Spirit is saying to the churches" (2:7; also 2:11, 17, 29; 3:6, 13, 22), even as the narrative trajectory of the prophecy is segmented by charismatically charged events. The manifestation of Jesus in the prologue was given to John while he was "in the spirit on the Lord's day" (1:9), even as John's seeing of the throne room and the events that "must take place after this" is facilitated while he "was in the spirit" (4:1–2). Later, the final destruction of Babylon is also unveiled to John "in the spirit in the wilderness" (17:3a), anticipating the unfolding of the New Jerusalem in the final vision (21:9).[26]

24. See also the final chapter on eschatology in Yong, *In the Days of Caesar*.

25. For a similar stance, albeit argued from an other-than-pentecostal site, see Rahner, "Hermeneutics of Eschatological Assertions."

26. Not surprisingly, pentecostal exegetes have approached the Apocalypses as divided at least in part by these pneumatological references; see, e.g., Skaggs and Benham, *Revelation*, 14–15; Thomas, *Apocalypse*, 2–6.

Pentecostal New Testament scholar and Revelation expert Robby Waddell suggests that there are additional warrants, of the intertextual variety, for understanding the book pneumatologically.[27] If readers are repeatedly urged to hear from the Spirit, then how might the Apocalypse's words resonate, in particular with regard to the upwards of five hundred allusions to the Old Testament canon prevalent across the prophecy?[28] More specifically, granting for the moment Waddell's discerning the vision of the two witnesses in Rev 11:1–13 as being at the heart of the major vision of the book (4:1—16:21),[29] he urges that the resonances between the "two olive trees and the two lampstands" in John's apocalypse (11:4) and in Zechariah's fifth vision (Zech 4:1–14) are unmistakable, and that the latter's clear pneumatological—perhaps more accurate: *ruah*-ological—reference thereby marks the former as well. So when Yahweh says to Zerubbabel, "Not by might, nor by power, but by my spirit" (Zech 4:6b), such carries over to the capacities of the two witnesses in Rev 11. More expansively, given that John's vision is mediated by the "spirit of prophecy" (19:10), the call is not only to attend to what the Spirit says but to carry out the witness of the Spirit. Hence, Waddell concludes, Rev 11 "enables John to express richly the role of the Spirit in the prophetic ministry of the church, whose primary task is to bear witness to Jesus in the world."[30] Even if we might want to argue about various aspects of Waddell's proposal, our colleague makes an important point that the witness of the Spirit is, even in Revelation, to inspire and enable the witness of its readers.[31]

My claim is that reading Revelation after Pentecost invites embrace of the eschatological promise of Christ in the Spirit. If a pentecostal hermeneutic applied to the book of Acts urges readers to receive the Spirit and live into the apostolic way, then such an interpretive perspective brought to Revelation similarly prompts readers to attend and embody the apocalyptic Spirit of prophecy. The closing verses to this book say as much: "The Spirit and the bride say, 'Come.' / And let everyone who hears say, 'Come.' / And let everyone who is thirsty come. / Let anyone who wishes take the water of life as a gift" (Rev 22:17). Hence Revelation

27. See Waddell, *Spirit in the Book of Revelation*.

28. Moyise, *Old Testament in Revelation*, 16; see also Beale, *John's Use of the Old Testament in Revelation*.

29. See Waddell, *Spirit in the Book of Revelation*, 148–50.

30. Waddell, *Spirit in the Book of Revelation*, 190.

31. See also Gorman, *Reading Revelation Responsibly*.

as a pneumatic and pentecostal text involves a response, indeed opens up space and creates an occasion for entry into the work of the Spirit that stretches back toward the beginning of time.[32] As such, even if "what is to take place after this" (1:19b) at least in part concerns what is future from our contemporary perspective, it certainly relates to the eschatological "last days" initiated on the Day of Pentecost. The fulfillment of Revelation's prophetic visions thereby depends in that sense on the response of those listening to and filled with the Spirit of prophecy as much as they are conditional on the final saving works of God.[33]

From this perspective, the redemption of the nations and kings, and the salvaging of their cultural glory and honor, are less eschatological pronouncements than they are contemporary tasks. What John sees apocalyptically, with all of the ambiguity surrounding the fate of the nations and their kings, can be received as a mandate for faithful messianic witness: the hope of the nations, rooted as such is in the revelatory promise, nevertheless involves Spirit-invited witness and persistence.[34] Hanging in the balance may be the destruction, or the salvation, of the nations, kings, and cultures of the world.

MANY TRIBES, LANGUAGES, PEOPLES, AND NATIONS: PERFORMING AN ESCHATOLOGICAL PNEUMATOLOGY OF CULTURE

Our modest goal is elaboration of a theology of culture that can inspire our own efforts to work for a multicultural church. Toward this end, we have hedged our bets that an eschatological imagination provides normative orientation for such a vision: what is finally promised to be, we have suggested, ought to guide what should be in the meanwhile. Yet although the nations and kings of the world bringing their glory and honor into

32. As signified also by development of themes from the First Testament that culminate in Revelation's epilogue; see Dumbrell, *End of the Beginning.*

33. The basic thesis here is not new. As Herms, *Apocalypse for the Church and for the World*, argued, the universalistic language in the book is hortatory, consistent with the apocalyptic genre, and is designed to encourage the faithful in anticipation of a final vindication. Whether universalism—of persons or, in our case, of nations and kings—is finally true or not is not a real question for John at this narrative and literary level.

34. As pentecostal scholars Chris Thomas and Frank Macchia put it: "A case can be made that the Spirit in Revelation is mainly directed to the conversion of the nations to the Lamb of God. . . . The Spirit is the global Spirit, who takes the blessings of God's grace beyond the borders of Israel to the nations"; see *Revelation*, 494–95.

the New Jerusalem is a potent image for a multicultural people of God, the overall ambiguity of these symbols across Revelation provides a less then coherent message for our purposes. We therefore turned to resourcing our task from a pentecostal perspective, exploring particularly how the universal horizon of the book of Acts in general and the Day of Pentecost narrative in particular invited not just a theoretical appreciation for the inclusion of the ends of the earth within the restoration of Israel but also practical commitments to enter into and embrace the inspiration and empowerment of the Spirit for universal witness. Will this more performative approach provide the needed recalibration for understanding apocalyptic kings and nations for contemporary multicultural praxis?

If what I am suggesting is a performative response to Revelation, however, then we must confront one important set of concerns before proceeding any further. The issue is that any call to enact the Apocalypse risks not just condoning but advocating its violence as well. Especially worrisome is that the violence is inflicted by the sword of the Lamb (19:15, 21) and consummated by heavenly fire (20:9b).[35] The problem is that even if Revelation clearly depicts the divine overthrow of the sinful systems of this world, this seems to happen precisely through the violent mechanisms undergirding what will soon be swept away. Hence to advocate a kind of living into the message of the Apocalypse is to commend a divine imperialism that mimics (even if it is also indicated to do away with) the imperial violence of the nations and kings of this world.[36] If such performance is inconceivable for those on the margins of history, then the larger history of Christendom warns us of how such perceptions of divinely sanctioned authority and exemplarity can be lethal when wielded by those at the centers of power.

Hence any pentecostal performance of Revelation will have to be discerning, not naively universalistic. Yet such particularism will have costs within current neo-imperial and neo-colonial context of global capitalism. On the one side, considering that those interested in maintaining

35. That the violence of Revelation has long been a concern of its readers is evidenced in Verheyden et al., *Ancient Christian Interpretation of "Violent Texts."*

36. "To construct God or Christ, together with their putatively salvific activities, from the raw material of imperial ideology is not to shatter the cycle of empire but merely to transfer it to a transcendental plane, thereby reifying and reinscribing it . . . creating an imperial divine 'essence' that is extremely difficult to dismantle or dislodge. . . . Revelation, locked as it is in visions of empires and counter-empires, emperors and counter-emperors, seems singularly powerless to provide: a conception of the divine sphere as other than empire writ large"; Moore, "Revelation to John," 452.

the status quo can resort to (now divinely underwritten violence) to keep the revolutionaries in their proper places, on the underside of empire, for instance, the question will inevitably need to be asked: Toward what are Spirit-inspired and empowered practices directed? On the other side, then, if Revelation can also comfort those who are persecuted, oppressed, and marginalized with promises of divine vindication in the coming inferno, is it possible for such consolation to be translated into praxis that works simultaneously for justice in this present world?[37] These are not merely theoretical or abstract questions since the Apocalypse itself explicitly narrates that the vindication of the disinherited of history involves the overturning of the social and economic mechanisms of the powers that be (Rev 17–18). As such, the final welcoming of the gifts and glory of the nations of the world follows from, rather than uncritically baptizes, their socio-economic achievements and accomplishments, and it is from out of recognition of the life-denying and destroying character of the imperial regimes of this world that divine judgment is pronounced. From this perspective, then, it is crucial to ask how the voice of the Spirit might enable faithful discipleship when it is just as possible for those of us who are now on the so-called upper side of history to appeal to this apocalyptic text for sanitizing the world of its impure elements as a way of preserving a more monocultural status quo rather than embracing a more multicultural community that simultaneously requires a resistant praxis toward the systems that support our way of life even as it welcomes the coming reign of God.

Revelation itself recognizes that not every voice echoes the salvific message of God. In fact, even at the heart of the book (if we followed Waddell), "members of the peoples and tribes and languages and nations" (11:9a) gloat over the death of the two divine witnesses as part of their revelry in their iniquities. Not surprisingly, then, the beast "was allowed to make war on the saints and to conquer them. It was given authority over every tribe and people and language and nation, and all the inhabitants of the earth will worship it, everyone whose name has not been written from the foundation of the world in the book of life of the Lamb that was slaughtered" (13:7–8). The many tongues of humankind, indeed all flesh, are just as capable of worshiping the beast as of witnessing to the Lamb (cf. 17:15).

37. As we see for instance in Boesak, *Comfort and Protest.*

Yet there is hope for the multitude, consistent with and expanding on the Pentecost miracle of the end-time gathering of the ends of the earth as the new people of God. John sees "another angel flying in mid-heaven, with an eternal gospel to proclaim to those who live on the earth—to every nation and tribe and language and people" (14:6; cf. 10:11). It is "from every tribe and language and people and nation" that saints have been redeemed for God by the blood of the Lamb (5:9),[38] and it is "from every nation, from all tribes and peoples and languages" that they stand "before the throne and before the Lamb, robed in white, with palm branches in their hands" (7:9). Richard Bauckham's analysis of these seven formulaic references to the many nations, et al., is that for John, "the nations which now serve Babylon will become, through the witness of the martyrs, God's peoples with whom he will be present in the New Jerusalem."[39] As "seven spirits of God [are] sent out into all the earth" (5:6b), so also will the nations—and their peoples and kings—be drawn into the new heavens and earth.

From this perspective, then, we can comprehend that the Apocalypse suggests perhaps two contrasting ultimate possibilities for the nations and their kings: damnation or salvation. "Both futures remain open; the question is how the world will respond."[40] More pointedly, this same question is posed for the churches: "Do these competing visions suggest divergent potentials for the future, that the nations may be either converted or destroyed, depending on the faithfulness of Christ's church?"[41] Put another way: Revelation's admonitions are not just for believers struggling against persecution or attempting to remain faithful amid the seductions of the world, whatever the *Sitz im Leben* of the original writing turns out to be. Rather, there are cosmic implications at stake: faithfulness has consequences beyond individual lives and extends to many nations and peoples, along with their kings.[42]

Read pentecostally, I suggest, the presence of nations and kings in the New Jerusalem, whatever else such might signify, also acts as a prod for messianic faithfulness. Traced across the apocalypse, the tension

38. On the saving blood of the Lamb, see also my "To Him Who Loves Us and Freed Us from Our Sins by His Blood . . ."

39. Bauckham, *Theology of the Book of Revelation*, 336.

40. Koester, *Revelation*, 833.

41. Keener, *Revelation*, 506.

42. See also Mathewson, *New Heaven and a New Earth*, 174–75, who notes that this rhetorical tension is indicative of the Apocalypse's hortatory design.

between national and regal judgment and salvation is retained in full force rather than absolved.[43] The point is practical rather than theoretical: not if and why the nations and kings are there but *how* did they get there. Answering the latter question implicates each reader—from every nation and ethnic group—in all of his or her existential situatedness and cultural embeddedness.

Hermeneutically, then, such a pentecostal angle searches for other textual cues that can inspire supportive praxis for the deity's redemptive works. Hence the already mentioned worship of the saints, drawn from the ends of the earth (5:9; 7:9), ought to be foregrounded: "every creature in heaven and on earth and under the earth and in the sea, and all that is in them, singing, 'To the one seated on the throne and to the Lamb, be blessing and honor and glory and might for ever and ever!'" (5:13).[44] The multicultural worship of the eschatological community is thereby not just an image to be yearned for but a call for enactment. Similarly, John envisions, in a recapitulation of Moses's song (see Exod 15:1–18):

> Great and amazing are your deeds,
> Lord God the Almighty!
> Just and true are your ways,
> King of the nations!
> Lord, who will not fear
> and glorify your name?
> For you alone are holy.
> *All nations will come*
> *and worship before you,*
> for your judgments have been revealed. (Rev 15:3–4, italics added)

The question for us is then this: How might such transnational or international worship be facilitated on this side of the eschaton? Can multinational and multicultural worship in the Spirit be fostered anticipating the final salvation? Can contemporary Pentecostalism, as a global and multinational worshiping communion, find inspiration in the Spirit through such a performative reading of worship in the book of Revelation so as to embrace, develop, and promote appropriate multicultural practices that can in turn underwrite a biblically and eschatologically oriented theology of culture for the twenty-first century?[45]

43. See Mathewson, "Destiny of the Nations in Revelation 21:1—22:5."

44. The centrality of worship is also unpacked by Kraybill, *Apocalypse and Allegiance*.

45. Archer, *"I Was in the Spirit on the Lord's Day,"* shows how early Pentecostals read Revelation in ways that also shaped their eschatological affections and worshipful

But authentic worship involves the divine shalom, which is peace with justice. Multinational worship in a postcolonial world will require justice not just between the nations but also between the haves and the have-nots. This is not to say that justice precedes worship but to enter into the hermeneutical circle that sees worship heralding justice and justice precipitating worship. Hence the haves will not be able to read Babylon and eschatological worship merely spiritually, just as the have-nots will inevitably read Babylon socially, politically, and economically as the spiritual powers and structures of persecution and oppression.[46] Yet the Spirit's outpouring was also on "slaves [*doulous*], both men and women" (Acts 2:18a), and this prompted both mutual sharing and common worship in the Spirit (Acts 2:42–47). Such a pentecostal approach to the Apocalypse ought to engender nothing less: a mutuality that bridges the gaps between kings and subjects, between governors and the governed, between those at the center and those on the historical underside of nations and peoples.

John surely recognized the audaciousness of the vision that involved the redemption of nations and kings so committed otherwise in pursuit of the sinfulness of Babylon. Perhaps for this reason he understood that the New Jerusalem would have to include the "tree of life with its twelve kinds of fruit, producing its fruit each month; and the leaves of the tree are for the healing of the nations" (22:2b).[47] Apart from their deep-rooted transfiguration and transformation—salvific reparation, no less—the new heavens and earth would be narrowly construed rather than constituted by the ends of the earth. It might be that even with the revelation of Jesus Christ in the Apocalypse we are still no less in need of a fresh Pentecost, a continual pentecostal revival that allows the many tongues to sing, the many languages to proclaim, the many nations to glorify God, the many kings to honor the deity, and the many cultures to live into and achieve their creational promise.[48]

---

experience of God; my claim is that contemporary Pentecostals in their second century need similar apocalyptic reorientation in order to further ecclesial thinking and practice in our multicultural world.

46. E.g., Waweru, "Postcolonial and Contrapuntal Reading of Revelation 22:1–5."

47. This text structures the argument of González, *For the Healing of the Nations*.

48. An earlier version of this essay was presented, thanks to Dale Coulter's invitation, at one of the plenary sessions at the 46th Annual Meeting of the Society for Pentecostal Studies, Florissant, Missouri, March 9–11, 2017, devoted to the theme "Pentecostalism and Culture"; I appreciate Melissa Archer for her constructive comments on a previous draft. Any errors of fact or interpretation remain my own responsibility.

INSTEAD OF A CONCLUSION

Was Paul a Missionary or an Undocumented Migrant?

Rethinking the Identity of the Apostle in Light of Mobility and Migration During the Roman Age

RODOLFO GALVAN ESTRADA III

THROUGHOUT THIS VOLUME, WE have explored various ways in which Amos Yong engages in a theological reading of Scripture—one that is deeply shaped by a pneumatological imagination. Yong invites us to read the Bible not merely to recover what happened in the world behind the text, but to discern the significance—and re-significance—of the text in light of our contemporary challenges and questions. We have traced how Yong's method shapes his reflections on public theology, social engagement, and culture, particularly as they emerge through careful and sustained readings of Acts. But the volume also widens the canonical lens, drawing on texts such as Revelation, James, and autobiographical readings of 1 Peter. His theological hermeneutic opens space for fresh opportunities, enabling us to return to familiar texts such as the book of Acts and read them from new interests and curiosities.

As I noted in the opening chapter, I do not write as a professional theologian. Yet through quiet stirrings and whispered promptings of the Spirit, I have found myself drawn to reconsider the historical significance of migration in the ancient world. These stirrings are what Yong describes as reading after Pentecost. That is, a particular pneumatological reading of Scripture that is intentionally engaged in a dynamic and relational involvement with the Spirit in our quest to find meaning. Yong offers an example of this in his reading of Lydia in Acts (see chapter 2), and his engagement with themes of exile and marginality in 1 Peter (see chapters 7–8). Indeed, one recurring theme we can glean from Yong's reading of Scripture in these studies is exile and migration—how the movement of people and presence in a foreign land contribute to an understanding of oneself and the mission of God. In this concluding chapter, I want to focus on this theme by offering an after-Pentecost reading of Paul as a migrant and question our cherished assumptions about his identity as a "missionary."

Rethinking the concept of missions for our time is not a new endeavor. In *Mission After Pentecost*, Amos Yong rightly characterizes our current moment as a post-missions era. He does so for three compelling reasons. First, we now inhabit a post-colonial reality. Since the modern missionary movement was historically "forged from the colonial enterprise" and served as a tool of "white supremacy and normativity," it is not only unraveling but must be fundamentally reimagined.[1] Second, we live in a post-Enlightenment society, where the alliance between Christian mission and Enlightenment rationalism—especially its view of the non-Western world as irrational—is no longer sustainable.[2] Third, we are situated in a post-Christian era in which Christianity has been decentered from the public square. In this age of multiculturalism and religious pluralism, a mission paradigm shaped by the assumption of Christian cultural dominance is no longer viable.[3] What is required, then, is not the abandonment of mission, but a renewed theological reflection on its purpose and practice. This includes a fresh engagement with Scripture—not from the inherited assumptions of past paradigms, but from new vantage points that speak to our contemporary moment and its complex realities.[4]

One way to begin such a reimagining is by reconsidering the identity of the apostle Paul. While he is often described in biblical scholarship as a "missionary,"[5] this label is shaped by the very paradigms that Yong

1. Yong, *Mission After Pentecost*, 2–3.

2. Yong, *Mission After Pentecost*, 4.

3. Yong, *Mission After Pentecost*, 4–5.

4. Yong, *Mission After Pentecost*, 6–7.

5. Albert Schweitzer reviews a history of interpreters on Paul, from F. C. Baur to the beginning of the twentieth century. He affirms that Paul's visionary experience

calls us to rethink. Is Paul really a missionary? Why do we describe Paul as a missionary if he never calls himself such? Is it even appropriate to define Paul with language that described a movement that emerged in the sixteenth century? What if, instead, we understood Paul as a migrant, and perhaps an undocumented one? Such a shift not only reframes Paul's theological and social identity but also opens up new possibilities for understanding mission in a world marked by movement, displacement, and cross-cultural encounter.

In this chapter, I want to reconsider Paul's identity and activity through a migrant lens. This initial idea came to me when I began to think about the role of missionaries and their diverse identities. As a member of the Assemblies of God Pentecostal Church, I found it strange that the missionaries our churches support are not simply White European men and women but people from all walks of life. In fact, many of those we support look no different than the undocumented migrants who live among us. For this reason, I began to rethink the language of a "missionary" and explore whether such a concept existed in antiquity. What I found instead, and as I will argue, is that describing Paul as a missionary is an anachronistic label that has been carried over from the colonial period of the sixteenth century. In fact, Paul's traveling activity would best fit the identity of a Mediterranean migrant—an undocumented one who has no ties or connection to the land in which he travels.

However, the contribution of this chapter is that I attempt to understand Paul, not solely within Latin American history or contemporary immigration issues, but within the context of migration in the first-century Roman world. It is my hope that by describing Paul as a migrant, we will not only reimagine the identity of perhaps the most written about person in Christian history but also rethink our own understanding of migrants and missionaries today.

---

contributed to his "call to be a missionary," an aspect neglected by those who psychologize Paul's experience. On other occasions, Schweitzer also describes Paul as one who engaged in "mission work." See Schweitzer, *Paul and His Interpreters*, 40, 126, 246; Schweitzer, *Mysticism of Paul*, 40, 148, 170, 178–81; Roetzel notices that both Acts and the Pauline letters agree that Paul was a "traveling missionary" in *Paul*, 10; McRay attempts to understand Paul, not as a "twenty-first-century evangelical missionary" yet still describes him as a "missionary" or one who engaged in "missionary journeys" in *Paul*, 11, 25 (esp. 148). Borg and Crossan describe Paul as having an "urban missionary strategy" though they do not explicitly describe Paul as a missionary in *First Paul*, 81–92. Campbell (in *Paul*, 23) asserts: "Apostles are basically missionaries. They take the good news of Jesus cross-culturally, and there are many challenges in this job that they must be especially gifted and skilled to navigate."

WHY DO WE CALL PAUL A MISSIONARY?

The term "missionary" warrants a more in-depth analysis than what I can provide here, but I do want to assert that this label should not be applied to Paul. Those in the Mediterranean world would not have understood Paul's traveling activities through a missionary category. As Paul Kollman asserts, before the sixteenth century, there was no such thing as a Christian mission.[6] In fact, the word "mission" and its related forms were not used to describe the spreading of Christianity until Ignatius of Loyola and the Jesuit leader José de Acosta were developing strategies for evangelizing the new world.[7] Kollman observes that early missiology emerged primarily to describe evangelism outside of Europe,[8] which was also during a time when Latin America was being conquered and plundered. Enrique Dussel, a historian of Latin American church history, finds that the church gave the Portuguese and Spanish governments the authority to lay claim to the Americas. Although the primary purpose of the conquest was missional, this goal was negated by economic and political concerns.[9] Eduardo Galeano says it best: "The sword and the cross marched together in the conquest and plunder of Latin America."[10]

Sixteenth-century missionary language contributed to European self-identity as people sent on a mission to a foreign land inhabited by indigenous people.[11] Said differently, the missionary terminology was part of a larger European political and religious climate that viewed non-Christians as objects to colonize and evangelize—and when necessary, with violence. Certainly, not all missionaries were colonialist. From Bartolomé de Las Casas to the missionary activities during the imperialistic era of the nineteenth century, there were missionaries who did not desire to be an extension of the empire.[12] The relationship between the church,

6. Kollman, "At the Origins of Mission," 425–26.

7. Kollman, "Defining Mission Studies," 48.

8. Kollman, "At the Origins of Mission," 432.

9. Dussel, *History of the Church in Latin America*, 38–44.

10. Galeano, *Open Veins of Latin America*, 20; the collaboration between church and empire continued throughout the history of missions. See Wu, "In the Shadow of Empire," 175–76; Rieger, "Theology and Mission Between Neocolonialism and Postcolonialism."

11. Kollman, "At the Origins of Mission," 436–39.

12. Indeed, it was also Bartolomé de Las Casas who, as a missionary, defended the rights and humanity of the indigenous people in Latin America. See de Las Casas, *Short Account of the Destruction of the Indies*. David Thomas Orique also traces the impact de

the missionary, and the empire is indeed complex. Yet, this missionary label imported upon Paul's identity ignores the history of European Christianity in its expansive mission and political conquest of indigenous people.[13] In a sense, it places Paul alongside the conquistador, traveling with those who come with a sword in hand to conquer and devour the natural resources of virgin lands.

When we turn to the late nineteenth and early twentieth centuries, missiology was becoming an academic discipline and being criticized for its colonial collusion.[14] In response, missionaries turned to the life of the apostle Paul and his evangelistic strategy to explain and justify their own missionary efforts to indigenous people. It was Roland Allen, an Anglican missionary to China, who viewed Paul as a "great missionary" and template for Western missionaries.[15] In his 1912 book, *Missionary Methods*, he harshly addresses his contemporary White missionaries who held paternalistic attitudes and a sense of racial superiority toward indigenous people.[16] Yet in Allen's descriptions of Paul, not once is Paul described as a migrant. According to Allen, Paul was a Jewish man of power and privilege who, as a result of being a citizen, had access to Roman protection whenever he traveled.[17] Later, Alice E. Luce, an Anglican missionary to India and Mexico, published three separate articles entitled "Paul's Missionary Methods" in the 1921 issues of *Pentecostal Evangel*.[18] Although

---

Las Casas had upon the notion of human rights and social justice in "Life, Labor, and Legacy of Bartolomé"; see also Christensen and Hutchison, *Missionary Ideologies in the Imperialist Era*.

13. One may object by saying that this depends on how we define these historically loaded terms, "mission" and "missionary." Certainly, David Bosch, a missiologist, admits that the term "mission" "remains undefinable" (*Transforming Mission*, 9).

14. See the classic work of Stephen Neill, who traces the collusion between imperial powers and missionaries in *Colonialism and Christian Mission*; Kyo Seong Ahn also highlights the impact of this book in "Christian Mission and Colonialism."

15. Allen, *Missionary Methods*, 94.

16. Allen describes these missionaries as having "racial and religious pride" and treating indigenous people as if they were inferior beings. This attitude and perspective toward indigenous people, as he concludes, is contrary to the Pauline missionary method. Allen states, "We have done everything for them except acknowledge any equality" in *Missionary Methods*, 90–96 (esp. 91).

17. Allen, *Missionary Methods*, 15–16.

18. See Luce, "Paul's Missionary Methods," January 8, 1921, 6–7; Luce, "Paul's Missionary Methods," January 22, 1921, 6, 11; and Luce, "Paul's Missionary Methods," February 5, 1921, 6–7. Luce explores some scriptural insights from the life of the apostle Paul for missionaries that include being connected to a home church, preaching the full gospel, and discipling new converts.

her articles continuously describe Paul as a missionary, it is in the final article that Paul is dubbed as the "great missionary" who did not make a distinction between race or nationality.[19]

Nonetheless, we can notice from these two missionaries in the early twentieth century that the life of the apostle Paul was being used to address the racist and paternalistic attitudes that missionaries had toward indigenous communities. They looked to Paul because he exemplified a non-paternalistic missionary who loves people of all races and class. Later missionary theologians such as Lesslie Newbigin and David Bosch trace the life of Paul and his methods in order to develop a theology of missions.[20] They describe Paul's activity as a missionary journey and simply interpret his identity through missiological lens, failing to explore his migration activity in the Roman world.

It is understandable why European missionaries would appeal to the life and identity of Paul in order to deal with their challenges, but by calling Paul a "missionary"—and when biblical scholars uncritically adopt this description—we are going back to a time when Paul was considered an ideal European missionary. Missionaries such as Allen and Luce projected upon Paul an identity that they wished their fellow missionary colleagues would embrace. Now, though, if contemporary missiologists are discussing the end of missions in the third millennium,[21] is it time to put an end to the portrayal of "Paul the missionary" that has been used as a model European missionary? How do we explain Paul's evangelistic travels and identity if not through a "missionary" lens?

19. Luce, "Paul's Missionary Methods," February 5, 1921, 6.

20. By the late 1970s, Newbigin was already drawing insights from the apostle Paul in his own exploration of a missions theology. Newbigin identifies Paul's missionary method to primarily include the establishment of a community within a specific region: "His task as a missionary is clear, limited, and literally—fundamental. He is sent to lay the foundation stone of the church, and that stone is Christ." See Newbigin, *Open Secret*, 128–30; Newbigin also notes that Paul never tells anyone to become a missionary, but Paul's missionary task was to create "believing communities in all the regions through which he has passed." See Newbigin, *Gospel in a Pluralist Society*, 94–95; Bosch describes Paul as the church's first missionary. In fact, he recognizes that it took biblical scholars several decades to finally realize what missionaries had already known—that Paul was a missionary. See Bosch, *Transforming Mission*, 125–41.

21. Yong, *Mission After Pentecost*, 1–14.

WHAT IS A MIGRANT?

Certainly, the terms "migrant" or "immigrant" never appear within the New Testament.[22] Before one proposes that since this "migrant" term did not exist in the ancient world and that I am making the same mistake that I point out with biblical scholars, I want to point out a few counters. First, David Noy recognizes that our English term for "migrant" does not really have a Latin equivalency, and the difference between an immigrant and a visitor in the Roman period is almost indistinguishable.[23] In other words, relying upon terminology alone will blind us from the mobility and migration of people in the Mediterranean world.

Second, we must be mindful that our understanding of immigration has been shaped by the rise of nation states and policing of borders. Even the term "alien" or the phrase "illegal alien," which is used in US immigration law, emerged from English law where it was presumed that one could give allegiance to the king or another sovereign nation.[24] As Roger Sanjek asserts, using a legally framed view of immigration "tends to obscure world historical continuities" between past migrations and present migrations.[25] For these reasons, it is therefore best to think about the role of migration and mobility in the ancient world rather than adopting uncritically modern views of a "missionary" in our understanding of the apostle Paul.

So, what does it mean to be a migrant in the Roman Mediterranean world? Noy points out that most foreigners were immigrants but were primarily known as having a home, a place of birth, and a religious or cultural loyalty somewhere other than Rome.[26] Laurens Tacoma, a lecturer in ancient history at Leiden University, identifies three forms of migration

22. The English term "migrant" originates from the Latin word *migratio*, translated as "a removal," or "a changing of one's habitation." The verb *migro*, likewise, describes the act of "removing," "departing," or "abandoning." See Lewis and Short, *Latin Dictionary*, s.v. "*migratio*," "*migro*."

23. Noy, *Foreigners in Rome*, 3; Claudia Moatti points out that the terms *advena*, *hospes*, *viator*, *inquilinus*, *qui morantur*, *consistentes*, *migrare*, and *peregrinari* correspond to situations of mobility even though there is no unitary concept in Latin. See Moatti, "Roman World, Mobility," 2.

24. Heimburger, *God and the Illegal Alien*, 26.

25. Sanjek, "Rethinking Migration, Ancient and Future," 316; Sailakshmi Ramgopal also notes that our own ease of movement in the Mediterranean world obscures the disconnectivity and difficult migration experiences of people in ancient Rome. See "Connectivity and Disconnectivity," 215–35.

26. Noy, *Foreigners in Rome*, xi, 2.

activity in the Roman Empire: "free mobility," "enforced mobility," and "state-organized movements."[27] Like Noy, Tacoma notes that it is difficult to draw a clear boundary between migration and other forms of mobility given that travelers also had the potential to become immigrants.[28] Regardless, migration in the Roman world, as Tacoma defines, is best understood as "the movement of persons by which they change their residence from one place to another on a permanent or semi-permanent basis."[29]

In Tacoma's study of migration in Rome, he identifies various immigrant groups who emerge in literature and inscriptions. These immigrant groups included the elite of the imperial aristocracy, Roman administrators, young elites seeking an education, intellectual philosophers and teachers, those seeking a permanent home in Rome, seasonal and temporary laborers, the poor seeking better economic conditions, those engaged in trade, slaves,[30] and the Roman military.[31] The various groups who migrated to Rome demonstrate the complexity and varied nature of migration and mobility. As Tacoma asserts, there was "no collective immigrant identity shared by all migrants," nor was there a "migrant community formation along ethnic lines."[32] People came to Rome for a variety of reasons, and often, it was not their final destination. Tacoma admits that few ancient sources explain the reasons for migration.[33]

PAUL THE MIGRANT IN THE ROMAN WORLD

What if, perhaps, Paul would not have been viewed as a missionary of the gospel, an anachronistic label which I think should be questioned, but someone traveling in every region and sharing the faith like a migrant preacher? What if the life and identity of a migrant today—one who is relentlessly pursued from city to city by the military agents of the empire,

27. Tacoma, *Moving Romans*, 7, 30–33.

28. De Ligt and Tacoma, "Approaching Migration," 6.

29. Tacoma, *Moving Romans*, 30; de Ligt and Tacoma, "Approaching Migration," 4, 8.

30. Philo describes how the Jewish people in Italy were the result of being prisoners of war in *Leg*, 155–57; David Noy also finds that as a result of the three Jewish revolts, the largest Jewish population movement occurred in the first and early second centuries CE. See Noy, "Jews in the Western Roman Empire," 175.

31. Tacoma, *Moving Romans*, 36–47.

32. Tacoma, *Moving Romans*, 246.

33. Tacoma, *Moving Romans*, 171.

who navigates borders and bureaucracies with uncertainty, who sleeps in shelters or open fields while constantly looking over their shoulder, who is harassed by mobs stirred up by fear and nationalism, who is barred from places of power and privilege, and who is marked as "other" because of the language they speak, the clothes they wear, the prayers they offer, and the culture they carry—is, in fact, the closest modern mirror to the life of the apostle Paul? What if it is in their movement, cultural marginality, and threat to nationalistic impulses that we see the clearest embodiment of Paul's own identity?

Indeed, focusing on the description of Paul's travel activities as a migrant is most suitable for a number of reasons. Within the letters of Paul, notably absent are any references to Tarsus, his birthplace or native land, which is solely found in Acts (9:11, 30; 11:25; 21:39; 22:3, 34). Additionally, never does Paul describe Rome as his home nor express any longing, desire, or connection to any specific territory. In fact, he explicitly states that he is ἀστατέω, "homeless" (1 Cor 4:11), a rare term found only once in the New Testament and also used by Plutarch to describe the constant movement of the sea.[34] This makes Paul emerge as someone traveling from town to town, finding a temporary stay only if there were converts to the Christian faith.

When Paul does discuss a common home, it is the "household" of God, a place of belonging that is spiritual and non-territorial. He discusses the responsibility believers have in working for the household of faith (Gal 6:10). He also reminds the gentiles that they were once separated from the people of God and not members of God's household (Eph 2:19). Paul's focus is not on a territory or region for himself or others. Nor does his homeland seem to be an important place for his own self-understanding and identity. Furthermore, Paul describes himself as a foreigner with citizenship to a heavenly city. He writes to the Philippians, "But our citizenship is in heaven, and it is from there that we are expecting a Savior, the Lord Jesus Christ" (Phil 3:20 NRSV). And while the gentiles may have citizenship rights from wherever they originate, he points out that they were "aliens from the citizenship [πολιτείας] of Israel" (Eph 2:12 NRSV) but, who, as a result of Christ, are now a dwelling place of God (v. 22).

Paul did not champion his citizenship but points the early followers of Jesus to their heavenly citizenship. Even more, he reminds the gentiles to recognize their new identification with the household of God.

34. Plutarch, *Crass.* 17.1 (trans. Perrin).

Certainly, Paul in Acts describes himself as a "Roman citizen" (22:27). However, I am curious if this was how Paul viewed himself. I suspect that we are adopting Luke's portrayal of Paul rather than Paul's self-understanding. In fact, when we explore Paul's letters and self-understanding, he never calls himself a Roman citizen. The letters to the Philippians and Romans would have been the most ideal place for Paul to draw his readers to this important fact. Why does Paul fail to remind the Romans that he too is a Roman? Maybe he was not a Roman citizen and this idea was invented by Luke in order to help assuage his readers of Acts that the early Christian movement was not being spread by a foreigner but someone who was their own?

Regardless of whether Paul viewed himself as a Roman citizen, it does not really matter when it comes to his immigrant identity. Within the Roman world, being a Roman citizen did not mean that one could not be a migrant or be deported. Roman citizens were exiled, were deported, and became foreigners—often at the whims of the emperor or whenever there was political unrest in Rome. Roman citizenship provided no such protections. Romans like Cicero, Ovid, and Julia (Caesar Augustus's daughter) were deported from Rome. In fact, the more political status that one had, the more than likely your mobility and migration were supervised and regulated. Dio Cassius remarks that during the Roman emperorship of Caesar Augustus, the right to travel was strictly enforced. He states:

> Apart from these measures, he forbade all members of the Senate to travel outside of Italy, unless he himself should order or give them leave to do so. This regulation is still observed to the present day, for no Senator is allowed to leave the country to visit any place except Sicily and Gallia Narbonensis. Because these regions are close to Rome, and their inhabitants are unarmed and peaceable, those who have any property are allowed to visit them as often as they wish without asking permission.[35]

In other words, the Roman senatorial class experienced tightly regulated movement. Senators could not travel freely across the empire without explicit imperial permission. Much like modern systems of border control, they required official authorization—akin to a passport or visa—particularly when traveling to politically sensitive or militarized provinces. In contrast, individuals of lower status—foreigners, non-citizens,

35. Dio Cassius, *Roman History* 54.42.

and the poor, or someone like the apostle Paul—faced fewer travel restrictions, though they lacked legal protections. Their movements were less monitored and escaped the scrutiny of the emperor, but their presence in unfamiliar regions was more precarious and subject to suspicion. Without the proper documentation, association to the land, or imperial right to travel—what we would today call "legal status" or "papers"—they had no formal authorization and could be deported at any time, without justification or recourse.

MIGRATION, TRAVEL, AND LAND

Migration was an empire phenomenon that had many causes and explanations. Sparse texts discuss the presence of foreigners and reasons why people migrate. Most notably, Virgil's first *Eclogue* describes the lament of an Italian farmer forced into migration during the Roman proscriptions. The Italian farmer states:

> We must go hence—some to the thirsty Africans, some to reach Scythia and the chalk-rolling Oaxes, and the Britons, wholly sundered from all the world. Ah, shall I ever, long years hence, look again on my country's bounds, on my humble cottage with its turf-clad roof—shall I, long years hence, look amazed on a few ears of corn, once my kingdom? Is a godless soldier to hold these well-tilled fallows? a barbarian these crops? See where strife has brought our unhappy citizens! For these have we sown our fields![36]

Others, like Caesar Augustus, react to the presence of migrants who pervade Rome. Augustus's moral reforms include a requirement of Roman bachelors to marry because of the fear that Rome would be inherited by Greeks and barbarians. Dio Cassius recounts the rationale that Augustus gave to the senate: "It is neither right nor honorable that our race should die out, the name of Romans disappears with us and the city be handed over to foreigners—to Greeks or even barbarians. . . . It is impossible for the city to maintain itself unless its population is replenished by a continual flow of new life."[37] Juvenal, likewise, laments the presence of foreigners in Rome and wonders why its citizens had not marched out of

36. Virgil, *Ecl.* 1.65–70.

37. Dio Cassius, *Roman History*, 56.7–8.

the city.[38] Indeed, the presence of migrants is notable whenever the elite of Rome anguish over the population and demographic changes in their city. Though there was no empire-wide mass deportation as we see today, there were several expulsions of foreigners, which served as a reminder of Rome's right to expel those whom they considered undesirable.

The most widely known source that discusses the rationale for migration is Seneca's letter to his mother, Helena. While Seneca attempts to comfort his mother, who was distressed over his exile, he provides some brief comments on why migrants travel, the nature of migration, and the pervasiveness of human migration:

> Some have been brought by ambition, some by the obligation of a public trust, some by an envoy's duty having been laid upon them, some, seeking a convenient and rich field for vice, by luxury, some by a desire for the higher studies, some by the public spectacles; some have been drawn by friendship, some, seeing the ample opportunity for displaying energy, by the chance to work; some have presented their beauty for sale, some their eloquence for sale—every class of person has swarmed into the city that offers high prizes for both virtues and vices.[39]

A variety of reasons exist for migrating to Rome. According to Seneca, foreigners come to Rome for personal desires, education, entertainment, social networks, and work opportunities. He also remarks that some who migrate to Rome do so because they are en route to another city.[40] Further, Seneca also notices a vast number of foreigners in Rome, making mention that it includes "more than half" of the population.[41]

In this same text, Seneca provides his mother with a rationale for human migration. He compares migration to the movement of celestial

38. Juvenal states, "My fellow-citizens, I cannot stand a Greekified Rome. Yet how few of our dregs are Achaeans? The Syrian Orontes has for a long time now been polluting the Tiber, bringing with it its language and customs, its slanting strings along with pipers, its native tom-toms too, and the girls who are told to offer themselves for sale at the Circus. Off you go, if your taste is a foreign whore in her bright headdress"; *Sat.* 3.62–65.

39. Seneca, *ad. Helv.* 6.2–3.

40. Seneca states, they "leave this city, which in a sense may be said to belong to all, and travel from one city to another; everyone will have a large proportion of foreign population" (*ad. Helv.* 6.4). See also Tacoma, *Moving Romans*, 48.

41. Seneca says, "Have all of them summoned by name and ask of each: 'Whence do you hail?' You will find that there are more than half who have left their homes and come to this city, which is truly a very great and a very beautiful one, but not their own. . . . Yet here resides more foreigners than natives" (*ad. Helv.* 6.3–4, 6).

bodies. He believes that since humanity is created from these same divine elements, and these elements are in constant movement, it is only natural that people too are always on the move. He believes that nature has planted within people a "certain restlessness" that makes them "find a new home."[42] To further emphasize this point, Seneca turns to the migration movements of the Greeks, Macedonians, Athenians, Spaniards, and others who reside in territories not founded by their ancestors.[43] He also reminds his mother that nations first emerged as colonies, including the Roman Empire, founded by refugees.[44] Seneca does admit that some migrate because of war, civil discord, excessive population, natural disasters, and famine.[45] He states, "at least this is clear—none has stayed in the place where it was born. The human race is constantly rushing to and fro; in this vast world some change takes place every day."[46]

Seneca, however, was not the only one who discussed migration. Those who also migrate include teachers who attempted to improve their economic situations and social standing. Suetonius does mention that during the reign of Nero, many teachers flocked to Rome and were able to socially advance.[47] Pliny, on the other hand, attempts to attract teachers to Tusculum so students would not have to travel to distant regions, including Rome.[48] While Paul would not neatly fit in this category of an aspiring teacher, we must recognize that not all migrants or migration activities were the same. Not all movements were motivated for the same reasons. To be an immigrant in ancient Rome had nothing to do with citizenship, social status, or agency. Most importantly, Paul would have blended in with the typical movement of migrants in the Mediterranean world, especially those who come to Rome for a temporary period and travel to other regions.

Again, not all migration was positively viewed. It was Lucian who discussed the common sentiment that people have toward their native land. He begins his *My Native Land* by quoting Homer's *Odyssey*, "Nothing is sweeter than one's native land."[49] From this quote he asserts that this

42. Seneca, *ad. Helv.* 6.6.
43. Seneca, *ad. Helv.* 7.1–2.
44. Seneca, *ad. Helv.* 7.7.
45. Seneca, *ad. Helv.* 7.4.
46. Seneca, *ad. Helv.* 7.5.
47. Suetonius, *Rhet.* 1.1.
48. Pliny, *Ep.* 4.1.
49. Lucian cites Homer's *Odyss.* 9.34 in *Patr.* 1.

is a common feeling among people—that they love their own homeland above all others. He then asks, "If nothing is sweeter, then is anything more holy and divine?" The short answer is no. One may ask, why? Lucian points out that one's native land is the reason why one exists—it is the place where they were educated and nurtured. There is something special about one's own home country. He states, "everyone loves his own country," including those who live in large cities.

As such, Lucian does not understand why those who are proud of being citizens fail to give their homeland proper respect.[50] Would one honor another father, or would a father neglect his son? he asks. By using this father's imagery, he asserts that "there is nothing closer than a father" and if one "pays his father proper honour, as the law and nature direct, then one should honour his fatherland still more, for his father himself belonged to it and his father's father and all their forbears, and the name of father goes back until it reaches the father-gods."[51] There is the recognition that land correlates with one's ancestors and the gods. Thus, for one to properly honor one's father, this must include honoring one's homeland. Yet what about those who travel to another land for education and learning? Lucian explains that even if this was the case, then one still needs to be thankful because if he had not been born there in his native land, he would not have known the need to study. In other words, one should not be ungrateful to the place where one was born even if one was educated elsewhere. We should honor our native land and contribute back to it with our education or with our resources.[52]

Lucian also remarks that many people who travel or migrate to foreign lands also long for their homeland. "No one," he remarks, forgets their homeland, especially those who experience difficult times. And those who do well also express one of the greatest hardships. That is, "that they do not live in their own country but sojourn in a strange land (ξενιτεύειν)."[53] For this reason, Lucian concludes that "to sojourn (ξενιτείας) is a reproach!"[54] These similar terms used here, "ξενιτεύειν" and "ξενιτείας," describe the experiences of one who migrates or lives like an exile or foreigner in a different land.[55] This is migration language.

50. Lucian, *Patr.* 2.
51. Lucian, *Patr.* 4.
52. Lucian, *Patr.* 5–7.
53. Lucian, *Patr.* 8.
54. Lucian, *Patr.* 8.
55. Montanari, *Brill Dictionary of Ancient Greek*, s.v. "ξενιτεύω," "ξενιτεία," 1417.

Indeed, he also notes that even those who have been praised or esteemed in a foreign land still desire to return to their home country. Again, he remarks, "even the young love their native land, but the aged men, being wiser, love it more."[56] Lucian also notices that aged men find it disastrous to die in a foreign land; to not be buried with one's ancestors suggests that one is still an "alien (ξενίας) even after death."[57] In other words, to live as a perpetual foreigner can extend even in life after death by not being buried in one's homeland.

PAUL WAS NOT A MISSIONARY

Paul expresses no attachment to a particular homeland, nor does he derive his identity from his Roman citizenship, assuming that he was a Roman citizen. And when we think about Paul as one traveling from city to city, this movement would not have been positively received within the Roman ethos. Now, migrants traveled for a variety of reasons—not just economic ones. As discussed earlier, some come for jobs, some come for entertainment, and others merely pass by en route to another city. Lucian emphasizes the importance of one's homeland and regards migration as a reproach. He even notes that to die in a foreign land is to die in perpetual exile. Paul expresses no affection for a homeland nor any desire to be buried in Tarsus. He does not find it a reproach to migrate and travel to unknown regions. Also, though he was educated in Jerusalem, he never once expresses a desire to return to Tarsus or even Judea, the home country of his ancestors. Judea plays a role in his migration activity—but it is one of sending monetary contributions (Rom 15:25–26, 31; 1 Cor 16:3) and his association with the Jewish Christian leadership (Acts 14–15).

Perhaps the point is that because Paul fully believes he was God's apostle to the gentiles, called to preach to people throughout the Mediterranean world, he could not have any particular longing or association to a homeland. His apostolic calling necessitated a migration identity given that he was constantly on the move to new cities and regions—a migration movement that required a detachment from a homeland. Said differently, as a result of Paul's evangelistic calling, the migrant life and identity were a necessity. He travels to a substantial number of cities and regions, including Jerusalem (Rom 15:25; Gal 1:18–19); Damascus

56. Lucian, *Patr.* 9.

57. Lucian, *Patr.* 9.

(2 Cor 11:32–33; Gal 1:17); Antioch (Gal 2:11–14); Philippi (Phil 4:15–16; 1 Thess 2:2); Troas (2 Cor 2:12–13); Thessalonica (Phil 4:16); Athens (1 Thess 3:1–6); and Corinth (2 Cor 1:19; 11:9; 12:14; 13:1). The regions include Judea (Rom 15:31); Arabia (Gal 1:16–17); Syria (Gal 1:21); Celicia (Gal 1:21); Galatia (1 Cor 16:1; Gal 4:13); Macedonia (1 Cor 16:5; 2 Cor 7:5; Phil 4:15–16); and Achaia (Rom 15:26). Paul also writes letters from Ephesus (1 Cor 16:8), mentions a travel to Illyricum (Rom 15:19), and desires to visit the far western part of the Roman Empire, which included Spain (Rom 1:11; 15:24, 28). Paul is always moving from one city to another without a permanent location. This movement can only be understood as being in perpetual migration.

In fact, Paul expresses to the Romans a desire to reach people who have never heard of the name Jesus. Notice what he tells the Romans and Corinthians:

> Thus I make it my ambition to proclaim the good news, not where Christ has already been named, so that I do not build on someone else's foundation, but as it is written, "Those who have never been told of him shall see, and those who have never heard of him shall understand." This is the reason that I have so often been hindered from coming to you. But now, with no further place for me in these regions, I desire, as I have for many years, to come to you when I go to Spain. For I do hope to see you on my journey and to be sent on by you, once I have enjoyed your company for a little while. (Rom 15:20–24 NRSV)

> We do not boast beyond limits, that is, in the labors of others; but our hope is that, as your faith increases, our sphere of action among you may be greatly enlarged, so that we may proclaim the good news in lands beyond you, without boasting of work already done in someone else's sphere of action. (2 Cor 10:15–16 NRSV)

Notice in the above letters how Paul's desire is simply to preach the gospel and continue to venture into new lands. However, we describe this migration activity as a missionary journey. We call him a missionary because this identity was popularly utilized in the nineteenth century to give Europeans a model on how they can evangelize non-Western people. This missionary identity, as I argue, would have not made sense in the ancient world. It only makes sense in a post–sixteenth-century world after the colonization of the Americas.

PAUL WAS AN UNDOCUMENTED IMMIGRANT

In the Roman world there was no such thing as a "missionary." Paul would have been viewed as a migrant given that he claims allegiance to another country besides the ones in which he travels. His allegiance is not to Tarsus or even Judea. Instead, it is to the household of God. Scholars of color have already suspected this. Efraín Agosto, in fact, describes Paul as a "'border' person and a 'migrant' worker with all his travels throughout the provinces and conquered territories of the Roman empire."[58] As a result, it is more appropriate to view Paul as a migrant disconnected from any fixed homeland, continuously traveling from one place to another on a permanent or semi-permanent basis—until he is forced to flee, like a refugee, for proclaiming unfamiliar and disruptive teachings (Acts 19). As Paul himself notes, "I only know that in every city the Holy Spirit warns me that prison and hardships are facing me" (Acts 20:23). Notice in the above quote how Paul admits that his presence in a foreign land will not be welcomed. Perhaps the only time Paul was ever truly "documented" was when he came under imperial custody and was transported to Rome for trial (Acts 25–28).[59] It is in this moment—under guard, in chains, and registered by the state—that Paul becomes documented to the imperial system. Otherwise, he closely resembles a modern undocumented migrant, whose presence often goes unnoticed until the machinery of the state intervenes—when detained, processed, deported, or forced to flee.

Does this presume that we must put an end to the idea of Paul as a missionary? Most certainly. But this is not to suggest that this is an end of missions. The goal of this essay is not to suggest that Paul was not an evangelist nor one who traveled to various regions to preach the gospel. Instead, this essay aims to challenge the contemporary understanding of his identity. If we attempt to understand Paul's identity, what scholars often describe as the "historical Paul," within the primary context of the Roman world, then the idea of Paul as a missionary needs to be abandoned. Instead, I propose that we view him as a migrant—foreigners who traveled to new lands and were identifiable by their different culture, speech, dress, religion, and way of life.

As a result, the best model to understand Paul and his identity is to look not at the fully funded missionaries who travel to foreign lands and own their SUVs so they may drive on unpaved roads. The best model

58. Agosto, "Islands, Borders, and Migration," 163.

59. I would like to thank Amos Yong for this insight!

that provides an insight into the real historical Paul is the undocumented migrant who is in constant movement—unwelcomed in most cities, misunderstood because of their speech and customs, and ostracized for having an allegiance to another kingdom. Paul was poor and depended upon his own hands to support himself. He was not funded by a missions board but bore the wounds of his ministry in his body and hands. He was imprisoned in inhuman conditions—akin to the migrant detention centers where the lights never turn off and the temperature is extremely cold.[60] If we are to envision Paul correctly, we must look to the faces of modern-day undocumented immigrants whose journeys are shaped by hope and embodied resistance. Uncovering this image is not just to correct our historical lens; it is to recover the true identity of the early Christian movement—an immigrant movement.

60. Undocumented migrants call the US immigration detention centers *hieleras* (freezers or iceboxes).

Bibliography

Achtemeier, Paul J. *1 Peter: A Commentary on First Peter*. Hermeneia. Minneapolis: Augsburg Fortress, 1996.

Adams, Edward. "Retrieving the Earth from the Conflagration: 2 Peter 3:5–13 and the Environment." In *Ecological Hermeneutics: Biblical, Historical, and Theological Perspectives*, edited by David G. Horrell et al., 108–19. London: T&T Clark, 2010.

Agosto, Efraín. "Islands, Borders, and Migration: Reading Paul in Light of the Crisis in Puerto Rico." In *Latinx, the Bible, and Migration*, edited by Efrain Agosto and Jacqueline Hidalgo, 149–70. Switzerland: Palgrave, 2018.

Ahn, Kyo Seong. "Christian Mission and Colonialism." In *The Oxford Handbook of Mission Studies*, edited by Kirsteen Kim and Alison Fitchett-Climenhaga, 330–47. New York: Oxford University Press, 2022.

Allen, Roland. *Missionary Methods: St. Paul's or Ours? A Study of the Church in the Four Provinces*. London: Scott, 1912.

Allison, Dale C., Jr. *A Critical and Exegetical Commentary on the Epistle of James*. New York: Bloomsbury, 2013.

Archer, Kenneth J. *A Pentecostal Hermeneutic for the Twenty-First Century: Spirit, Scripture and Community*. Journal of Pentecostal Theology Supplement 28. London: T&T Clark, 2004.

———. *A Pentecostal Hermeneutic: Spirit, Scripture, and Community*. Cleveland, TN: CPT, 2009.

Archer, Kenneth J., and L. William Oliverio Jr., eds. *Constructive Pneumatological Hermeneutics in Pentecostal Christianity*. New York: Palgrave Macmillan, 2016.

Archer, Melissa L. *"I Was in the Spirit on the Lord's Day": A Pentecostal Engagement with Worship in the Apocalypse*. Cleveland, TN: CPT, 2015.

———. "Pentecostals and the Apocalypse: A Survey of Recent Pentecostal Biblical Scholarship on the Apocalypse." *Journal of Pentecostal Theology* 24 (2015) 57–91.

Aymer, Margaret. *James: Diaspora Rhetoric of a Friend of God*. T&T Clark Study Guides to the New Testament. London: Bloomsbury, 2015.

Baines, Matthew Charles. "The Identity and Fate of the Kings of the Earth in the Book of Revelation." *Reformed Theological Review* 75 (2016) 73–88.

Barreto, Eric D. *Ethnic Negotiations: The Function of Race and Ethnicity in Acts 16*. WUNT 2.294. Tübingen: Mohr Siebeck, 2010.

———. "A Gospel on the Move: Practice, Proclamation, and Place in Luke-Acts." *Interpretation* 72 (2018) 175–87.

Barton, Stephen. "Historical Criticism and Social-Scientific Perspectives in New Testament Study." In *Hearing the New Testament: Strategies for Interpretation*, edited by Joel Green, 34–64. Grand Rapids: Eerdmans, 2010.

Bauckham, Richard. *The Climax of Prophecy: Studies in the Book of Revelation*. 1993. Repr., London: T&T Clark, 2005.

———. "James and Jesus." In *The Brother of Jesus: James the Just and His Mission*, edited by Bruce Chilton and Jacob Neusner, 100–137. Louisville: Westminster John Knox, 2001.

———. "The Story of the Earth According to Paul: Romans 8:18–23." *Review and Expositor* 108 (2011) 91–97.

———. *The Theology of the Book of Revelation*. Cambridge: Cambridge University Press, 2003.

Bauman-Martin, Betsy. "Speaking Jewish: Postcolonial Aliens and Strangers in First Peter." In *Reading First Peter with New Eyes: Methodological Reassessment of the Letter of First Peter*, edited by Robert L. Webb and Betsy Bauman-Martin, 144–77. LNTS 364. London: T&T Clark, 2007.

Beale, G. K. *The Book of Revelation: A Commentary on the Greek Text*. Grand Rapids: Eerdmans, 1999.

———. *John's Use of the Old Testament in Revelation*. LNTS 166. 1998. Repr., London: Bloomsbury T&T Clark, 2015.

———. *The Use of Daniel in Jewish Apocalyptic Literature and in the Revelation of St. John*. Lanham, MD: University Press of America, 1984.

Bertone, John A. "The Experience of Glossolalia and the Spirit's Empathy: Romans 8:26 Revisited." *Pneuma* 25 (2003) 54–65.

Bjørndal, Silje Kvamme. *The Church in a Secular Age: A Pneumatological Reconstruction of Stanley Hauerwas's Ecclesiology*. Eugene, OR: Wipf & Stock, 2018.

Blount, Brian K. *Revelation: A Commentary*. NTL. Louisville: Westminster John Knox, 2009.

Bock, Darrell L. *A Theology of Luke and Acts: God's Promised Program, Realized for All Nations*. Grand Rapids: Zondervan, 2012.

Bockmuehl, Markus. "Antioch and James the Just." In *James the Just and Christian Origins*, edited by Bruce Chilton and Craig A. Evans, 155–98. NovTSup 98. Leiden: Brill, 1999.

Boesak, Allan. *Comfort and Protest: The Apocalypse from a South African Perspective*. Louisville: Westminster John Knox, 1987.

Borg, Marcus, and John Dominic Crossan. *The First Paul*. New York: HarperOne, 2010.

Bosch, David. *Transforming Mission: Paradigm Shifts in Theology of Mission*. Maryknoll, NY: Orbis, 1991.

Bredin, Mark. *Jesus, Revolutionary of Peace: A Nonviolent Christology in the Book of Revelation*. Carlisle: Paternoster, 2003.

Brinks, C. L. "'Great Is Artemis of the Ephesians': Acts 19:23–41 in Light of Goddess Worship in Ephesus." *Catholic Biblical Quarterly* 71 (2009) 776–94.

Brown, Raymond E., and John P. Meier. *Antioch and Rome: New Testament Cradles of Catholic Christianity*. New York: Paulist, 1983.

Bucur, Bogdan G. "Hierarchy, Prophecy, and the Angelomorphic Spirit: A Contribution to the Study of the Book of Revelation's *Wirkungsgeschichte*." *Journal of Biblical Literature* 127 (2008) 173–94.

Bultmann, Rudolf. "Is Exegesis Without Presuppositions Possible?" In *New Testament and Mythology and Other Basic Writings*, edited by Schubert Miles Ogden, 145–53. Philadelphia: Fortress, 1989.

Busto, Rudy V. "The Gospel According to the Model Minority? Hazarding an Interpretation of Asian American Evangelical College Students." In *New Spiritual Homes: Religion and Asian Americans*, edited by David K. Yoo, 169–87. Honolulu: University of Hawaii Press, 1999.

Byrne, Brendan. "An Ecological Reading of Rom. 8:19–22: Possibilities and Hesitations." In *Ecological Hermeneutics: Biblical, Historical and Theological Perspectives*, edited by David G. Horrell et al., 83–93. London: T&T Clark, 2010.

Calpino, Teresa J. *Women, Work, and Leadership in Acts*. WUNT 2.361. Tübingen: Mohr Siebeck, 2014.

Campbell, Douglas. *Paul: An Apostle's Journey*. Grand Rapids: Eerdmans, 2018.

Cargal, Timothy B. *Restoring the Diaspora: Discursive Structure and Purpose in the Epistle of James*. SBLDS 144. Atlanta: Scholars, 1993.

Carroll, John T. "Creation and Apocalypse." In *God Who Cares: Essays in Honor of W. Sibley Towner*, edited by William P. Brown and S. Dean McBride Jr., 251–60. Grand Rapids: Eerdmans, 2000.

Carson, D. A. *Exegetical Fallacies*. 2nd ed. Grand Rapids: Baker Academic, 1996.

Chang, Derek. *Citizens of a Christian Nation: Evangelical Missions and the Problem of Race in the Nineteenth Century*. Philadelphia: University of Pennsylvania Press, 2010.

Christensen, Torben, and William Hutchison. *Missionary Ideologies in the Imperialist Era: 1880–1920*. Denmark: Christensen Bogyrykkeri, 1982.

Christerson, Brad, et al. *God's Resistance: Mobilizing Faith to Defend Immigrants*. New York: New York University Press, 2023.

Chung, Paul S. *Hermeneutical Theology and the Imperative of Public Ethics: Confessing Christ in Post-Colonial World Christianity*. Eugene, OR: Pickwick, 2013.

———. *Public Theology in an Age of World Christianity: God's Mission as Word-Event*. New York: Palgrave Macmillan, 2010.

Coker, K. Jason. *James in Postcolonial Perspective: The Letter as Nativist Discourse*. Minneapolis: Fortress, 2015.

Conner, Benjamin T. *Disabling Mission, Enabling Witness: Exploring Missiology Through the Lens of Disability Studies*. Missiological Engagements. Downers Grove, IL: IVP Academic, 2018.

Copan, Paul, and Kenneth D. Litwak. *The Gospel in the Marketplace of Ideas: Paul's Mars Hill Experience for Our Pluralistic World*. Downers Grove, IL: IVP Academic, 2014.

Cruse, C. F., trans. *Eusebius' Ecclesiastical History*. Updated ed. Peabody, MA: Hendrickson, 1998.

Curley, Edwin, ed. *The Collected Works of Spinoza, Volume 2*. Princeton: Princeton University Press, 2016.

Davids, Peter H. "Controlling the Tongue and the Wallet: Discipleship in James." In *Patterns of Discipleship in the New Testament*, edited by Richard N. Longenecker, 225–47. Grand Rapids: Eerdmans, 1996.

Day, Keri. *Azusa Reimagined: A Radical Vision of Religious and Democratic Belonging*. Stanford: Stanford University Press, 2022.

de Las Casas, Bartolomé. *A Short Account of the Destruction of the Indies*. Translated by Nigel Griffin. New York: Penguin, 2004.

de Ligt, Luuk, and Laurens Tacoma. "Approaching Migration in the Early Roman Empire." In *Migration and Mobility in the Early Roman Empire*, edited by Luuk de Ligt and Laurens Tacoma, 1–22. Leiden: Brill, 2016.

de Smidt, Kobus. "Hermeneutical Perspectives on the Spirit in the Book of Revelation." *Journal of Pentecostal Theology* 7 (1999) 27–47.

de Villiers, Pieter. "Love in the Revelation of John." In *Seeing the Seeker: Explorations in the Discipline of Spirituality—A Festschrift for Kees Waaijman on the Occasion of His 65th Birthday*, edited by Hein Blommestijn et al., 155–68. Titus Brandsma Institute Studies in Spirituality Supplement 19. Leuven: Peeters, 2008.

Desch, Michael C., ed. *Public Intellectuals in the Global Arena: Professors or Pundits?* Notre Dame: University of Notre Dame Press, 2016.

Dio Cassius. *The Roman History: The Reign of Augustus*. Translated by Ian Scott-Kilvert. New York: Penguin, 1987.

Draper, Jonathan. "Apostles, Teachers, and Evangelists: Stability and Movement of Functionaries in Matthew, James, and the Didache." In *Matthew, James, and Didache: Three Related Documents in Their Jewish and Christian Settings*, edited by Huub van de Sandt and Jürgen Zangenberg, 139–76. SBL Symposium Series 45. Leiden: Brill, 2008.

Dubis, Mark. *Messianic Woes in First Peter: Suffering and Eschatology in 1 Peter 4:12–19*. StBibLit 33. New York: Lang, 2002.

Dumbrell, William J. *The End of the Beginning: Revelation 21–22 and the Old Testament*. Grand Rapids: Baker, 1985.

du Preez, J."Exegetical Notes: People and Nations in the Kingdom of God According to the Book of Revelation." *Journal of Theology for Southern Africa* 49 (1984) 49–51.

du Rand, Jan A. "'. . . Let Him Hear What the Spirit Says. . .': The Functional Role and Theological Meaning of the Spirit in the Book of Revelation." *Ex Auditu* 12 (1997) 43–58.

Dussel, Enrique. *A History of the Church in Latin America: Colonialism to Liberation 1492–1979*. Grand Rapids: Eerdmans, 1981.

Edgar, William. *Created and Creating: A Biblical Theology of Culture*. Downers Grove, IL: IVP Academic, 2017.

Edwards, Denis. "Final Fulfilment: The Deification of All Creation." *SEDOS Bulletin* 41 (2009) 181–95.

Eller, Vernard. "How the Kings of the Earth Land in the New Jerusalem: 'The World' in the Book of Revelation." *Katallagete—Be Reconciled* 5 (1975) 21–27.

Elliot, John. *What Is Social-Scientific Criticism?* Philadelphia: Fortress, 1993.

Estrada, Rodolfo Galvan, III. "Blaspheming Angels: The Presence of Magicians in Jude 8–10." *Journal of the Evangelical Theological Society* 63 (2020) 739–58.

———. "Is a Contextualized Hermeneutic the Future of Pentecostal Readings? The Implications of a Pentecostal Hermeneutic for a Chicano/Latino Community." *Pneuma* 37 (2015) 341–55.

———. *A Latino Reading of Race, Kinship, and the Empire: John's Prologue*. Switzerland: Palgrave Macmillan, 2023.

———. *A Pneumatology of Race in the Gospel of John: An Ethnocritical Study*. Eugene, OR: Pickwick, 2020.

———. *Race and the Foreigner in the New Testament: A Hermeneutical Guide*. Grand Rapids: Eerdmans, forthcoming.

———. "The Racial Significance of Paul's Clothing Metaphor (Romans 13:14; Galatians 3:27; Ephesians 4:24; Colossians 3:10)." *Religions* 14 (2023) https://doi.org/10.3390/rel14060684.

———. "Spirit in Jude 19–20." *Journal of Pentecostal Theology* 25 (2016) 43–57.

———. "What Does the Paraclete Have to Do with Dreamers? A Pneumatological Paradigm for Latino/a Social–Political Advocacy." *Perspectivas* 16 (2019) 67–81.

———. "What Does the Spirit Have to Do with Foreigners? Reading Acts 10:28–48 with Diodorus of Sicily and Tacitus." *Pneuma* 39 (2017) 272–91.

Etzioni, Amatai, and Alyssa Bowditch, eds. *Public Intellectuals: An Endangered Species?* Lanham, MD: Rowman & Littlefield, 2006.

Fallon, Michael. *The Apocalypse: A Call to Embrace the Love That Is Stronger Than Death*. 1990. Repr., Bangalore: Asia Trading Corporation, 2005.

Farganis, Sondra. "A Public or Dissenting Intellectual?" In *The Changing Role of the Public Intellectual*, edited by Dolan Cummings, 157–71. New York: Routledge, 2005.

Farley, Lawrence R. *The Apocalypse of St. John: A Revelation of Love and Power*. Chesterton, IN: Conciliar, 2011.

Fee, Gordon. *Revelation: A New Covenant Commentary*. Eugene, OR: Cascade, 2011.

Fekkes, Jan, III. *Isaiah and Prophetic Traditions in the Book of Revelation: Visionary Antecedents and Their Development*. JSNTSup 93. Sheffield: Sheffield Academic, 1994.

Fitzmyer, Joseph A. *To Advance the Gospel: New Testament Studies*. 2nd ed. Grand Rapids: Eerdmans, 1998.

Fleming, Kenneth. *Buddhist-Christian Encounter in Contemporary Thailand*. Religionswissenschaft 19. New York: Lang, 2014.

Ford, J. M. *Revelation*. AB 38. Garden City, NY: Doubleday, 1975.

Fournier, Marianne. *The Episode at Lystra: A Rhetorical and Semiotic Analysis of Acts 14:7–20a*. AUS 197. New York: Lang, 1997.

Fowl, Stephen E. *Philippians*. Two Horizons New Testament Commentary. Grand Rapids: Eerdmans, 2005.

Francis, Richard Shiningthunder. *The Apocalypse of Love: Mystical Symbolism in Revelation*. Martinsville, IN: Bookman, 2004.

Fudge, Thomas A. *Christianity Without the Cross: A History of Salvation in Oneness Pentecostalism*. Parkland, FL: Universal, 2003.

Furnish, Victor Paul. *The Love Command in the New Testament*. Nashville: Abingdon, 1972.

Galeano, Eduardo. *Open Veins of Latin America: Five Centuries of the Pillage of a Continent*. Translated by Cedric Belfrage. New York: Monthly Review, 1997.

Gause, Hollis. *Revelation: God's Stamp of Sovereignty on History*. Cleveland, TN: Pathway, 1983.

Gaventa, Beverly Roberts, ed. *Apocalyptic Paul: Cosmos and Anthropos in Romans 5–8*. Waco, TX: Baylor University Press, 2013.

Gelpi, Donald L. *The Divine Mother: A Trinitarian Theology of the Holy Spirit*. Lanham, MD: University Press of America, 1984.

Glahn, Sandra L. *Nobody's Mother: Artemis of the Ephesians in Antiquity and the New Testament*. Downers Grove, IL: IVP Academic, 2023.

Goh, Elaine Wei-Fun, et al., eds. *From Malaysia to the Ends of the Earth: Southeast Asian and Diasporic Contributions to Biblical and Theological Studies*. Claremont, CA: Claremont, 2021.

González, Justo L. *For the Healing of the Nations: The Book of Revelation in an Age of Cultural Conflict*. Maryknoll, NY: Orbis, 1999.

Gorman, Michael J. *Elements of Biblical Exegesis: A Basic Guide for Students and Ministers*. Grand Rapids: Baker, 2020.

———. "Majority-Culture Biblical Interpretation: Reading While White." In *The New Testament in Color*, edited by Esau McCaulley et al., 35–42. Downers Grove, IL: InterVarsity, 2024.

———. *Reading Revelation Responsibly: Uncivil Worship and Witness Following the Lamb into the New Creation*. Eugene, OR: Cascade, 2011.

Green, Chris E. W. *Pentecostal Ecclesiology: A Reader*. Leiden: Brill, 2016.

Green, Joel B. *1 Peter*. Two Horizons New Testament Commentary. Grand Rapids: Eerdmans, 2007.

———. "Living in Exile: The Church in the Diaspora in 1 Peter." In *Holiness and Ecclesiology in the New Testament*, edited by Kent E. Brower and Andy Johnson, 311–25. Grand Rapids: Eerdmans, 2007.

———. *Practicing Theological Interpretation: Engaging Biblical Texts for Faith and Formation*. Grand Rapids: Baker Academic, 2012.

Green, Joel B., and David F. Watson, eds. *Wesley, Wesleyans, and Reading Bible as Scripture*. Waco, TX: Baylor University Press, 2012.

Grey, Jacquline. "Biblical Hermeneutics: Reading Scripture with the Spirit in Community." In *The Routledge Handbook of Pentecostal Theology*, edited by Wolfgang Vondey, 129–39. Oxon: Routledge, 2020.

———. *Three's a Crowd: Pentecostalism, Hermeneutics, and the Old Testament*. Eugene, OR: Wipf & Stock, 2011.

Gruca-Macauley, Alexandra. *Lydia as a Rhetorical Construct in Acts*. Emory Studies in Early Christianity 18. Atlanta: SBL, 2016.

Gutiérrez, Gustavo. *Power of the Poor in History*. Eugene, OR: Wipf & Stock, 2004.

Habets, Myk, ed. *Third Article Theology: A Pneumatological Dogmatics*. Minneapolis: Fortress, 2016.

Hartin, Patrick J. *James of Jerusalem: Heir to Jesus of Nazareth*. Collegeville, MN: Liturgical, 2004.

Hayford, Jack. *E-Quake: A New Approach to Understanding the End Times Mysteries in the Book of Revelation*. Nashville: Nelson, 1999.

Heimburger, Robert. *God and the Illegal Alien: United States Immigration Law and a Theology of Politics*. New York: Cambridge University Press, 2018.

Heltzel, Peter Goodwin. *Resurrection City: A Theology of Improvisation*. Grand Rapids: Eerdmans, 2012.

Herms, Ronald. *An Apocalypse for the Church and for the World: The Narrative Function of Universal Language in the Book of Revelation*. BZNW 143. Berlin: de Gruyter, 2006.

———. "Invoking the Spirit and Narrative Intent in John's Apocalypse." In *Spirit and Scripture: Exploring a Pneumatic Hermeneutic*, edited by Kevin L. Spawn and Archie T. Wright, 99–114. London: T&T Clark, 2012.

Hertig, Young Lee. "Cross-Cultural Mediation: From Exclusion to Inclusion." In *Mission in Acts: Ancient Narratives in Contemporary Contexts*, edited by Robert L. Gallagher and Paul Hertig, 59–72. Maryknoll, NY: Orbis, 2004.

Heufelder, Emmanuel M. *The Spirit Prays in Us: Reflections on Romans 8:26–27*. Translated by Gregory J. Roettger. Collegeville, MN: Liturgical, 1976.

Hidalgo, Jacqueline. *Revelation in Aztlán: Scriptures, Utopias, and the Chicano Movement*. New York: Palgrave Macmillan, 2016.

Hopkins, Dwight N., ed. *Black Faith and Public Talk: Critical Essays on James H. Cone's Black Theology and Black Power*. Waco, TX: Baylor University Press, 2007.

Horrell, David G. "Between Conformity and Resistance: Beyond the Balch-Elliott Debate Towards a Postcolonial Reading of First Peter." In *Reading First Peter with New Eyes: Methodological Reassessment of the Letter of First Peter*, edited by Robert L. Webb and Betsy Bauman-Martin, 109–43. LNTS 364. London: T&T Clark, 2007.

Houston, Graham. *Leading by Example: Peter's Way for the Church Today*. Milton Keynes: Paternoster, 2008.

Hutchinson Edgar, David. *Has God Not Chosen the Poor? The Social Setting of the Epistle of James*. JSNTSup 206. Sheffield: Sheffield Academic, 2001.

Im, Chandler H., and Amos Yong, eds. *Global Diasporas and Mission*. Regnum Edinburgh Centenary Series 23. Oxford: Regnum, 2014.

Immendörfer, Michael. *Ephesians and Artemis: The Cult of the Great Goddess of Ephesus as the Epistle's Context*. WUNT 2.436. Tübingen: Mohr Siebeck, 2017.

Ingalls, Monique, and Amos Yong, eds. *The Spirit of Praise: Music and Worship in Global Pentecostal-Charismatic Christianity*. University Park, PA: Pennsylvania State University Press, 2015.

Intan, Benyamin Fleming. *"Public Religion" and the Pancasila-Based State of Indonesia: An Ethical and Sociological Analysis*. AUS 238. New York: Lang, 2006.

Isasi-Díaz, Ada María, et al., eds. *Theological Perspectives for Life, Liberty, and the Pursuit of Happiness: Public Intellectuals for the Twenty-First Century*. New York: Palgrave Macmillan, 2013.

Jackman, David. *The Message of John's Letters: Living in the Love of God*. Downers Grove, IL: InterVarsity, 1988.

Jacoby, Russell. *The Last Intellectuals: American Culture in the Age of Academe*. New York: Basic, 2000.

Jenkins, Philip. *The Next Christendom: The Coming of Global Christianity*. 3rd ed. Oxford: Oxford University Press, 2011.

Jersak, Bradley. *Her Gates Will Never Be Shut: Hope, Hell, and the New Jerusalem*. Eugene, OR: Wipf & Stock, 2009.

Johns, Cheryl Bridges. *Re-Enchanting the Text: Discovering the Bible as Sacred, Dangerous, and Mysterious*. Grand Rapids: Baker, 2023.

Johns, Loren L. *The Lamb Christology of the Apocalypse of John: An Investigation into Its Origins and Rhetorical Force*. WUNT 2.167. Tübingen: Mohr Siebeck, 2003.

Johnson, Andy. *1 and 2 Thessalonians*. Two Horizons New Testament Commentary. Grand Rapids: Eerdmans, 2016.

Johnson, Luke Timothy. *The Letter of James: A New Translation with Introduction and Commentary*. AB 37A. New York: Doubleday, 1995.

Josephus, Flavius. *The Complete Works*. Translated by William Whiston. Philadelphia: Potter, 1905.

Juvenal and Persius. *Juvenal and Persius*. Edited and translated by Susanna Morton Braund. LCL 91. Cambridge: Harvard University Press, 2004.

Kärkkäinen, Veli-Matti. *Toward a Pneumatological Theology: Pentecostal and Ecumenical Perspectives on Ecclesiology, Soteriology and Theology of Mission*. Edited by Amos Yong. Lanham, MD: University Press of America, 2002.

Kärkkäinen, Veli-Matti, et al., eds. *Interdisciplinary and Religio-Cultural Discourses on a Spirit-Filled World: Loosing the Spirits*. New York: Palgrave Macmillan, 2013.

Keenan, John P. *The Wisdom of James: Parallels with Mahāyāna Buddhism*. New York: Newman, 2005.

Keener, Craig S. *Acts: An Exegetical Commentary*. Vol. 1, *Introduction and 1:1—2:47*. Grand Rapids: Baker Academic, 2012.

———. *Acts: An Exegetical Commentary*. Vol. 3, *15:1—23:35*. Grand Rapids: Baker Academic, 2014.

———. "Pentecostal Biblical Interpretation/Spirit Hermeneutics." In *Scripture and Its Interpretation: A Global, Ecumenical Introduction to the Bible*, edited by Michael Gorman, 270–83. Grand Rapids: Baker Academic, 2017.

———. *Revelation*. NIVAC. Grand Rapids: Zondervan, 2000.

———. *Spirit Hermeneutics: Reading Scripture in Light of Pentecost*. Grand Rapids: Eerdmans, 2016.

Kilcrease, Jack. "Creation's Praise: A Short Liturgical Reading of Genesis 1–2 and the Book of Revelation." *Pro Ecclesia* 21 (2012) 314–25.

Klutz, Todd. *The Exorcism Stories in Luke-Acts: A Sociostylistic Reading*. SNTSMS 129. Cambridge: Cambridge University Press, 2004.

Koester, Craig R. *Revelation: A New Translation with Introduction and Commentary*. AYB 38A. New Haven: Yale University Press, 2014.

Kollman, Paul. "At the Origins of Mission and Missiology: A Study in the Dynamics of Religious Language." *Journal of the American Academy of Religion* 79 (2011) 425–58.

———. "Defining Mission Studies for the Third Millennium of Christianity." In *The Oxford Handbook of Mission Studies*, edited by Kirsteen Kim and Alison Fitchett-Climenhaga, 37–55. New York: Oxford University, 2022.

Kraftchick, Steve. "Paul's Use of Creation Themes: A Test of Romans 1–8." *Ex Auditu* 3 (1987) 72–87.

Kraybill, J. Nelson. *Apocalypse and Allegiance: Worship, Politics, and Devotion in the Book of Revelation*. Grand Rapids: Brazos, 2010.

Krentz, Edgar. *The Historical-Critical Method*. Philadelphia: Fortress, 1975.

Kurz, William J. *Acts of the Apostles*. Catholic Commentary on Sacred Scripture. Grand Rapids: Baker Academic, 2013.

Lawrence, Louise J. *Sense and Stigma in the Gospels: Depictions of Sensory-Disabled Characters*. Oxford: Oxford University Press, 2013.

Le, Vince. "The Pentecostal Movement in Vietnam." In *Global Renewal Christianity*. Vol. 1, *Asia and Oceania*, edited by Amos Yong and Vinson Synan, 181–95. Lake Mary, FL: Charisma, 2016.

———. *Vietnamese Evangelicals and Pentecostalism: The Politics of Divine Intervention*. Leiden: Brill, 2019.

Lee, Hee Youl. *A Dynamic Reading of the Holy Spirit in Revelation: A Theological Reflection on the Functional Role of the Holy Spirit in the Narrative*. Eugene, OR: Wipf & Stock, 2014.

Lee, Sang Hyun. *From a Liminal Place: An Asian American Theology*. Minneapolis: Fortress, 2010.

Lee, Younghoon. *The Holy Spirit Movement in Korea: Its Historical and Theological Development*. London: Regnum, 2009.

Lee, Younghoon, et al., eds. *Pentecostal Mission and Global Christianity: An Edinburgh Centenary Reader*. Regnum Edinburgh Centenary Series. London: Regnum, 2012.

Lennartsson, Göran. *Refreshing and Restoration: Two Eschatological Motifs in Acts 3:19–21*. Lund: Lund University Centre for Theology and Religious Studies, 2007.

Lewis, Charlton T., and Charles Short. *Latin Dictionary*. New York: American Book Company, 1879.

Luce, Alice E. "Paul's Missionary Methods." *Pentecostal Evangel*, January 8, 1921.

———. "Paul's Missionary Methods." *Pentecostal Evangel*, January 22, 1921.

———. "Paul's Missionary Methods." *Pentecostal Evangel*, February 5, 1921.

Lucian. *Phalaris. Hippias or The Bath. Dionysus. Heracles. Amber or The Swans. The Fly. Nigrinus. Demonax. The Hall. My Native Land. Octogenarians. A True Story. Slander. The Consonants at Law. The Carousal (Symposium) or The Lapiths*. Translated by A. M. Harmon. LCL 14. Cambridge: Harvard University Press, 1913.

Lussier, Ernest. *God Is Love According to Saint John*. New York: Alba, 1977.

Lyke, Larry L. *I Will Espouse You Forever: The Song of Songs and the Theology of Love in the Hebrew Bible*. Nashville: Abingdon, 2007.

Macchia, Frank D. *Baptized in the Spirit: A Global Pentecostal Theology*. Grand Rapids: Zondervan, 2006.

———. *Justified in the Spirit: Creation, Redemption, and the Triune God*. Grand Rapids: Eerdmans, 2010.

Marschner, Walter. "Ritual and the Holy in Social Struggles: The Mysticism of Peasant Movements as a Challenge to Public Theology." In *Public Theology in Brazil: Social and Cultural Challenges*, edited by Eneida Jacobsen et al., translated by Luís Marcos Sander and Hedy L. Hofmann, 115–30. Theologie in der Öffentlichkeit [Theology in the Public Square] 6. Berlin: LIT, 2013.

Marsden, George M. *Reforming Fundamentalism: Fuller Seminary and the New Evangelicalism*. Grand Rapids: Eerdmans, 1987.

Martin, Lee Roy, ed. *Pentecostal Hermeneutics: A Reader*. Leiden: Brill, 2013.

Mathewson, Dave. "The Destiny of the Nations in Revelation 21:1—22:5: A Reconsideration." *Tyndale Bulletin* 53 (2002) 121–42.

———. *A New Heaven and a New Earth: The Meaning and Function of the Old Testament in Revelation 21:1—22:5*. JSNTSup 238. Sheffield: Sheffield Academic, 2003.

Matson, David Lertis. *Household Conversion in Acts: Pattern and Interpretation*. JSNTSup 123. Sheffield: Sheffield Academic, 1996.

Mauck, John W. *Paul on Trial: The Book of Acts as a Defense of Christianity*. Nashville: Nelson Reference, 2001.

Maynard-Reid, Pedrito U. *Poverty and Wealth in James*. Maryknoll, NY: Orbis, 1987.

Mbuvi, Andrew M. *Temple, Exile, and Identity in 1 Peter*. LSNT 345. London: T&T Clark, 2007.

McGinn, Sheila E. "All Creation Groans in Labor: Paul's Theology of Creation in Romans 8:18–23." In *Earth, Wind, and Fire: Biblical and Theological Perspectives on Creation*, edited by Carol J. Dempsey and Mary Margaret Pazdan, 114–23. Collegeville, MN: Liturgical, 2004.

McIlraith, Donal A. *The Reciprocal Love Between Christ and the Church in the Apocalypse*. Rome: Columbian Fathers, 1989.

McKnight, Scot. *The Letter of James*. NICNT. Grand Rapids: Eerdmans, 2011.
McNicol, Allan J. *The Conversion of the Nations in Revelation*. LNTS 438. London: T&T Clark, 2011.
McRay, John. *Paul: His Life and Teaching*. Grand Rapids: Baker Academic, 2007.
Menzies, Robert P. "Was John the Revelator Pentecostal?" In *But These Are Written . . . : Essays on Johannine Literature in Honor of Professor Benny C. Aker*, edited by Craig S. Keener et al., 221–34. Eugene, OR: Pickwick, 2014.
Michael, John. *Anxious Intellects: Academic Professionals, Public Intellectuals, and Enlightenment Values*. Durham, NC: Duke University Press, 2000.
Michaels, J. Ramsey. *1 Peter*. WBC 49. Waco, TX: Word, 1988.
Mittelstadt, Martin W. *Reading Luke-Acts in the Pentecostal Tradition*. Cleveland, TN: CPT, 2010.
Moatti, Claudia. "Roman World, Mobility." In vol. 4 of *The Encyclopedia of Global Human Migration*, edited by Immanuel Ness. Malden, MA: Wiley-Blackwell, 2013. https://doi.org/10.1002/9781444351071.wbeghm459.
Moffatt, James. *Love in the New Testament*. London: Hodder & Stoughton, 1929.
Moltmann, Jürgen. *The Coming of God: Christian Eschatology*. Translated by Margaret Kohl. Minneapolis: Fortress, 1996.
———. *God for a Secular Society: The Public Relevance of Theology*. Translated by Margaret Kohl. Minneapolis: Fortress, 1999.
Montanari, Franco. *The Brill Dictionary of Ancient Greek*. Edited by Madeleine Goh and Chad Schroeder. Leiden: Brill, 2015.
Moore, Rickie. "Canon and Charisma in the Book of Deuteronomy." *Journal of Pentecostal Theology* 1 (1992) 75–92.
———. "Deuteronomy and the Fire of God: A Critical Charismatic Interpretation." *Journal of Pentecostal Theology* 7 (1995) 11–33.
———. *The Spirit of the Old Testament*. Journal of Pentecostal Theology Supplement Series 35. Dorset: Deo, 2011.
Moore, Rickie D., and Brian Neil Peterson. *Voice, Word, and Spirit: A Pentecostal Old Testament Survey*. Nashville: Abingdon, 2017.
Moore, Stephen D. "The Revelation to John." In *A Postcolonial Commentary on the New Testament Writings*, edited by Fernando F. Segovia and R. S. Sugitharajah, 436–54. The Bible and Postcolonialism 13. London: T&T Clark, 2009.
Morris, Leon. *Testaments of Love: A Study of Love in the Bible*. Grand Rapids: Eerdmans, 1981.
Moule, C. F. D. *The Holy Spirit*. Grand Rapids: Eerdmans, 1978.
Mouw, Richard J. *When the Kings Come Marching In: Isaiah and the New Jerusalem*. Rev. ed. Grand Rapids: Eerdmans, 2002.
Moy, Russell G. "Resident Aliens of the Diaspora: 1 Peter and Chinese Protestants in San Francisco." *Semeia* 90–91 (2002) 51–67.
Moyise, Steve. *The Old Testament in the Book of Revelation*. 1995. Repr., London: Bloomsbury T&T Clark, 2015.
Nañez, Rick. *Full Gospel, Fractured Minds: A Call to Use God's Gift of the Intellect*. Grand Rapids: Zondervan, 2010.
Nebelsick, Harold P. "Ecclesia Reformata Semper Reformanda." *Reformed Liturgy and Music* 18 (1984) 59–63.
Neill, Stephen. *Colonialism and Christian Mission*. New York: McGraw-Hill, 1966.
Newbigin, Lesslie. *Gospel in a Pluralist Society*. Grand Rapids: Eerdmans, 1978.

———. *The Open Secret: An Introduction to the Theology of Mission*. Grand Rapids: Eerdmans, 1978.

Newton, Jon K. *Revelation Reclaimed: The Use and Misuse of the Apocalypse*. Milton Keynes: Paternoster, 2009.

———. *The Revelation Worldview: Apocalyptic Thinking in a Postmodern World*. Eugene, OR: Wipf & Stock, 2015.

Noel, Bradley Truman. *Pentecostal and Postmodern Hermeneutics: Comparisons and Contemporary Impact*. Eugene, OR: Wipf & Stock, 2010.

Noll, Mark A. *The Scandal of the Evangelical Mind*. Grand Rapids: Eerdmans, 1995.

Noy, David. *Foreigners in Rome: Citizens and Strangers*. Swansea: Classic Press of Wales, 2022.

———. "Jews in the Western Roman Empire in Late Antiquity: Migration, Integration, Separation." *Veleia* 30 (2013) 169–77.

Oord, Thomas Jay. *The Uncontrolling Love of God: An Open and Relational Account of Providence*. Downers Grove, IL: IVP Academic, 2015.

Orique, David Thomas. "The Life, Labor, and Legacy of Bartolomé de Las Casas." *Peace Review* 26 (2014) 325–33. https://doi.org/10.1080/10402659.2014.937988.

Osborn, Grant. *The Hermeneutical Spiral*. Downers Grove, IL: InterVarsity, 2006.

Painter, John. "James and Peter: Models of Leadership and Mission." In *The Missions of James, Peter, and Paul: Tensions in Early Christianity*, edited by Bruce Chilton and Craig Evans, 143–209. NovTSup 115. Leiden: Brill, 2005.

Palmer, Earl F. *Love Has Its Reasons: An Inquiry into New Testament Love*. Waco, TX: Word, 1977.

Parsons, Mikael C. *Body and Character in Luke and Acts: The Subversion of Physiognomy in Early Christianity*. Grand Rapids: Baker Academic, 2006.

Partridge, Christopher. *The Re-Enchantment of the West: Alternative Spiritualities, Sacralization, Popular Culture, and Occulture*. 2 vols. London: T&T Clark, 2005.

Penna, Angelo. *St. Paul the Apostle*. Translated by K. C. Thompson. London: St. Paul, 1960.

Perkins, Pheme. "Apocalyptic Sectarianism and Love Commands: The Johannine Epistles and Revelation." In *The Love of Enemy and Nonretaliation in the New Testament*, edited by Willard M. Swartley, 287–96. Louisville: Westminster John Knox, 1992.

Peter, Rowan. *Proclaiming the Peacemaker: The Malaysian Church as an Agent of Reconciliation in a Multicultural Society*. Oxford: Regnum, 2012.

Peterson, Cheryl M. *Who Is the Church? An Ecclesiology for the 21st Century*. Minneapolis: Fortress, 2013.

Phan, Peter C. *Christianities in Asia*. Malden, MA: Wiley-Blackwell, 2010.

———. *Christianity with an Asian Face: Asian American Theology in the Making*. Maryknoll, NY: Orbis, 2003.

Philo. *On the Embassy to Gaius. General Indexes*. Translated by F. H. Colson. LCL 379. Cambridge: Harvard University Press, 1962.

Pinnock, Clark. *Flame of Love: A Theology of the Holy Spirit*. Downers Grove, IL: InterVarsity, 1996.

Pliny the Younger. *Letters*. Vol. 1, *Books 1–7*. Translated by Betty Radice. LCL 55. Cambridge: Harvard University Press, 1969.

Plutarch. *Lives*. Vol. 3, *Pericles and Fabius Maximus. Nicias and Crassus*. Translated by Bernadotte Perrin. LCL 65. Cambridge: Harvard University Press, 1916.

Poon, Michael Nai-Chiu, ed. *Christian Movements in Southeast Asia: A Theological Exploration*. Singapore: Genesis, 2010.

Posner, Richard A. *Public Intellectuals: A Study of Decline*. 2nd ed. Cambridge: Harvard University Press, 2003.

Powell, Mark Allan. *What Is Narrative Criticism?* Philadelphia: Fortress, 1990.

Price, Robert M. *The Widow Traditions in Luke-Acts: A Feminist-Critical Scrutiny*. SBLDS 155. Atlanta: Scholars, 1997.

Rahner, Karl. "The Hermeneutics of Eschatological Assertions." In *Theological Investigations*. Vol. 4, *More Recent Writings*, translated by Kevin Smyth, 323–46. Baltimore: Helicon, 1966.

Ramachandra, Vinoth. *Subverting Global Myths: Theology and the Public Issues Shaping Our World*. Downers Grove, IL: IVP Academic, 2008.

Ramgopal, Sailakshmi. "Connectivity and Disconnectivity in the Roman Empire." *Journal of Roman Studies* 112 (2022) 215–35. https://doi.org/10.1017/S0075435822000466.

Reese, Ruth Ann. *2 Peter and Jude*. Two Horizons New Testament Commentary. Grand Rapids: Eerdmans, 2007.

Reimer, Ivoni Richter. *Women in the Acts of the Apostles: A Feminist Liberation Perspective*. Translated by Linda A. Maloney. Minneapolis: Fortress, 1995.

Reimer, Reg. *Vietnam's Christians: A Century of Growth in Adversity*. Pasadena, CA: William Carey Library, 2011.

Rhoads, David, ed. *From Every People and Nation: The Book of Revelation in Intercultural Perspective*. Minneapolis: Fortress, 2005.

Richard, Earl J. *Reading 1 Peter, Jude, and 2 Peter: A Literary and Theological Commentary*. Macon, GA: Smyth & Helwys, 2000.

Richards, Hubert J. *What the Spirit Says to the Churches: A Key to the Apocalypse*. New York: Kenedy & Sons, 1967.

Richards, Randolph, and Brandon J. O'Brien. *Misreading Scripture with Western Eyes: Removing Cultural Blinders to Better Understand the Bible*. Downers Grove, IL: InterVarsity, 2012.

Rieger, Joerg. "Theology and Mission Between Neocolonialism and Postcolonialism." In *Critical Readings in the History of Christian Mission*, edited by Martha Frederiks and Dorottya Nagy, 2:531–54. Leiden: Brill, 2021.

Robinson, Anthony B., and Robert W. Wall. *Called to Be Church: The Book of Acts for a New Day*. Grand Rapids: Eerdmans, 2006.

Roetzel, Calvin. *Paul: The Man and the Myth*. Minneapolis: Fortress, 1999.

Rogers, Eugene F., Jr. *After the Spirit: A Constructive Pneumatology from Resources Outside the Modern West*. Grand Rapids: Eerdmans, 2005.

Rothschild, Clare K. *Paul in Athens: The Popular Religious Context of Acts 17*. WUNT 341. Tübingen: Mohr Siebeck, 2014.

Rowe, C. Kavin. *World Upside Down: Reading Acts in the Graeco-Roman Age*. Oxford: Oxford University Press, 2009.

Royalty, Robert M., Jr. *The Streets of Heaven: The Ideology of Wealth in the Apocalypse of John*. Mason, GA: Mercer University Press, 1998.

Ruiz, Jean-Pierre. *Ezekiel in the Apocalypse: The Transformation of Prophetic Literature in Revelation 16:17—19:10*. European University Studies 23. New York: Lang, 1989.

Salvatierra, Alexia, and Peter G. Heltzel. *Faith Rooted Organizing: Mobilizing the Church in Service of the World*. Downers Grove, IL: InterVarsity, 2014.

Sanjek, Roger. "Rethinking Migration, Ancient and Future." *Global Networks* 3 (2003) 315–36.

Schauf, Scott. *Theology as History, History as Theology: Paul in Ephesus in Acts 19*. BZNW 133. Berlin: de Gruyter, 2005.

Schleiermacher, Friedrich. *Hermeneutics: The Handwritten Manuscripts*. Translated by James Duke and Jack Forstman. Missoula, MT: Scholars, 1977.

Schmithals, Walther. *Paul and James*. Translated by Dorothea M. Barton. SBT 46. Chatham: SCM, 1965.

Schnabel, Ekhard J. "John and the Future of the Nations." *Bulletin for Biblical Research* 12 (2002) 243–71.

Schüssler Fiorenza, Elisabeth. "The First Letter of Peter." In *A Postcolonial Commentary on the New Testament Writings*, edited by Fernando F. Segovia and R. S. Sugitharajah, 379–403. London: T&T Clark, 2009.

———. *Revelation: Vision of a Just World*. Minneapolis: Fortress, 1991.

Schweitzer, Albert. *The Mysticism of Paul the Apostle*. Translated by William Montgomery. Baltimore, MD: Johns Hopkins University Press, 1998.

———. *Paul and His Interpreters: A Critical History*. Translated by William Montgomery. London: Adam and Charles Black, 1912.

Segovia, Fernando. "And They Began to Speak in Other Tongues: Competing Modes of Discourse in Contemporary Biblical Criticism." In *Readings from This Place: Social Location and Biblical Interpretation in the United States*, edited by Fernando Segovia and Mary Ann Tolbert, 1:1–32. Minneapolis: Fortress, 1995.

———. *Decolonizing Biblical Studies: A View from the Margins*. Maryknoll, NY: Orbis, 2000.

Seneca. *Moral Essays*. Vol. 2, *De Consolatione ad Marciam. De Vita Beata. De Otio. De Tranquillitate Animi. De Brevitate Vitae. De Consolatione ad Polybium. De Consolatione ad Helviam*. Translated by John W. Basore. LCL 254. Cambridge: Harvard University Press, 1932.

Skaggs, Rebecca, and Priscilla C. Benham. *Revelation*. Pentecostal Commentary Series. Dorset: Deo, 2009.

Smalley, Stephen S. *The Revelation to John: A Commentary on the Greek Text of the Apocalypse*. Downers Grove, IL: InterVarsity, 2005.

———. *Thunder and Love: John's Revelation and John's Community*. Milton Keynes: Nelson Word, 1994.

Smith, James K. A. *Awaiting the King: Reforming Public Theology*. Grand Rapids: Baker Academic, 2017.

Smith, Mitzi J. *The Literary Construction of the Other in the Acts of the Apostles: Charismatics, the Jews, and Women*. 2011. Repr., Cambridge: Clarke, 2012.

Smith, Shively T. J. *Strangers to Family: Diaspora and 1 Peter's Invention of God's Household*. Waco, TX: Baylor University Press, 2016.

Spawn, Kevin. "The Principle of Analogy and Biblical Interpretation in the Renewal Tradition." In *Spirit and Scripture: Exploring a Pneumatic Hermeneutic*, edited by Kevin L. Spawn and Archie T. Wright, 46–72. New York: Bloomsbury, 2013.

Spawn, Kevin L., and Archie T. Wright, eds. *Spirit and Scripture: Exploring a Pneumatic Hermeneutic*. New York: Bloomsbury, 2013.

Stenschke, Christoph. "Migration and Mission According to the Book of Acts." *Missionalia* 44 (2016) 129–51.

Stephens, Mark B. *Annihilation or Renewal? The Meaning and Function of New Creation in the Book of Revelation*. WUNT 2.307. Tübingen: Mohr Siebeck, 2011.

Strelan, Rick. *Paul, Artemis, and the Jews in Ephesus*. BZNW 80. Berlin: de Gruyter, 1996.

Suetonius, *Lives of the Caesars*. Vol. 2, *Claudius. Nero. Galba, Otho, and Vitellius. Vespasian. Titus, Domitian. Lives of Illustrious Men: Grammarians and Rhetoricians. Poets (Terence. Virgil. Horace. Tibullus. Persius. Lucan). Lives of Pliny the Elder and Passienus Crispus*. Translated by J. C. Rolfe. LCL 38. Cambridge: Harvard University Press, 1914.

Swinton, John. *Becoming Friends of Time: Disability, Timefullness, and Gentle Discipleship*. Studies in Religion, Theology, and Disability. Waco, TX: Baylor University Press, 2017.

———. "From Inclusion to Belonging: A Practical Theology of Community, Disability and Humanness." *Journal of Religion, Disability, and Health* 16 (2012) 172–90.

Tacoma, Laurens. *Moving Romans: Migration to Rome in the Principate*. New York: Oxford University Press, 2016.

Tamez, Elsa. *The Scandalous Message of James: Faith Without Works Is Dead*. Translated by John Eagleson. New York: Crossroad, 1990.

Tanner, Cullen. "Climbing the Lampstand-Witness-Trees: Revelation's Use of Zechariah 4 in Light of Speech Act Theory." *Journal of Pentecostal Theology* 20 (2011) 81–92.

Tanner, Tom. "Tenure and Other Faculty Facts at ATS Member Schools." *Association of Theological Schools*, August 20, 2015. https://www.ats.edu/files/galleries/tenure-and-other-faculty-facts-part-2.pdf?utm_content=buffer6a8c9&utm_medium=social&utm.

Thiselton, Anthony C. *New Horizons in Hermeneutics*. Grand Rapids: Zondervan, 1992.

———. *The Two Horizons: New Testament Hermeneutics and Philosophical Description*. Grand Rapids: Eerdmans, 1980.

Thomas, John Christopher. *The Apocalypse: A Literary and Theological Commentary*. Cleveland, TN: CPT, 2012.

———. *The Devil, Disease, and Deliverance: Origins of Illness in New Testament Thought*. Journal of Pentecostal Theology Supplement Series 13. Sheffield: Sheffield Academic, 1998.

———. *Footwashing in John 13 and the Johannine Community*. JSNTSup 61. Sheffield: JSOT, 1991.

———. *He Loved Them Until the End: The Farewell Materials in the Gospel According to John*. Pune: Fountain, 2003.

———. "New Jerusalem and the Conversion of the Nations: An Exercise in Pneumatic Discernment (Rev. 21:1—22:5)." In *The Spirit and Christ in the New Testament and Christian Theology: Essays in Honor of Max Turner*, edited by I. Howard Marshall et al., 228–45. Grand Rapids: Eerdmans, 2012.

———. *The Pentecostal Commentary on 1 John, 2 John, 3 John*. Cleveland: Pilgrim, 2004.

———. *The Spirit of the New Testament*. Dorset: Deo, 2005.

Thomas, John Christopher, and Frank D. Macchia. *Revelation*. Two Horizons New Testament Commentary. Grand Rapids: Eerdmans, 2016.

Thompson, Marianne Meye. *Colossians and Philemon*. Two Horizons New Testament Commentary. Grand Rapids: Eerdmans, 2005.

Toenges, Elke. "'See, I Am Making All Things New': New Creation in the Book of Revelation." In *Creation in Jewish and Christian Tradition*, edited by Henning Graf Reventlow and Yair Hoffman, 138–52. JSOTSup 319. London: Sheffield Academic, 2002.

Tonstad, Sigve K. *Saving God's Reputation: The Theological Function of* Pistis Iesou *in the Cosmic Narratives of Revelation*. LNTS 337. London: T&T Clark, 2006.

Toyama, Nikki A., and Tracey Gee, eds. *More Than Serving Tea: Asian American Women on Expectations, Relationships, Leadership, and Faith*. Downers Grove, IL: InterVarsity, 2006.

Trebilco, Paul. *The Early Christians in Ephesus from Paul to Ignatius*. Grand Rapids: Eerdmans, 2007.

Tu, Wei-Ming. *Way, Learning, and Politics: Essays on the Confucian Intellectual*. Albany, NY: State University of New York Press, 1993.

Turner, Max. *Power from on High: The Spirit in Israel's Restoration and Witness in Luke-Acts*. Journal of Pentecostal Theology Supplement Series 9. Sheffield: Sheffield Academic, 1996.

van Tilborg, Sjef. *Imaginative Love in John*. BibInt 2. Leiden: Brill, 1993.

Verheyden, Joseph, et al., eds. *Ancient Christian Interpretation of "Violent Texts" in The Apocalypse*. NTOA 92. Gottingen: Vandenhoeck & Ruprecht, 2011.

Virgil. *Eclogues. Georgics. Aeneid: Books 1–6*. Translated by H. Rushton Fairclough. Revised by G. P. Goold. LCL 63. Cambridge: Harvard University Press, 1916.

Virkler, Henry. *Hermeneutics: Principles and Processes of Biblical Interpretation*. Grand Rapids: Baker Academic, 2007.

Volf, Miroslav. *A Public Faith: How Followers of Christ Should Serve the Common Good*. Grand Rapids: Brazos, 2011.

Waddell, Robby. "Revelation and the (New) Creation: A Prolegomenon on the Apocalypse, Science, and Creation." In *The Spirit Renews the Face of the Earth: Pentecostal Forays in Science and Theology of Creation*, edited by Amos Yong, 30–50. Eugene, OR: Pickwick, 2009.

———. *The Spirit in the Book of Revelation*. Journal of Pentecostal Theology Supplement Series 30. Dorset: Deo, 2006.

Walaskay, Paul W. *"And So We Came to Rome": The Political Perspective of St. Luke*. SNTSMS 49. Cambridge: Cambridge University Press, 1984.

Wall, Robert W. *Community of the Wise: The Letter of James*. The New Testament in Context. Valley Forge, PA: Trinity, 1997.

Wall, Robert W., and Eugene E. Lemcio. *The New Testament as Canon: A Reader in Canonical Criticism*. JSNTSup 76. Sheffield: JSOT, 1992.

Wall, Robert W., with Richard B. Steele. *1 and 2 Timothy and Titus*. Two Horizons New Testament Commentary. Grand Rapids: Eerdmans, 2012.

Walton, Steve. "Evil in Ephesus: Acts 19:8–40." In *Evil in Second Temple Judaism and Early Christianity*, edited by Chris Keith and Loren T. Stuckenbruck, 224–34. WUNT 2.417. Tübingen: Mohr Siebeck, 2016.

Ware, James. "Paul's Hope and Ours: Recovering Paul's Hope of the Renewed Creation." *Concordia Journal* 3 (2009) 129–39.

Warner, Marina. "Angels and Engines: The Culture of Apocalypse." *Raritan* 25 (2005) 12–41.

Waweru, Humphry. "Postcolonial and Contrapuntal Reading of Revelation 22:1–5." *Churchman* 121 (2007) 23–38, 139–62.

Wernle, Paul. *Paulus als Heidenmissionar.* Basil: Mohr Siebeck, 1899.

Westhelle, Vitor. *Eschatology and Space: The Lost Dimension in Theology Past and Present.* New York: Palgrave Macmillan, 2012.

Whiteley, D. E. H. *The Theology of St. Paul.* Philadelphia: Fortress, 1964.

Williams, Travis B. *Good Works in 1 Peter: Negotiating Social Conflict and Christian Identity in the Greco-Roman World.* WUNT 337. Tübingen: Mohr Siebeck, 2014.

———. *Persecution in 1 Peter: Differentiating and Contextualizing Early Christian Suffering.* NovTSup 145. Leiden: Brill, 2012.

Wilson, Mark W. "The New Love of the Ephesians: Who Could It Be?" Paper presented at the Evangelical Theological Society, Providence, RI, November 15–17, 2017.

———. "Revelation 19:10 and Contemporary Interpretation." In *Spirit and Renewal: Essays in Honor of J. Rodman Williams*, edited by Mark W. Wilson, 191–202. Journal of Pentecostal Theology Supplement Series 5. Sheffield: Sheffield Academic, 1994.

———. *The Victor Sayings in the Book of Revelation.* Eugene, OR: Wipf & Stock, 2007.

Witetschek, Stephen. "Artemis and Asiarchs: Some Remarks on Ephesian Local Colour in Acts 19." *Biblica* 90 (2009) 334–54.

Witherington, Ben, III. *Letters and Homilies for Jewish Christians: A Socio-Rhetorical Commentary on Hebrews, James, and Jude.* Downers Grove, IL: IVP Academic, 2007.

Wood, A. Skevington. *Paul's Pentecost: Studies in the Life of the Spirit from Romans 8.* Exeter: Paternoster, 1963.

Wu, Albert. "In the Shadow of Empire: Josef Schmidlin and Protestant-Catholic Ecumenism Before the Second World War." *Journal of Global History* 13 (2018) 165–87. https://doi.org/10.1017/S1740022818000037.

Yep, Jeanette, et al. *Following Jesus Without Dishonoring Your Parents.* Downers Grove, IL: InterVarsity, 1998.

Yong, Amos. "The Affective Spirit: Historiographic Revitalization in the Christian Theological Tradition." In *The Spirit, the Affections, and the Christian Tradition*, edited by Dale M. Coulter and Amos Yong, 293–302. Notre Dame: University of Notre Dame Press, 2016.

———. "American Political Theology in a Post-al Age: A Perpetual Foreigner and Pentecostal Stance." In *Faith and Resistance in the Age of Trump*, edited by Miguel A. De La Torre, 107–14. Maryknoll, NY: Orbis, 2017.

———. "Apostolic Evangelism in the Postcolony: Opportunities and Challenges." *Mission Studies* 34 (2017) 147–67.

———. "Asian American Religion: A Review Essay." *Nova Religio* 9 (2006) 92–107.

———. "'As the Spirit Gives Utterance . . .': Pentecost, Intra-Christian Ecumenism, and the Wider *Oekumene*." *International Review of Mission* 92 (2003) 299–314.

———. "Between the Local and the Global: Autobiographical Reflections on the Emergence of the Global Theological Mind." In *Shaping a Global Theological Mind*, edited by Darren C. Marks, 187–94. Aldershot: Ashgate, 2008.

———. *Beyond the Impasse: Toward a Pneumatological Theology of Religions.* 2003. Repr., Eugene, OR: Wipf & Stock, 2014.

———. *The Bible, Disability, and the Church: A New Vision of the People of God.* Grand Rapids: Eerdmans, 2011.

———. "Christological Constants in Shifting Contexts: Jesus Christ, Prophetic Dialogue, and the *Missio Spiritus* in a Pluralistic World." In *Mission on the Road to Emmaus: Constants, Contexts, and Prophetic Dialogue*, edited by Stephen B. Bevans and Cathy Ross, 19–33. London: SCM, 2015.

———. "Come Holy Spirit: Global and Cosmic Yearnings." Paper presented at the Annual Study Days of the Studienzentrum für Glaube und Gesellschaft, Fribourg, Switzerland, June 19–20, 2017.

———. "The Coming Spirit of Theology: Moltmann, Pneumatology, and Trinitarian Eschatology for the Third Millennium." In *Jürgen Moltmann and the Work of Hope: The Future of Christian Theology*, edited by M. Douglas Meeks, 53–75. Lanham, MD: Lexington, 2018.

———. *The Cosmic Breath: Spirit and Nature in the Christianity-Buddhism-Science Trialogue*. Philosophical Studies in Science and Religion 4. Leiden: Brill, 2012.

———. "*Creator Spiritus* and the Spirit of Christ: Toward a Trinitarian Theology of Creation." In *The Work of the Holy Spirit*, edited by Jeffrey Barbeau and Beth Jones, 168–82. Downers Grove, IL: IVP Academic, 2015.

———. "Culture." In *Dictionary of Mission Theology: Evangelical Foundations*, edited by John Corrie, 82–87. Downers Grove, IL: InterVarsity, 2007.

———."The Demonic in Pentecostal-Charismatic Christianity and in the Religious Consciousness of Asia." In *Asian and Pentecostal: The Charismatic Face of Christianity in Asia*, edited by Allan Anderson and Edmond Tang, 93–127. London: Regnum International, 2005.

———. *The Dialogical Spirit: Christian Reason and Theological Method for the Third Millennium*. Eugene, OR: Cascade, 2014.

———. *The Dialogical Spirit II: Contextual God, Pluralistic Selves, and Dialectical Imagination After Pentecost*. Edited by Spencer Moffatt. Eugene, OR: Cascade, 2024.

———. "Diasporic Discipleship from West Asia Through Southeast Asia and Beyond: A Dialogue with 1 Peter." *Asia Journal of Theology* 32 (2018) 3–21.

———. *Discerning the Spirit(s): A Pentecostal-Charismatic Contribution to Christian Theology of Religions*. Journal of Pentecostal Theology Supplement Series 20. 2000. Repr., Eugene, OR: Wipf & Stock, 2018.

———. "Evangelism and the Political in Southeast Asia: A Pentecostal Perspective." *Evangelical Review of Theology and Politics* 4 (2016) EF18–20.

———. "From Demonization to Kin-domization: The Witness of the Spirit and the Renewal of Missions in a Pluralistic World." In *Global Renewal, Religious Pluralism, and the Great Commission: Toward a Renewal Theology of Mission and Interreligious Encounter*, edited by Amos Yong and Clifton Clarke, 157–74. Asbury Theological Seminary Series in World Christian Revitalization Movements in Pentecostal/Charismatic Studies 4. Lexington, KY: Emeth, 2011.

———. "From Every Tribe, Language, People, and Nation: Diaspora, Hybridity, and the Coming Reign of God." In *Global Diasporas and Mission*, edited by Chandler H. Im and Amos Yong, 253–61. Regnum Edinburgh Centenary Series 23. Oxford: Regnum, 2014.

———. *The Future of Evangelical Theology: Soundings from the Asian American Diaspora*. Downers Grove, IL: IVP Academic, 2014.

———. "Glocalization and the Gift-Giving Spirit: Informality and Shalom Beyond the Political Economy of Exchange." *Journal of Youngsan Theology* 25 (2012) 7–29.

———. "Guests, Hosts, and the Holy Ghost: Pneumatological Theology and Christian Practices in a World of Many Faiths." In *Lord and Giver of Life: Perspectives on Constructive Pneumatology*, edited by David H. Jensen, 71–86. Louisville: Westminster John Knox, 2008.

———. *The Hermeneutical Spirit: Theological Interpretation and the Scriptural Imagination for the Third Christian Millennium*. Eugene, OR: Cascade, 2017.

———. *The Heteroglossic Spirit: Unruly Tongues and Translations After Pentecost*. Edited by Ekaputra Tupamahu. Eugene, OR: Cascade, forthcoming.

———."Homily: From the Jewish Diaspora to the Indian (Christian) Diaspora: An Autobiographical Look at 1 Peter's Message to West Asia." Edited by John Alex. *New Life Theological Journal* 9 (2019) 7–18.

———. *Hospitality and the Other: Pentecost, Christian Practices, and the Neighbor*. Faith Meets Faith. Maryknoll, NY: Orbis, 2008.

———. "I Believe in the Holy Spirit: From the Ends of the Earth to the Ends of Time." In *The Spirit over the Earth: Pneumatology in the Majority World*, edited by K. K. Yeo et al., 13–33. Majority World Theology 3. Grand Rapids: Eerdmans, 2016.

———. "The Im/Migrant Spirit: De/Constructing a Pentecostal Theology of Migration." In *Theology of Migration in the Abrahamic Religions*, edited by Peter C. Phan and Elaine Padilla, 133–53. Christianities of the World. New York: Palgrave Macmillan, 2014.

———. "Improvisation, Indigenization, and Inspiration: Theological Reflections on the Sound and Spirit of Global Renewal." In *The Spirit of Praise: Music and Worship in Global Pentecostal-Charismatic Christianity*, edited by Monique Ingalls and Amos Yong, 279–88. University Park, PA: Penn State University Press, 2015.

———. "Incarnation, Pentecost, and Virtual Spiritual Formation: Renewing Theological Education in Global Context." In *A Theology of the Spirit in Doctrine and Demonstration: Essays in Honor of Wonsuk and Julie Ma*, edited by Teresa Chai, 27–38. Baguio City: Asia Pacific Theological Seminary, 2014.

———. "Informality, Illegality, and Improvisation: Theological Reflections on Money, Migration, and Ministry in Chinatown, NYC, and Beyond." In *New Overtures: Asian North American Theology in the 21st Century—Essays in Honor of Fumitaka Matsuoka*, edited by Eleazar S. Fernandez, 248–68. Upland, CA: Sopher, 2012.

———. *In the Days of Caesar: Pentecostalism and Political Theology—The Cadbury Lectures 2009*. Sacra Doctrina: Christian Theology for a Postmodern Age. Grand Rapids: Eerdmans, 2010.

———. "Jubilee, Liberation, and Pentecost: The Preferential Option of the Poor on the Apostolic Way." In *Evangelical Theologies of Liberation*, edited by Elise Mae Cannon and Andrea Smith, 306–24. Downers Grove, IL: IVP Academic, 2019.

———. *The Kerygmatic Spirit: Apostolic Preaching in the 21st Century*. Edited by Josh Samuel. Eugene, OR: Cascade, 2018.

———. "Kings, Nations, and Cultures on the Way to the New Jerusalem: A Pentecostal Witness to an Apocalyptic Vision." In *The Pastor and the Kingdom: Essays Honoring Jack W. Hayford*, edited by S. David Moore and Jonathan Huntzinger, 231–51. Dallas: The King's University Press, 2017.

———. *Learning Theology: Tracking the Spirit of Christian Faith*. Louisville: Westminster John Knox, 2018.

———. "Liberating and Diversifying Theological Education: A Subversive or Empowering Aspiration?" *CrossCurrents* 69 (2019) 10–17.

———. "'The Light Shines in the Darkness': Johannine Dualism and the Challenge of Christian Theology of Religions Today." *Journal of Religion* 89 (2009) 31–56.

———. "Many Tongues, Many Practices: Pentecost and Theology of Mission at 2010." In *Mission After Christendom: Emergent Themes in Contemporary Mission*, edited by Ogbu U. Kalu et al., 43–58. Louisville: Westminster John Knox, 2010.

———. "The Many Tongues of Asian and Oceanian Pentecostalisms: An Introduction and Some Theological Prognostications." In *Global Renewal Christianity*. Vol. 1, *Asia and Oceania*, edited by Vinson H. Synan and Amos Yong, 392–98. Lake Mary, FL: Charisma, 2015.

———. *The Missiological Spirit: Christian Mission Theology for the Third Millennium Global Context*. Eugene, OR: Cascade, 2014.

———. *Mission After Pentecost: The Witness of the Spirit from Genesis to Revelation*. Mission in Global Community. Grand Rapids: Baker Academic, 2019.

———. "Missional Renewal: Pentecostal Perspectives to and from the Ends of the Earth." *Quadrum* 1 (2018) 133–56.

———. "The *Missio Spiritus*: Towards a Pneumatological Missiology of Creation." In *Creation Care in Christian Mission*, edited by Kapya J. Kaoma, 121–33. Regnum Edinburgh Centenary Series 29. Oxford: Regnum, 2015.

———. "'Not Many of You Should Become Teachers . . .': Whose (Established) Professoriate? Which (Diasporic) Faculty?" In *Now to God Who Is Able: Vocation, Justice, and Ministry—Essays in Honor of Mark Labberton*, edited by Neal D. Presa and Anne E. Zaki, 139–54. Eugene, OR: Wipf & Stock, 2023.

———. "Pentecostal Christianities and Their Political Lives: Many Tongues, Many Political Practices." In *Politischer Pentekostalismus: Transformation des globalen Christentums im Spiegel theologischer Motive und pluraler Normativität*, edited by Leandro L. B. Fontana and Markus Luber, 183–96. Weltkirche und Mission 18. Regensburg: Pustet, 2023.

———. "Pentecostal Health and Wealth: A Theology of Economics." In *Recent Developments in the Economics of Religion*, edited by Paul Oslington et al., 295–303. The International Library of Critical Writings in Economics 341. Cheltenham: Edward Elgar, 2018.

———. "Pentecostal Witness in the Neighborhood: Acts 16:11–15." Sermon, Assembleia de Deus, Gramado, Brazil, July 15, 2023.

———. "Pluralism, Secularism, and Pentecost: Newbigin-ings for *Missio Trinitatis* in a New Century." In *The Gospel and Pluralism Today: Reassessing Lesslie Newbigin for the 21st Century*, edited by Scott W. Sunquist and Amos Yong, 147–70. Missiological Engagements: Church, Theology and Culture in Global Contexts 1. Downers Grove, IL: IVP Academic, 2015.

———. "The Pneumatological Imagination: The Logic of Pentecostal Theology." In *The Routledge Handbook of Pentecostal Theology*, edited by Wolfgang Vondey, 152–62. New York: Routledge, 2020.

———. *Pneumatology and the Christian-Buddhist Dialogue: Does the Spirit Blow Through the Middle Way?* Studies in Systematic Theology 11. Leiden: Brill, 2012.

———. "The Power of Language: The Implications of Pentecost for Global Worship." *Reformed Worship* 119 (2016) 28–33. https://www.reformedworship.org/article/march-2016/power-language.

———. "Race and the Political in 21st Century Evangelical America: A Review Essay." *Evangelical Review of Theology and Politics* 5 (2017) RA1–11.

———. "Race and Racialization in a Post-Racist Evangelicalism: A View from Asian America." In *Aliens in the Promised Land: Why Minority Leadership Is Overlooked in White Christian Churches and Institutions*, edited by Anthony B. Bradley, 45–58. Phillipsburg, NJ: P&R, 2013.

———. *Renewing Christian Theology: Systematics for a Global Christianity*. Images and commentary by Jonathan A. Anderson. Waco, TX: Baylor University Press, 2014.

———. *Renewing the Church by the Spirit: Theological Education After Pentecost*. Theological Education Between the Times. Grand Rapids: Eerdmans, 2020.

———. *Revelation*. Belief: A Theological Commentary on the Bible. Louisville: Westminster John Knox, 2021.

———."Revelation and the Political in the 21st Century: A Review Essay." *Evangelical Review of Theology and Politics* 4 (2016) 1–10.

———. "Salvation, Society, and the Spirit: Pentecostal Contextualization and Political Theology from Cleveland to Birmingham, from Springfield to Seoul." *Pax Pneuma* 5 (2009) 22–34.

———."The Spirit, the Body, and the Sacraments: Pentecostal-Catholic Dialogue and the 'Pneumatological-Sacramental' Imagination." In *Renewal History and Theology: Essays in Honor of H. Vinson Synan*, edited by S. David Moore and James M. Henderson, 241–64. Cleveland, TN: CPT, 2014.

———. "The Spirit, the Common Good, and the Public Sphere: The 21st Century Public Intellectual in Apostolic Perspective." In *Public Intellectuals and the Common Good: Christian Thinking for Human Flourishing*, edited by Todd C. Ream et al., 21–41. Downers Grove, IL: IVP Academic, 2021.

———. *The Spirit of Creation: Modern Science and Divine Action in the Pentecostal-Charismatic Imagination*. Pentecostal Manifestos 4. Grand Rapids: Eerdmans, 2011.

———. *Spirit of Love: A Trinitarian Theology of Grace*. Waco, TX: Baylor University Press, 2012.

———. *The Spirit Poured Out on All Flesh: Pentecostalism and the Possibility of Global Theology*. Grand Rapids: Baker Academic, 2005.

———. "The Spirit, Vocation, and the Life of the Mind: A Pentecostal Testimony." In *Pentecostals in the Academy: Testimonies of Call*, edited by Steven M. Fettke and Robby Waddell, 203–20. Cleveland, TN: CPT, 2012.

———. *Spirit-Word-Community: Theological Hermeneutics in Trinitarian Perspective*. New Critical Thinking in Religion, Theology, and Biblical Studies. Burlington, VT: Ashgate, 2002.

———. "Theological and Scientific Perspectives on Signs, Wonders, and Miracles: Toward a Full(er) Gospel Account." In *Signs, Wonders, and Miracles: Pentecostal and Scientific Reflections*, edited by Simo Frestadius and Claire Williams, 221–40. Cleveland, TN: CPT, 2025.

———. *Theology and Down Syndrome: Reimagining Disability in Late Modernity*. Waco, TX: Baylor University Press, 2007.

———. "'To Him Who Loves Us and Freed Us from Our Sins by His Blood . . .': A Pentecostal-Canonical Interpretation of Apocalyptic Love." In *Spirit and Story: Pentecostal Readings of Scripture—Essays in Honor of John Christopher Thomas*, edited by Blaine Charette and Robby Waddell, 117–34. Sheffield: Sheffield Phoenix, 2020.

———. "A Typology of Prosperity Theology: A Religious Economy of Global Renewal or a Renewal Economics?" In *Pentecostalism and Prosperity: The Socioeconomics of the Global Charismatic Movement*, edited by Amos Yong and Katherine Attanasi, 15–33. Christianities of the World 1. New York: Palgrave Macmillan, 2012.

———. "Understanding and Living the Apostolic Way: Oral Culturality and Hermeneutics After Pentecost." In *International Conference on the Catholic Church and Pentecostalism: Challenges in the Nigerian Context—Proceedings, Presentations and Final Report*, edited by Raphael Madu et al., 87–103. Abuja: Catholic Secretariat of Nigeria, 2016.

———. "Unveiling Interpretation After Pentecost: Revelation, Pentecostal Reading, and Christian Hermeneutics of Scripture—A Review Essay." *Journal of Theological Interpretation* 11 (2017) 147–63.

———. *Who Is the Holy Spirit? A Walk with the Apostles.* Brewster, MA: Paraclete, 2011.

———. "Worship in Many Tongues: The Power of Praise in the Vernacular." *Worship Leader* 122 (2015) 14–17.

Yong, Amos, and Dale M. Coulter. *The Holy Spirit and Higher Education: Renewing the Christian University.* Waco, TX: Baylor University Press, 2023.

Yong, Amos, and Cecil M. Robeck, Jr., eds. *The Cambridge Companion to Pentecostalism.* Cambridge: Cambridge University Press, 2014.

Yong, Amos, and James K. A. Smith, eds. *Science and the Spirit: A Pentecostal Engagement with the Sciences.* Bloomington: Indiana University Press, 2010.

Yu, Frank W. *Yellow: Race in America Beyond Black and White.* New York: Basic, 2002.

Zetterholm, Magnus. "'And Abraham Believed': Paul, James, and the Gentiles." *Nordisk judaistik* 24 (2003) 109–21.

Subject Index

Scripture Index

www.ingramcontent.com/pod-product-compliance
Lightning Source LLC
LaVergne TN
LVHW100521110826
845146LV00002B/728

* 9 7 9 8 3 8 5 2 5 1 5 4 4 *